CONTENTS

UNIT 3: VISIONS OF HUMANITY

UNIT 4: NATURE AND OUR ENVIRONMENT

POEMS
American Themes

SECOND EDITION

WILLIAM C. BASSELL

Amsco School Publications, Inc.
315 Hudson Street/New York, N.Y. 10013

William C. Bassell is the Principal of Long Island City High School in New York City. Prior to that he served as an Assistant Principal and as an English teacher. He has also taught at the college level. A longtime advocate of interdisciplinary and multicultural instruction, Mr. Bassell has brought his experience to bear in his writing.

When ordering this book, please specify:
R 620 S *or* POEMS: AMERICAN THEMES, SOFTBOUND
  or
R 620 H *or* POEMS: AMERICAN THEMES, HARDBOUND

ISBN 1-56765-023-6 (Softbound edition)
  NYC Item 56765-023-5
ISBN 1-56765-027-9 (Hardbound edition)
  NYC Item 56765-027-8

Printed in the United States of America

7 8 9 10 11   04 03 02

UNIT 5: VALUES

UNIT 6: THIS LAND OF OURS

UNIT 7: GOOD TIMES—BAD TIMES

ACKNOWLEDGMENTS

Grateful acknowledgment is made to the following sources for permission to use copyrighted materials. Every effort has been made to obtain permission to use previously published material; any errors or omissions are unintentional.

Samuel Allen: "To Satch" by Samuel Allen.

Elizabeth Barnett: "God's World," "Lament," "Love Is Not All," "Pity Me Not," "Recuerdo," and "On Hearing a Symphony of Beethoven" by Edna St. Vincent Millay. From *Collected Poems*, HarperCollins. Copyright © 1917, 1921, 1922, 1923, 1928, 1931, 1945, 1948, 1950, 1951, 1955, 1958 by Edna St. Vincent Millay and Norma Millay Ellis. Reprinted by permission of Elizabeth Barnett, literary executor.

Brandt & Brandt Literary Agency, Inc.: From *John Brown's Body* by Stephen Vincent Benét, Henry Holt and Company, Inc. copyright 1927, 1928 by Stephen Vincent Benét, copyright renewed © 1955, 1956 by Rosemary Carr Benét.

Gwendolyn Brooks: "Truth" by Gwendolyn Brooks © copyright 1991, from her book *Blacks*, published by Third World Press, Chicago, 1991.

Carcanet Press Limited: "Underwater" by Michael Schmidt.

Molly Malone Cook Literary Agency, Inc.: "The Swimming Lesson," from *No Voyage and Other Poems* (Houghton Mifflin). Copyright © 1965 by Mary Oliver. Used by permission of the Molly Malone Cook Literary Agency.

Mrs. Gwendolyn Crosscup: "To James" by Frank Horne.

Curtis Brown, Ltd.: "Dick Szymanski," copyright © 1968 by Ogden Nash, reprinted by permission of Curtis Brown, Ltd.

Babette Deutsch: "Morning Work-out" by Babette Deutsch.

Dodd, Mead & Company, Inc.: "The Skater of Ghost Lake" from *Golden Fleece* by William Rose Benét, copyright 1933, 1935 by Dodd, Mead & Company, Inc., copyright renewed.

Doubleday: "I See a Star" by Alonzo Lopez from *Whispering Wind* by Terry Allen. Copyright © 1972 by the Institute of American Indian Arts. "My Papa's Waltz," copyright 1942 by Hearst Magazines, Inc. "Night Journey," copyright 1940 by Theodore Roethke, from *The Collected Poems of Theodore Roethke* by Theodore Roethke. Used by permission of Doubleday, a division of Bantam Doubleday Dell Publishing Group, Inc.

Dave Etter: "The Fact" from *The Last Train to Prophetstown* by Dave Etter, University of Nebraska Press, 1968.

Mari Evans: "When in Rome" by Mari Evans.

Farrar, Straus & Giroux, Inc.: "Losses" from *The Complete Poems* by Randall Jarrell, copyright 1948 by Mrs. Randall Jarrell, renewed copyright © 1975 by Mary von Schrader Jarrell. "Water" from *For the Union Dead* by Robert

TO THE TEACHER

This second edition of *Poems: American Themes* addresses the need to add high quality multicultural poetry to the canon of classics traditionally read in the classroom. Thus, the teacher will now find, in addition to many tried and true classics of American poetry, a healthy assortment of poems by African-American, Asian-American, Hispanic-American, Italo-American, Judeo-American, and Native-American poets, many of whom are women. Most of these poets are twentieth century, some are actively writing as of 1994, while one is a nineteenth-century abolitionist. Consequently, the mosaic of American poetry as presented in *Poems: American Themes* has been considerably enhanced.

The late Wilbert J. Levy wrote in his introduction to the first edition, "Poetry is the keenest perception of experience and the rendering of that perception in the most richly articulate language." I believe that poetry has a unique place in literature because it affords the reader the opportunity to experience a poet's perceptions and emotions and to appreciate the beauty of language. While motivational links with students' experiences are essential springboards for analysis and discussion, poetry, since it is such a personal art form, should be taught with a view towards achieving empathy with the poet and an appreciation of the poet's "richly articulate" use of language. This second edition of *Poems: American Themes* affords the student the opportunity to encounter the emotions and ideas of poets, male and female, of many ethnic backgrounds who have in common a desire to express themselves in highly personal terms. Lest the teacher think that emotions have taken over the lessons at the expense of the technical, let me reassure him or her that those aspects of poetry have not been neglected either in the lessons, the introduction, or the Reader's Guide to Poetic Terms and Devices. Indeed, I believe that the fullest appreciation of poetry comes with an understanding of both the artistic and technical aspects of the genre.

Writing activities have taken a more prominent place than before in this second edition. Predicated upon the belief that students should write thoughtfully about what they read, each poem has a writing assignment attached to it. The assignments, which relate to the poem just read and often refer back to previously read poems in order to make appropriate connections, have deliberately been left in a general form, i.e., "write a brief essay," "write a paragraph," "compose a poem," etc. This allows the teacher maximum flexibility in choosing an approach to writing. The activities herein can be used with and adapted to many approaches including, but not limited to, the writing process, portfolio assessment, cooperative learning, and so on. Again, the assignments are presented as a foundation for writing; the teacher has, as a teacher should, the freedom and flexibility to build upon them as he or she sees fit.

The poems have once again been grouped by themes which relate to the American experience. This approach was retained because of my belief (bolstered by experience) that poetry, as a result of its unique way of exploring the human condition, is highly accessible to students when presented in groups of poems dealing with the same broad theme. Nevertheless, I have included in the Teacher's Manual a chronological table of contents for the instructor who prefers to integrate this text into a chronologically arranged survey course. The questions in each lesson have been phrased in such a way as to require, usually, a sustained response, often provoked by the words "how" or "why," thus insuring that the student think critically about what he or she has read. Since I believe that interdisciplinary instruction and enrichment are important in any English class, the link between poetry and art has been retained because these genres have so much in common; linkages with music, mostly American, have been added to approximately one third of the lessons. Also, the Unit Reviews have been overhauled to allow for more specific, analytical responses in numerous places. The Teacher's Manual now includes brief biographies of the poets.

Every writer has numerous muses, and I would like to dedicate this volume to four of mine: my wife Alison and my father Robert whose provocative intellectual discussions and humanistic encouragement made this possible, and my two sons, Joseph and Phillip, whose love and smiles are all that any proud father could desire.

William C. Bassell

AN INTRODUCTION

WHY READ POETRY?

Reading poetry is different from all other reading. Poetry raises your consciousness about many, many things. Through poetry, you can know yourself better, know all people better, and know the world better. Through poetry, you can experience and appreciate how poets feel about life, living, the world around them, and the issues that concern them.

The first important steps in learning to read poetry are very easy. Let's take a look at two sides of poetry. First, we'll examine what poems are written about; then we'll study the language of poetry. Believe it or not, you know more about both than you probably think.

First, what are poems written about? Are the subjects unfamiliar and unusual? Not at all. There is nothing closer or more familiar to you than the subject matter of poetry.

Have you ever jogged, or swum, or danced, or played a sport and experienced inexpressible delight at the feel of your muscles in well-coordinated action? Have you enjoyed the smell of freshly cut grass in the springtime? Have you ever seen a terrible accident, the sight of which has haunted you with feelings of dread and horror? Have you ever felt that the daily routine of your life was unbearably monotonous and meaningless? Have you yearned for love until it hurt beyond words? Have you laughed? Have you cried? Have you ever felt uplifted, ecstatic, patriotic, confident, hopeful, guilty, worried, upset, insecure?

Of course, your answer to many of these questions will be "yes!" These basic feelings that we all share and these common experiences are what poetry is written about. You know them as well as you know your own face in the mirror. The subject matter of poetry is you. You have expert knowledge of it because you know yourself.

You also know something about the language of poetry. When you describe in graphic detail something that happened, when you speak feelings of love, when you cheer at a sporting or musical event, when you explain how you feel about something important to you, when you say or do anything that involves powerful expression of or appeal to emotion, you are using the language of poetry. Under these circumstances, people are not interested in using words only for their dictionary meanings. Rather, we use other qualities of words—rhythm, rhyme, repetition, figurative language—to convey our emotions and to engage those of others. These special qualities have technical names—such as rhyme, alliteration, image, metaphor, symbol, connotation—terms you will learn more about as you go on.

You are already familiar with the use of these special qualities of words because they are sometimes used in ordinary language to lend interest or color to what is being said. This, however, is only a helpful beginning. Ordinary language is one-dimensional. The purpose of ordinary language is to establish meaning, to make things perfectly clear. However, the most important things about us as human beings are not at all perfectly clear. They are complex, murky, contradictory, and uncontainable. To express the subject matter of his or her poems, the poet uses all of the qualities of words in subtle, complex ways. The poet artistically combines the dictionary meanings of words with such devices as rhythm, metaphor, and symbol to capture the essence of human experiences and human feelings. Therefore, the language of poetry is multidimensional, expressive, creative, and suggestive. This kind of language must be studied and learned.

THE SOUND OF POETRY

Poetry is meant to be read aloud. The sounds of the words are an important element in the enjoyment and understanding of any poem. Reading aloud can convey a poem's happiness, energy, humor, seriousness, or intensity simply through the sound of the human voice. The expression of these feelings and moods in words is also enhanced through the rhythm, rhymes, and sound patterns of the oral reading.

In poetry, sound qualities of words are used to help express meaning and feeling. Poems should always be read aloud. When you read poetry for enjoyment or when you study a poem in this collection, read it aloud two or three times. But, before you read, remember these simple rules which will make your reading come alive. Read the poem for the meaning of the words, adjusting your pauses and your rhythm to the meaning, not the sound of the words, the line endings, or the rhymes. You should not pause at the end of each line unless the meaning makes it sensible to do so or unless it is indicated by punctuation. Also, don't read any poem in a singsong rhythm. The sound effects and the rhythm of the poem will come through naturally, by themselves, and enrich the meaning when you read in a straightforward way. If you read to emphasize sounds, the meaning will get lost.

THE IMAGERY OF POETRY

Besides word sounds, poetry is made up of word pictures, or imagery. Imagery is an important element of poetry. Imagery is the use of words by a poet to recreate the sensory impressions of actual experience. Imagery is most often visual, but imagery also includes words of sound, smell, taste, and touch. Imagery may be literal, directly describing sense experiences, or it may be figurative, using comparisons such as metaphors and similes to make its effect.

Careful readers of poetry look for these images, see them in their minds' eye and react to them. These readers will not only see, hear, feel, taste, and smell the sensual impressions of the poem but will add to them whatever is consistent to make the image even more complete. An important part of the richly suggestive meaning of poems is grasped by the reader's active and exact response to imagery, both literal and figurative.

THE SUGGESTED MEANINGS OF POETRY

We like to know just what the meaning is of anything we read. The meaning of a poem is the capturing, largely through suggestion, of a feeling, a mood, an understanding, an event that is part of the world of human experience. This meaning is often suggested through images and sounds. Meaning in a poem is also suggested through other qualities of words. Poets carefully choose words so that their connotations, or associations, as well as their denotations, or direct meanings, contribute to the suggested meaning of the poem as a whole.

Each of the three foregoing characteristics of poetry occurs in the form of a variety of devices that have technical names.

The sounds of poetry may be shaped through alliteration, assonance, cacophony, consonance, euphony, meter, onomatopoeia, repetition, rhyme, and rhythm.

The imagery of poetry can occur in the form of analogy, metaphor, metonymy, personification, simile, and synecdoche.

The suggested meanings of poetry can be achieved by allusion, ambiguity, anticlimax, antithesis, apostrophe, connotation, diction, hyperbole, irony, paradox, and understatement.

The Study Questions for each poem will help you to see how these and other devices are used to help make meaning in each poem. The Reader's Guide to Poetic Terms and Devices gives you clear explanations of these and other terms. Refer to it as often as you need to while studying each poem. You may wish to spend a few minutes now looking up some of the terms that have been listed above.

Next, let's take a look at another important point about reading poetry. The key to unlocking meaning is to look closely and carefully at the words of the poem in order to answer the question, "Who is the speaker and what are the circumstances?" Sometimes, it is true, the words of the poem represent a poet speaking directly to us as a fellow human being. More often, however, the speaker is a fictional person speaking in fictional circumstances. It is essential to grasping the poem that we learn from it all we can about that person and those circumstances. Having answered the question above, ask yourself several others. What word sounds help to express the meaning? What images occur? What is the suggested meaning of the poem?

You have learned so far, four key points about reading poetry:

1. Read the poem for word sounds. To do this, read the poem aloud, not once but several times.

2. Read the poem for imagery. To do this, read the poem several times so that the images, or word pictures, become clearer and clearer.
3. Read the poem for rich, suggested meaning, realizing that the meaning of a poem is the capturing of a feeling, a mood, an understanding, an event that is part of your own familiar experience as a human being. To do this, read the poem several times.
4. Read the poem closely to answer the question, "Who is the speaker and what are the circumstances?" To get the richest answer to this question, read the poem several times.

To these four key points, we can add a fifth:

5. A poem must be read not once but many times for you to achieve fullest understanding and appreciation of it.

You now have a working knowledge of five important techniques for reading poetry. You are ready to study the poems in this book, enjoy them for themselves, and become a better and better reader of poetry as you go along.

In the book, you will find a number of aids to your reading of the poems. Here is an explanation of the best way to use these aids:

THEMES

The poems are arranged in units according to themes, or broad ideas, that will be familiar to you and whose importance you will recognize. The seven themes are "Sports," "Freedom and Diversity," "Visions of Humanity," "Nature and Our Environment," "Values," "This Land of Ours," and "Good Times/Bad Times." Each theme is introduced by a discussion that sets the poems of the unit in a broad context and gives you some starting points for studying the poems. Read each of these introductions carefully and react to them with your own thinking.

POEM INTRODUCTIONS

Each poem is accompanied by a short introductory discussion to provide you with background information that you may not have or to direct your attention to a problem or question that will lead into the poem, or to give you some other help in getting started with a successful reading. Read the poem's introduction before you read the poem.

DEFINITIONS AND EXPLANATIONS

Most poems are accompanied by a set of notes about words and phrases in the poem with which you may need assistance. These notes offer various kinds of important help. In many cases, they will help you to understand the connotation of a word used by the poet and to appreciate the richness of the writing.

Sometimes the notes will give you a definition of a word with which you may not be familiar. The definition will be one which fits the particular shade of meaning intended by the poet. At other times, the notes will help you with the fullest comprehension of a specific reference in the poem.

Before you read each poem, study the notes of the "Definitions and Explanations." Use the line reference to pick out the word or phrase in the poem and look at it in its context. When you get to reading the poem, glance at the notes whenever necessary.

STUDY QUESTIONS

After you have read the poem several times with the aids just mentioned, you will understand and enjoy it on a basic level. But, for a good reader, that is not enough. You will want to go further to realize the fullest comprehension and know the deepest pleasure of the poem. You will want to explore its meaning in greater depth and to react more fully to its meaning for *you*. You will want to have a fuller appreciation of the art of the poem, of the way its sounds, its images, and its other language devices work. The study questions will help you to achieve these goals, to make you an expert reader of the poem. In answering the study questions, you will sometimes want to refer to the Reader's Guide to Poetic Terms and Devices. When you come across terms in the questions whose meanings are unfamiliar to you, refer to the Reader's Guide for explanations. After a while, you won't need to, and you will have a real, active understanding of the meaning of these terms, not just a collection of memorized definitions.

WRITING

Writing is an important means of communication. It helps us say what we mean and can help clarify our thinking. It is also an opportunity for us to be creative and expressive. Every poem is followed by a writing activity which is designed to help you expand your own reactions to the poem you have just studied, to reinforce your knowledge of and response to the issues the poem has raised, and (occasionally) to help you make connections between poems. Your assignments can be part of a journal, a portfolio, general classwork or homework, a formal essay or composition, or a creative writing assignment. No matter what, the writing assignments will be valuable in helping you to enjoy and understand the poem and its message to the fullest.

MUSIC

Music is an important part of our lives and is artistic and poetic in its own way. Some poems have music listening activities connected to them; these activities will introduce you to different kinds of music and show you how the music and the poetry are interrelated.

UNIT REVIEWS

You will want some of the poems and some of the things you have learned from the poems to stay with you, to give you memories and renewed pleasure in years to come. Each section of the book concludes with a "Unit Review." The exercises of the "Unit Review" are designed to reinforce and perhaps make permanent the strong memories of some of the poems you have read. They also include several art works for you to react to, write about, and link to the poems. Art is a powerfully emotional genre as is poetry. Indeed, art and poetry, like music and poetry, have many similarities which warrant exploration.

Welcome to the world of American poetry. May you find it inspiring and rewarding!

Sports  14

Among our greatest national events are baseball's World Series, football's Super Bowl, basketball's playoffs, tennis' U.S. Open, golf's Master's Tournament, horse racing's Kentucky Derby, and boxing's heavyweight championships. We also celebrate with much enthusiasm excellence in track and field, swimming, ice skating, and auto racing. Our national heroes include many, many figures from the world of athletics, indicating the important place they hold in the lives of Americans. We pay our top athletes more than we pay almost anybody else in American society.

Sports are the center of life for many youngsters and adults as they both participate in and watch the events on television or in the stadium. Sports are recreation, relaxation, discipline, health, comradeship, patriotism, and big business. Obviously, sports are a central part of the American experience.

It is the role of poets to capture both experience and the meaning of experience. Various aspects of the sports experience have captured the attention of American poets.

TO SATCH

Samuel Allen

Sometimes I feel like I will *never* stop
Just go on forever
Till one fine mornin
I'm gonna reach up and grab me a handfulla stars
Throw out my long lean leg 5
And whip three hot strikes burnin down the heavens
And look over at God and say
How about that!

The greatest athletes end up in professional sports. But, even among the pros, there are those whose unique careers and personalities make them legendary figures. One such legend of baseball is LeRoy "Satchel" Paige (1906–1982). Paige began pitching in the Negro Leagues in 1924. Because the majors were open to whites only, Paige received little of the media coverage that he would have otherwise gotten. Yet, by word of mouth, his reputation grew; and because of his excellence and the length of his pitching career, he became a living legend. In 1934, he reportedly won 104 of 105 games and pitched, over the course of his career, 55 no-hitters. In 1947, when Paige was 41, an age when most pitchers have already retired, the majors were integrated and Paige pitched, over the next 18 seasons, for the Cleveland Indians, the St. Louis Browns, and the Kansas City Athletics. In 1962, he is alleged to have said, "Maybe I'll pitch forever." In the 1965 season, at the age of 59, Paige won 28 and lost 31 games. He was elected to the baseball Hall of Fame in 1971.

Samuel Allen, a black poet, captures the spirt of Satchel Paige's career in this short but exciting poem.

STUDY QUESTIONS

1. In this tribute to Satch, why does the poet make Satch the speaker of the poem rather than use a narrator? How does this make the poem more effective?

2. Why does the longevity of Satch's career receive the greatest emphasis?

3. What qualities of Satch's personality and character are brought out? When answering, bear in mind the frustrations he felt and the obstacles he faced.

4. How do the **diction** and **rhythm** of the poem capture the spirit of an athlete whose heart and soul are in what he does?

5. In what "league" is Satch going to do his final pitching? How does the poet use **imagery** to capture Satch's pitching in the "heavenly league"? How does Satch feel about his career and his life as a pitcher?

WRITING

1. Why is a legendary sports hero like Satch an inspiration to so many people? Write a paragraph that explains your point of view.

2. Some athletes keep playing long after others of their age have retired. Name two other athletes and explain why they hold a special appeal for their fans.

THE BASE STEALER

Robert Francis

Poised between going on and back, pulled
Both ways taut like a tightrope-walker,
Fingertips pointing the opposites,
Now bouncing tiptoe like a dropped ball
Or a kid skipping rope, come on, come on,   5
Running a scattering of steps sidewise,
How he teeters, skitters, tingles, teases,
Taunts them, hovers like an ecstatic bird,
He's only flirting, crowd him, crowd him,
Delicate, delicate, delicate, delicate—now!   10

One of the most exciting moments in a baseball game is when a runner steals a base, that is, he runs from one base to another before the ball has been hit by the batter; or, sometimes, before it has even left the pitcher's hand. Stealing a base requires great skill, speed, agility, and the ability to "fake out" the key players on the other team. Notice how Robert Francis captures the delicious tenseness surrounding a runner about to steal a base.

DEFINITIONS AND EXPLANATIONS

taut (line 2)   Tightly drawn.

teeters (line 7)   Moves unsteadily.

skitters (line 7)   Glides lightly or quickly.

ecstatic (line 8)   Full of overpowering emotion.

STUDY QUESTIONS

1. How is the base stealer compared to a tightrope walker? Why is this comparison appropriate?

2. Why does the poet compare the runner to "a dropped ball," "a kid skipping rope," and "an ecstatic bird"? Are these comparisons effective? What **figure of speech** is the poet using when making these comparisons?

3. How does the poet use language to create the tenseness of the runner about to try to steal a base?

4. What effect is created by the poem's being only one sentence long?

5. How would you read the last line of the poem? Why?

WRITING

Think of a situation which made you unusually tense. In a creative poem that uses "The Base Stealer" as a model, try to recapture the tension.

THE DOUBLE PLAY

Robert Wallace

In his sea-lit
distance, the pitcher winding
like a clock about to chime comes down with

the ball, hit
sharply, under the artificial   5
banks of arc lights, bounds like a vanishing string

over the green
to the shortstop magically
scoops to his right whirling above his invisible

shadows   10
in the dust redirects
its flight to the running poised second baseman

pirouettes
leaping, above the slide, to throw
from mid-air, across the colored tightened interval,   15

to the leaning-
out first baseman ends the dance
drawing it disappearing into his long brown glove

continued

The expression "poetry in motion" can be used to describe the flight of a sea gull, the movements of an athlete, or the performance of a dancer. It expresses the deeply felt excitement aroused by the beauty of perfect grace, coordination, and timing. In "The Double Play," Robert Wallace is inspired by poetry in motion on the baseball diamond.

DEFINITIONS AND EXPLANATIONS

banks of arc lights (line 6)   Clusters of powerful artificial lights used in night games to light the field.

invisible shadows (lines 9–10)   The artificial lights are positioned so that shadows are canceled out.

poised (line 12)   Balanced in position.

pirouettes (line 13)   Spins around gracefully; pivots.

casual (line 23)   Cool; nonchalant.

STUDY QUESTIONS

1. Who is the speaker of the poem? Where is he located? How do you know?

2. Summarize, in a narrative paragraph, the poem's sequence of action.

3. How do you know that there was one out before the double play?

4. How do lines 1–2 suggest the distance between a point high up in the stands and the pitcher's mound? How does the phrase "sea-lit" imply a comparison between the view of the mound from above and a diver's view of the sea lit by a diving lamp?

5. According to the **simile** in line 6, how is the moving ball like a vanishing string?

6. How are words like "ball," "shortstop," "second baseman," and "first baseman" used to reflect the speed and uninterrupted movement of the double play? How do the line endings reflect the flowing action of the double play? What is the effect of the odd break between lines 16 and 17?

7. Why do you think the poet chose to describe the shortstop's actions with the phrase "redirects its flight"?

8. The poet **metaphorically** compares the double play to a dance in line 17, line 9 ("whirling") and line 12 ("poised"). Where else does the poet use dance images? What kind of dance seems to be suggested?

stretches. What
is too swift for deception 20
is final, lost, among the loosened figures

jogging off the field
(the pitcher walks), casual
in the space where the poem has happened.

9. How does most of the team leave the field? How does the pitcher leave? Why is there a difference? Explain.

10. What is "the poem" that "has happened" (line 24)?

WRITING

1. Choose a sport that you like and know well. Write a paragraph or two describing the most exciting actions of the sport. Then, convert the prose into poetic form.

2. How could this poem be compared to "The Base Stealer" in terms of style, imagery, approach, and tone?

MUSIC

Listen to a recording of "Take Me Out To the Ballgame." How do the words of the song capture the excitement of baseball?

EX-BASKETBALL PLAYER
John Updike

Pearl Avenue runs past the high-school lot,
Bends with the trolley tracks, and stops, cut off
Before it has a chance to go two blocks,
At Colonel McComsky Plaza. Berth's Garage
Is on the corner facing west, and there,   5
Most days, you'll find Flick Webb, who helps Berth
    out.

Flick stands tall among the idiot pumps—
Five on a side, the old bubble-head style,
Their rubber elbows hanging loose and low.
One's nostrils are two S's, and his eyes   10
An E and O. And one is squat, without
A head at all—more of a football type.

Once Flick played for the high-school team, the
    Wizards.
He was good: in fact, the best. In '46
He bucketed three hundred ninety points,   15
A county record still. The ball loved Flick.
I saw him rack up thirty-eight or forty
In one home game. His hands were like wild birds.

He never learned a trade, he just sells gas,
Checks oil, and changes flats. Once in a while,   20
As a gag, he dribbles an inner tube,
But most of us remember anyway.

continued

Football, basketball, and baseball are the most popular team spectator sports in America. From little leagues to the pros, these sports are big-time, complex, highly organized, extremely competitive, and expensive. The wild enthusiasm of millions of fans, the pressures of owners, alumni, managers, and coaches, the opinions of sportswriters and commentators swirl like gales around most athletes. Questions have been raised about the effect of all this on the athlete as a person. For some, it may be a rich and rewarding life. For others it may be punishing and destructive. "Ex-Basketball Player" tells about a case in which the player, after four years of high-school hero-worship, honor, and glory, suddenly finds it all gone. In addition, he has made no more progress with either his sport or his education.

DEFINITIONS AND EXPLANATIONS

Flick (line 6)   The word "flick" means a light, quick movement.

coiled (line 26)   Tensed as though ready to leap or spring.

tiers (line 29)   Rows of seats.

Necco Wafers, Nibs, and Juju Beads (line 30)   These are the brand names of small candies that come in a mixture of bright colors.

STUDY QUESTIONS

1. Describe Flick Webb's achievements and status as a high-school basketball player. Why was he given the name Flick?

2. What is meant by the **personification** "The ball loved Flick" (line 16) and the **simile** "His hands were like wild birds" (line 18)?

3. What is Flick doing now? What is his status?

4. How does the poet describe Pearl Avenue, the street on which Flick works? How is Pearl Avenue a **symbol** of Flick's life?

His hands are fine and nervous on the lug wrench.
It makes no difference to the lug wrench, though.

Off work, he hangs around Mae's Luncheonette.   25
Grease-gray and kind of coiled, he plays pinball,
Sips lemon cokes, and smokes those thin cigars;
Flick seldom speaks to Mae, just sits and nods
Beyond her face toward bright applauding tiers
Of Necco Wafers, Nibs, and Juju Beads.   30

5. Read the description of the gasoline pumps in the second **stanza**. How are "the idiot pumps/Five on a side" connected to Flick's past life? How do they **ironically** contrast Flick's old life and his present one?

6. The most important element of this poem is what it suggests about Flick's feelings about his present condition. How do each of the following lines show how Flick feels:

Lines 19–21: Is dribbling the inner tube really a gag or only a pretended gag, expressing inner despair?

Lines 23–24: What unhappy contrast is Flick feeling?

Lines 25–26: Why is Flick "coiled"?

Lines 28–30: Note Flick's behavior and the phrase "bright applauding tiers." What is going on in his mind? What terrible **irony** is there in the last line?

Summarize Flick's mental state by explaining how he feels and why he feels that way.

WRITING

1. How might Flick's life have been different had he not been a star athlete? How does the poem answer the question? Explain.

2. Write a journal entry describing how it feels to have had something valuable (whether emotionally or materially) and to have lost it. What is it like to know how things used to be?

THE GREAT SCARF OF BIRDS
John Updike

Playing golf on Cape Ann in October,
I saw something to remember.

Ripe apples were caught like red fish in the nets
of their branches. The maples
were colored like apples,   5
part orange and red, part green.
The elms, already transparent trees,
seemed swaying vases full of sky. The sky
was dramatic with great straggling V's
of geese streaming south, mare's-tails above them.   10
Their trumpeting made us look up and around.
The course sloped into salt marshes,
and this seemed to cause the abundance of birds.

As if out of the Bible
or science fiction,   15
a cloud appeared, a cloud of dots
like iron filings which a magnet
underneath the paper undulates.
It dartingly darkened in spots,
paled, pulsed, compressed, distended, yet   20
held an identity firm: a flock
of starlings, as much one thing as a rock.
One will moved above the trees
the liquid and hesitant drift.

continued

Why are so many people attracted to outdoor sports such as baseball, football, soccer, golf, swimming, surfing, skating, cycling, and jogging? Of course, they are attracted by the fun and challenge of the sport itself. However, as you probably know from your own experience, the outdoor setting is an important part of the pleasure. In this poem, John Updike, an important American author, writes about a beautiful, inspiring October day on the golf course.

DEFINITIONS AND EXPLANATIONS

Cape Ann (line 1) Cape Ann is a picturesque peninsula on the northern coast of Massachusetts. The sea makes its presence felt everywhere on Cape Ann.

V's of geese (lines 9–10) In the autumn, wild geese migrate from northern Canada to the south. In vast numbers, they fly established routes that carry them over the New England coast. They travel at altitudes as high as 9,000 feet above sea level, in V-shaped formations, the leader at the point. They fly rapidly, and they sound wild honks and cackles as they knife across the sky.

mare's-tails (line 10) Long, narrow formations of clouds, appearing very high in the sky and resembling a horse's flying tail in shape.

undulates (line 18) Moves in waves; pulsates.

compressed (line 20) Pressed together; compact.

distended (line 20) Stretched out.

starlings (line 22) These black birds travel in flocks consisting of enormous numbers of birds.

legible (line 26) Readable; able to be made out easily.

Lot's wife (line 29) In the Bible, Lot's wife was turned into a pillar of salt as punishment when she defied the command not to turn and look at the wicked cities of Sodom and Gomorrah, which were being destroyed by the angels of God.

fairway (line 33) The long, grassy stretch of a golf course between the tee and the green. The golfer tries to keep the ball in play along the fairway.

casual (line 43) Unplanned; unpredictable.

billow (line 43) A great surge or swelling.

negligently (line 47) Carelessly.

Come nearer, it became less marvellous,   25
more legible, and merely huge.
''I never saw so many birds!'' my friend exclaimed.
We returned our eyes to the game.
Later, as Lot's wife must have done,
in a pause of walking, not thinking   30
of calling down a consequence,
I lazily looked around.

The rise of the fairway above us was tinted,
so evenly tinted I might not have noticed
but that at the rim of the delicate shadow   35
the starlings were thicker and outlined the flock
as an inkstain in drying pronounces its edges.
The gradual rise of green was vastly covered;
I had thought nothing in nature could be so broad
      but grass.

And as   40
I watched, one bird,
prompted by accident or will to lead,
ceased resting; and, lifting in a casual billow,
the flock ascended as a lady's scarf,
transparent, of gray, might be twitched   45
by one corner, drawn upward and then,
decided against, negligently tossed toward a chair:
the southward cloud withdrew into the air.

Long had it been since my heart
had been lifted as it was by the lifting of that scarf.   50

1. The golfer uses **imagery** to describe the colorful autumn setting. How does he picture the apples in the trees? How does this **simile** reinforce the setting suggested in lines 1 and 12? Why does the golfer say the elm trees are ''transparent'' (line 7)? What are the elm trees compared to? Why is this an effective image? How might you describe the smell and feel of the air as suggested by the images in the poem?

2. How do the **allusions** to the Bible and science fiction (lines 14–15) suggest the effect of the flock on the golfer? Why does the poet refer to Lot's wife, another biblical allusion? Why do you think the golfer is reminded of the Bible as he walks the course?

3. In lines 19–21, how do the words ''paled'' and ''distended'' get at the same meaning in two different ways? Read the lines aloud. How does the poet use **alliteration** to reinforce the description of the flock? Give two examples.

4. Why is the flock compared to iron filings in the **simile** in lines 16–17? How does the phrase ''one will'' (line 23) convey the idea of unity of purpose?

5. Why does the poet say that when the flock comes closer, it becomes ''more legible, and merely huge'' (line 26)? How does the **connotation,** or suggested meaning, of these words contrast with the connotation of the words the golfer uses when he first sees the flock?

6. Why is the flock compared to a scarf (lines 40–48)? How does this **simile** emphasize and describe the movement of the flock?

7. How did the golfer react to seeing the flock lift and ascend? Why?

WRITING

Select another sport in which a natural setting is an important attraction to the participant. Describe the sport and explain why the outdoors would be such a key element.

MUSIC

Play a recording of Ottorino Respighi's *The Birds*. How does the music capture in sound the flight of a flock?

UNDERWATER
Michael Schmidt

Underwater, this is the cathedral
sea. Diving, our bubbles rise
as prayers are said to do, and burst
into our natural atmosphere—
occupying, from this perspective,   5
the position of a heaven.

The ceiling is silver, and the air
deep green translucency. The worshippers
pray quietly, wave their fins.
You can see the color of their prayer   10
deep within their throats: scarlet, some,
and some fine-scaled vermilion; others

pass tight-lipped with moustaches
trailing and long paunches, though
they are almost wafer-thin seen sideways,   15
or unseen except for whiskers.
Further down, timorous sea-spiders
slam their doors, shy fish disappear

into their tenement of holes, and eels
warn that they have serpent tails.   20
Deep is wild, with beasts one meets
usually in dreams. Here the giant octopus
drags in its arms. We meet it.
We are hungry in the upper air, and you

continued

How do you account for the appeal of underwater sports such as scuba diving and snorkeling? What is the unique attraction of these sports as compared with other outdoor sports? How might the feeling a diver experiences be different from what a golfer experiences? In the haunting and powerful poem "Underwater," Michael Schmidt helps the reader to develop a strong sense of the scuba diver's experience by comparing the sea to a cathedral.

DEFINITIONS AND EXPLANATIONS

cathedral (line 1) The great Gothic cathedrals of Europe are among the most notable of all human structures. Their majestic, soaring interiors were designed to express the deep religious spirit of the Middle Ages. Great blocks of stone were used to create reaches of horizontal and vertical spaces that spread outward and upward in splendid archways. Stained glass windows filled the reaches of space with special qualities of light and color.

perspective (line 5) A particular point of view from which a scene is observed.

translucency (line 8) The quality of letting just enough light through so that objects are seen as shadowy and dim.

vermilion (line 12) Bright, yellowish red.

paunches (line 14) Protruding bellies.

timorous (line 17) Timid; afraid.

tenement (line 19) A building with many apartments, usually overcrowded and rundown.

conflagration (line 26) A big, destructive fire.

sanctuary (line 31) Any place of refuge or protection; a holy place. (At one time, fugitives were immune from arrest or punishment in a church or other sacred place and were said to have "sanctuary" when so protected.)

bland (line 34) Soft; mild.

STUDY QUESTIONS

1. Who is the speaker in this poem? Who is the "you" (line 24)?

2. The underwater setting is compared in a **metaphor** to a cathedral (lines 1–2). Why is this an appropriate comparison?

have the sea-spear that shoots deep;   25
you fire accurately, raising a conflagration
of black ink. The animal grabs stone
in slow motion, pulls far under a ledge
and piles the loose rock there as if
to hide might be enough. It holds tight,   30

builds sanctuary, and I think cries
"sanctuary!"—it dies at your second shot.
We come aboveboard then, with our eight-armed
dinner and no hunger left, pursued by the bland
eyes of fish who couldn't care, by black   35
water and the death we made there.

3. How does the scuba diver extend the cathedral **metaphor** with respect to prayers, heaven, the worshippers, and sanctuary? What do the words "ceiling" and "air" (line 7) actually refer to?

4. In the "cathedral sea," the divers commit a sin or desecration. Describe in your own words what they do and what happens. Why do they commit this act, and what is the result? What is the special emotional impact of the crime of murder in a cathedral?

5. Where in the poem does the mood change from a feeling of mystical peace and order to a feeling of chaotic danger, violence, and guilt? In your judgment, why did the poet include these two clashing, contradictory feelings?

WRITING

1. Write a journal entry describing in detail a personal experience you have had with scuba diving, snorkeling, or the sea. How did the experience affect you?

2. Look at photographs of the interiors of some of the great cathedrals of the world (Notre Dame in Paris, Westminster Abbey in London, St. Patrick's in New York). Write a description of the cathedral in which you compare it to the underwater experience (that is, reverse the comparison which Schmidt makes in this poem).

MUSIC

Listen to the first fifteen minutes or so of Wagner's opera *Das Rheingold*, which takes place in the depths of the Rhine river. How does the music capture the grandeur of the river? How do the instruments Wagner chose convey this majesty? How could this music also convey the grandeur of a cathedral?

THE DIVER
Robert Hayden

Sank through easeful
azure. Flower
creatures flashed and
shimmered there—
lost images   5
fadingly remembered.
Swiftly descended
into canyon of cold
nightgreen emptiness.
Freefalling, weightless   10
as in dreams of
wingless flight,
plunged through infra-
space and came to
the dead ship,   15
carcass that swarmed with
voracious life.
Angelfish, their
lively blue and
yellow prised from   20
darkness by the
flashlight's beam,
thronged her portholes.
Moss of bryozoans
blurred, obscured her   25
metal. Snappers,
gold groupers explored her,
fearless of bubbling
manfish. I entered
the wreck, awed by her silence,   30

continued

Scuba diving to study sunken vessels and to observe the sea life surrounding the vessel is a popular sport. There is a feeling of wonder which many divers experience as they enter a special world created by nature but also containing objects made by people. Images of diving also occur again and again in dreams. This poem seems at first to describe a diver's awe as he floats downward towards a sunken ship. But, is that all it means?

DEFINITIONS AND EXPLANATIONS

azure (line 2)   The blue color of the clear sky.

infraspace (lines 13–14)   Literally "below space." In this case, the word refers to the sea.

voracious (line 17)   Ravenous or insatiably eager; here, the word refers to the vast amount of sea life and its almost frenzied activity.

prised (line 20)   Captured, as in a prize.

bryozoans (line 24)   These are sea animals which attach themselves to wrecks and other undersea objects in branched or mossy colonies. They reproduce by budding.

ectoplasmic (line 37)   Here, ghostly mysteriousness.

eldritch (line 43)   Weird or eerie; mysterious.

languid (line 54)   Slow and sluggish.

STUDY QUESTIONS

1. What **image** does the opening of the poem create? How is the voyage to the ship like a dream?

2. How is the "dead ship" still alive? What effect does it have on the diver?

3. How is the past reflected in what the diver sees? How does he react to his visions?

4. Explain the phrase "in languid/ frenzy strove, as/one freezing fights off/ sleep desiring sleep." What does the diver seem to want?

5. How does the use of the phrase "respirator's brittle belling" at the end of the poem change the poem's meaning suddenly? What does "reflex of life-wish" mean?

feeling more keenly
the iron cold.
With flashlight probing
fogs of water
saw the sad slow   35
dance of gilded
chairs, the ectoplasmic
swirl of garments,
drowned instruments
of buoyancy,   40
drunken shoes. Then
livid gesturings,
eldritch hide and
seek of laughing
faces. I yearned to   45
find those hidden
ones, to fling aside
the mask and call to them,
yield to rapturous
whisperings, have   50
done with self and
every dinning
vain complexity.
Yet in languid
frenzy strove, as   55
one freezing fights off
sleep desiring sleep;
strove against the
cancelling arms that
suddenly surrounded   60
me, fled the numbing
kisses that I craved.
Reflex of life-wish?
Respirator's brittle
belling? Swam from   65
the ship somehow;
somehow began the
measured rise.

6. Based upon your answer to question 5, explain how the ship and the diver are used as **symbols**.

7. Why does the poet compare the actions and emotions of this sport to a near-death experience?

8. How does the pattern of the lines (**rhythm** and length) create the effect of a diver sinking down into the deep?

WRITING

This poem uses imagery very effectively to create a mood of mystery and "otherworldliness." In an essay, explain exactly how imagery is used throughout the poem.

THE SWIMMING LESSON

Mary Oliver

Feeling the icy kick, the endless waves
Reaching around my life, I moved my arms
And coughed, and in the end saw land.

Somebody, I suppose,
Remembering the medieval maxim,   5
Had tossed me in,
Had wanted me to learn to swim,

Not knowing that none of us, who ever came back
From that long lonely fall and frenzied rising,
Ever learned anything at all   10
About swimming, but only
How to put off, one by one,
Dreams and pity, love and grace—
How to survive in any place.

What is the best way to learn how to swim? Should a child be given lessons and gradually introduced into the water, or should the youngster be thrown in and expected to fend for himself or herself? How do you feel about the sink-or-swim philosophy of teaching somebody to swim? How could this approach to swimming or, for that matter, to life be damaging? Mary Oliver, in "The Swimming Lesson," has something to say about this.

DEFINITIONS AND EXPLANATIONS

medieval (line 5)   Belonging to the Middle Ages. The word sometimes has the meaning of lacking knowledge, understanding, or enlightenment.

maxim (line 5)   A rule or principle of conduct.

frenzied (line 9)   Excited and fearful; frantic.

STUDY QUESTIONS

1. Who might the "somebody" in line 4 have been?

2. Explain the method for teaching a child to swim alluded to by the **alliterative** phrase "medieval maxim" in line 5. Why does the speaker describe the process as "medieval"? How do you think she feels about it? How do you feel about the method?

3. In lines 1–3, an adult recalls an early childhood experience. How do you know the memory is clear and vivid? How did the original experience probably affect the young child? What does the speaker mean when she says "reaching around my life" in line 2?

4. How did the shock of being thrown into the water shape the child's view of life? How did this view result from the experience? Explain how the action can also be a **metaphor** for the betrayal of the trusting bond which exists between a youngster and his or her parents.

5. How did the adult in the poem probably feel about the wisdom of tossing the child into the water? How did the child feel about it? Why?

WRITING

Describe other experiences children have in their relationships with adults that can result in distrust or dislike. What is the ideal relationship for children to have with adults? How can that be established?

THE SKATER OF GHOST LAKE
William Rose Benét

Ghost Lake's a dark lake, a deep lake and cold:
Ice black as ebony, frostily scrolled;
Far in its shadows a faint sound whirrs;
Steep stand the sentineled deep, dark firs.

A brisk sound, a swift sound, a ring-tinkle-ring;　　5
Flit-flit,—a shadow, with a stoop and a swing,
Flies from a shadow through the crackling cold.
Ghost Lake's a deep lake, a dark lake and old!

Leaning and leaning, with a stride and a stride,
Hands locked behind him, scarf blowing wide,　　10
Jeremy Randall skates, skates late,
Star for a candle, moon for a mate.

Black is the clear glass now that he glides,
Crisp is the whisper of long lean strides,
Swift is his swaying—but pricked ears hark.　　15
None comes to Ghost Lake late after dark!

Cecily only,—yes, it is she!
Stealing to Ghost Lake, tree after tree,
Kneeling in snow by the still lake side,
Rising with feet winged, gleaming, to glide.　　20

Dust of the ice swirls. Here is his hand.
Brilliant his eyes burn. Now, as was planned,
Arm across arm twined, laced to his side,
Out on the dark lake lightly they glide.

Dance of the dim moon, a rhythmical reel,　　25
A swaying, a swift tune,—skurr of the steel;
Moon for a candle, maid for a mate,
Jeremy Randall skates, skates late.

Black as if lacquered the wide lake lies;
Breath is a frost-fume, eyes seek eyes;　　30
Souls are a sword-edge tasting the cold.
Ghost Lake's a deep lake, a dark lake and old!

continued

Have you ever gone ice skating on a pond or lake on a clear, crisp winter night? What sights stand out in your mind? What sounds? What sensations? What do you remember as the dominant mood of the experience? Is night skating an ideal romantic setting for two sweethearts? This is a story poem about two night skaters, a poem that will haunt your memory for a long time.

DEFINITIONS AND EXPLANATIONS

ebony (line 2)   A hard, black wood.

scrolled (line 2)   Etched or carved with curved designs.

sentineled (line 4)   Standing like guards.

firs (line 4)   Tall, straight evergreen trees.

reel (line 25)   A dance characterized by circular and gliding movements.

skurr (line 26)   This is an **onomatopoeic** word imitating the sound of skate blades on ice.

lacquered (line 29)   Having a highly polished, smooth surface.

bound (line 35)   Edge; boundary.

veers (line 43)   Changes direction.

STUDY QUESTIONS

1. How does the poet create a mysterious opening for the poem? How does he first indicate the presence of a human being? Describe Jeremy's appearance and movements. Why are Cecily's feet described as "winged" (line 20)?

2. Why do you think Cecily and Jeremy are meeting secretly at night? What do they say and do when they meet? What words and sounds indicate the first warning of danger? How does the poet use language to hint at the death of the lovers?

3. The reader must use his or her imagination to complete this mysterious story of two lovers meeting late at night to skate on a dark, lonely, dangerous lake. Who do you think Jeremy and Cecily are? Why are they meeting in such a secretive way? How does the poet create the atmosphere of danger which seems to surround them?

4. Mystery, suspense, and danger are suggested by the name "Ghost Lake." The tall fir trees around the lake are described in line 4 as standing like senti-

Far in the shadows hear faintly begin
Like a string pluck-plucked of a violin,
Muffled in mist on the lake's far bound,   35
Swifter and swifter, a low singing sound!

Far in the shadows and faint on the verge
Of blue cloudy moonlight, see it emerge,
Flit-flit,—a phantom, with a stoop and a swing . . .
Ah, it's a night bird, burdened of wing!   40

Pressed close to Jeremy, laced to his side,
Cecily Culver, dizzy you glide.
Jeremy Randall sweepingly veers
Out on the dark ice far from the piers.

"Jeremy!" "Sweetheart?" "What do you fear?"   45
"Nothing, my darling,—nothing is here!"
"Jeremy?" "Sweetheart?" "What do you flee?"
"Something—I know not; something I see!"

Swayed to a swift stride, brisker of pace,
Leaning and leaning, they race and they race;   50
Ever that whirring, that crisp sound thin
Like a string pluck-plucked of a violin;

Ever that swifter and low singing sound
Sweeping behind them, winding them round;
Gasp of their breath now that chill flakes fret;   55
Ice black as ebony,—blacker—like jet!

Ice shooting fangs forth—sudden—like spears;
Crackling of lightning,—a roar in their ears!
Shadowy, a phantom swerves off from its prey . . .
No, it's a night bird flit-flits away!   60

Low-winging moth-owl, home to your sleep!
Ghost Lake's a still lake, a cold lake and deep.
Faint in its shadows a far sound whirrs.
Black stand the ranks of its sentinel firs.

nels, alert and on guard. List other words and phrases that suggest mystery, suspense, and danger. Explain how the poet uses them effectively.

5. How does the poet use both **rhythm** and **rhyme** scheme to reinforce musically the movement of the characters across the lake? How does he express the sounds that break the silence of the lake at night? Why do the sounds of the letters ''s'' and ''z'' dominate in the words of the poem? How else does the poet use **alliteration** and **onomatopoeia** to contribute to the total impact of the poem?

WRITING

Obviously, this poem is the tragic end to a love story. Write your own story about the events leading up to the poem. Try to make your characters as vivid as possible.

TO JAMES
Frank Horne

Do you remember
How you won
That last race . . . ?
How you flung your body
At the start . . .   5
How your spikes
Ripped the cinders
In the stretch . . .
How you catapulted
Through the tape . . .   10
Do you remember . . . ?
Don't you think
I lurched with you
Out of those starting holes . . . ?
Don't you think   15
My sinews tightened
At those first
Few strides . . .
And when you flew into the stretch
Was not all my thrill   20
Of a thousand races
In your blood . . . ?
At your final drive
Through the finish line
Did not my shout   25
Tell of the
Triumphant ecstasy
Of victory . . . ?

continued

$\mathbf{T}$hough running has become a very popular sport in recent years, it is, in fact, one of the oldest. When the Olympic games first started in ancient Greece, the contests consisted almost entirely of a variety of footraces. Though the modern Olympics are much more varied, the track events are still the core of this athletic competition. In "To James," Frank Horne, an African-American poet, compares winning a race to succeeding in life.

DEFINITIONS AND EXPLANATIONS

spikes (line 6)   In outdoor racing, the runners' shoes may be equipped with spikes that can dig into the ground without any slipping and give the athletes the fullest return on their efforts.

cinders (line 7)   The outdoor track is sometimes surfaced with cinders to give the runner a dry, firm foothold.

stretch (line 8)   On a curved track, the stretch is the straight length leading to the finish line. In all cases, the stretch is the final part of the race when runners put forth all the strength and effort left in them.

catapulted (line 9)   Hurled forward with great force.

tape (line 10)   The string stretched across the track at the finish line. The victor breaks the tape with his or her chest when crossing the finish line.

lurched (line 13)   Suddenly shot forward.

starting holes (line 14)   At the starting point, the runners are in a tense, crouched position, ready to spring forward at the firing of the starting gun. They lean forward on their fingertips. Their legs are behind them with toes braced into holes for the fastest possible kick from the starting line. Nowadays, special blocks are often used instead of starting holes.

sinews (line 16)   The tough fibers that connect muscle to bone.

STUDY QUESTIONS

1. Who is James? What is the relationship of the speaker to James? How do lines 12–14, lines 20–22, and lines 29–31 add to the reader's impressions of the speaker?

2. How do the line lengths and the **rhythms** of this poem (as well as the words) reveal this to be a sprint?

Live
As I have taught you   30
To run, Boy—
It's a short dash
Dig your starting holes
Deep and firm
Lurch out of them   35
Into the straightaway
With all the power
That is in you
Look straight ahead
To the finish line   40
Think only of the goal
Run straight
Run high
Run hard
Save nothing   45
And finish
With an ecstatic burst
That carries you
Hurtling
Through the tape   50
To victory . . .

3. The poem is about two races, a real one and a **metaphorical** one. At what point does the speaker begin to talk about the metaphorical race? How do each of the following lines have both a literal and metaphorical meaning?

"It's a short dash" (line 32)

"Dig your starting holes
  Deep and firm" (lines 33–34)

"Think only of the goal" (line 41)

"To victory" (line 51)

4. Why might the speaker have wanted to say the words of this poem to James?

5. How does knowing that the poet is black affect the way one might respond to question 4?

WRITING

1. Describe an incident in your life in which you worked very hard to succeed. How does the incident you selected parallel "To James"?

2. Write a brief essay in which you persuade a friend not to give up on something but to keep on trying to succeed. Explain why the person shouldn't give up, and make a comparison between his or her efforts and a sport.

3. Write a vivid description of the speaker of "To James." Before writing, make decisions about the speaker's age, build, facial appearance, voice, mannerisms, style of dress, etc.

DICK SZYMANSKI
Ogden Nash

The life of an offensive center
Is one that few could wish to enter.
You'll note that that of Dick Szymanski
Is not all roses and romanski.
He centers the ball, he hears a roar — 5
Is it a fumble, or a score?
What's happening he can only wonder.
Because he's upside down, down under.
He accomplishes amazing feats.
And what gets photographed? His cleats. 10

Are you a football fan? How many outstanding quarterbacks or running backs can you name? On the other hand, how many offensive linemen, particularly centers, can you name? The sad, sad fact is that all the fame and glory go to the passers and the runners. The center, who takes all the fierce crunch of the pileup as the two teams clash at the line, is unnoticed and unknown, literally and figuratively buried in the heap. Ogden Nash, a well-known humorous poet, has a little fun with this fact.

EXPLANATION

Dick Szymanski (title)   Szymanski was one of the outstanding centers in pro football during the 1950's. At the height of his career, he played for the Baltimore Colts.

STUDY QUESTIONS

1. Explain the humor of lines 5–6.

2. Why can Szymanski "only wonder" (line 7)?

3. Explain the **anticlimax** in lines 9–10.

4. How does Nash use questions to add to the humor of the poem?

5. Nash is especially known for clever, funny, often highly inventive **rhymes.** Give one example. Why is it funny?

WRITING

1. Write a brief, humorous poem. Feel free to use unusual rhymes or alter words as Ogden Nash does.

2. In this poem, Ogden Nash pokes gentle fun at one aspect of football. Have you ever seen a sporting event where something humorous occurred? Write a brief paragraph describing the humorous incident. Be as detailed as possible in your narrative, and try to write with a humorous slant.

MUSIC

The song "Pass the Football" from Leonard Bernstein's musical *Wonderful Town* (Lyrics by Betty Comden and Adolph Green) presents a different view of football from the poem. Explain this view and react to it.

MORNING WORK-OUT
Babette Deutsch

The sky unfolding its blanket to free
The morning.
Chill on the air. Clean odor of stables.
The grandstand green as the turf,
The pavilion flaunting its brilliance   5
For no one.
Beyond hurdles and hedges, swans, circling, cast
A contemplative radiance over the willow's shadows.
Day pales the toteboard lights,
Gilds the balls, heightens the stripes of the poles.   10
Dirt shines. White glisten of rails.
The track is bright as brine.
Their motion a flowing.
From prick of the ear to thick tail's shimmering drift,
The horses file forth.   15
Pink nostrils quiver, as who know they are showing
      their colors.
Ankles lift, as who hear without listening.
The bay, the brown, the chestnut, the roan have
      loaned
Their grace to the riders who rise in the stirrups, or
      hunch
Over the withers, gentling with mumbled song.   20
A mare ambles past, liquid eye askance.
Three, then four, canter by: voluptuous power
Pours through their muscles,
Dancing in pulse and nerve.
They glide in the stretch as on skis.   25

continued

Horse racing has been called "the sport of kings and the king of sports." For some the attraction is merely the thrill of gambling, for others the social occasion, for still others the glamour of the race-track setting. For the true lover of the sport, however, the central lure is the spectacle of the animal itself, the pure power and grace of the magnificent thoroughbred in action. This poem, whose setting is the racetrack during workout time in the early morning, savors the beauty of the racing thoroughbred.

DEFINITIONS AND EXPLANATIONS

contemplative (line 8) Quietly thoughtful; pensive.

radiance (line 8) Glowing or shining light.

toteboard (line 9) The board that displays in lights the betting status of the horses.

brine (line 12). Salt water; the ocean.

withers (line 20) The highest part of the back of a horse, located between the shoulder blades.

canter (line 22) Move at a slow, easy gallop.

voluptuous (line 22) Giving pleasure to the senses.

Centaur (line 28) In Greek mythology, a creature with a man's head, chest, and arms and a horse's body and legs.

wuthering (line 29) Galloping with the head and neck turned slightly sideways.

unsyllabled (line 31) Unbroken; flowing smoothly.

eloquence (line 31) Verbal expression that is forceful, fluent, and graceful.

girths (line 36) The bands around the bellies of the horses which hold the saddles in place.

haunches (line 36) Hindquarters of the horse.

paradigm (line 38) An example; a perfect model.

azuring (line 41) Turning blue.

Two
Are put to a drive:
Centaur energy bounding as the dirt shudders, flies
Under the wuthering pace,
Hushes the hooves' thunders,   30
The body's unsyllabled eloquence rapidly
Dying away.
Dark-skinned stable-boys, as proud as kin
Of their display of vivacity, elegance,
Walk the racers back.   35
Foam laces the girths, sweaty haunches glow.
Slowly returning from the track, the horse is
Animal paradigm of innocence, discipline, force.
Blanketed, they go in.
Odor of earth   40
Enriches azuring air.

1. How do the opening twelve lines set the scene in sharp, sense-appealing **images**? What is the effect of "For no one" (line 6)?

2. How does the poet describe the first appearance of the horses? What activities follow? What relationship between horse and rider is suggested in lines 18–20 and line 28?

3. How are "unsyllabled" and "eloquence" (line 31) used **metaphorically** to express the velocity of the two horses on the track?

4. Why does the odor of earth enrich the air after the workout?

WRITING

Line 38 suggests that the horse is the perfect model of "innocence, discipline, force." Can human athletes be put into the same category? Explain in an expository paragraph or two.

Sports

1. **Memorable lines** Poetry offers the pleasure of memorable or quotable lines. Begin to make your own collection of memorable lines. From the poems in this unit, select two passages of one line or several lines with which to begin your collection. The basis of your selection may be strength of image, music of line, depth of emotion, appeal of theme, or any combination of these. Write the passages in your notebook with title and author. Memorizing the lines will give you added pleasure.

2. Briefly review the poems in this unit. Then, answer the following questions:

    a. How is "To Satch" a true tribute to a real sports figure?

    b. How does "Underwater" deal with violence in sports?

    c. How does "The Great Scarf of Birds" emphasize the beauty of the natural setting of a sport?

    d. How does "The Double Play" delight in "poetry in motion"?

    e. How do "Ex-Basketball Player" and "The Swimming Lesson" probe a negative aspect of sports other than violence? What point do they make?

    f. How are "The Diver" and "Underwater" alike?

3. Show your knowledge of terms in poetry. Here are five short passages from the poems in this unit. Choosing from the list of terms that follows, name the term applicable to the passage and explain why the passage is an example of the term you selected.

        simile   onomatopoeia
        metaphor   anticlimax
        alliteration

    a. "He accomplishes amazing feats.
       And what gets photographed? His cleats."
      —Ogden Nash: "Dick Szymanski"

    b. "... a string pluck-plucked of a violin,"
      —William Rose Benét: "The Skater of Ghost Lake"

c. "... at the rim of the delicate shadow
    the starlings were thicker and outlined the flock
    as an inkstain in drying pronounces its edges."
    —John Updike: "The Great Scarf of Birds"

d. "Underwater, this is the cathedral sea."
    —Michael Schmidt: "Underwater"

e. "How he teeters, skitters, tingles, teases,"
    —Robert Francis: "The Base Stealer"

4. Review your knowledge of vocabulary by choosing the numbered word or phrase whose meaning is closest to the underlined word.

a. bland   (1) exciting (2) quiet (3) mild
                (4) active (5) unaware

b. casual   (1) deliberate (2) specific (3) autocratic
                (4) nonchalant (5) mendacious

c. catapult   (1) hurl forward (2) pull backwards (3) ease
                ahead
                (4) grab swiftly (5) attack quickly

d. frenzied   (1) frantic (2) fanatical (3) frothy
                (4) fatuous (5) familiar

e. distended   (1) concluded (2) involved (3) enlarged
                (4) compressed (5) deleted

f. The writer's favorite maxim was "A penny saved is a penny earned."
                (1) ideal (2) belief (3) rhyme (4) rule (5) summary

g. The ballet dancer was very adept at the pirouette.
                (1) leap (2) pivot (3) grand duet
                (4) waltz (5) cakewalk

h. The school building served as a sanctuary for those escaping the violent hurricane.
                (1) enclosure (2) ideal location (3) change of pace
                (4) safe place (5) place of doom

i. The appearance of ghosts in the mist was an eldritch experience for the young archaeologist.
                (1) unusual (2) new (3) frightening
                (4) unnerving (5) eerie

j. The excellent work served as a paradigm for all to follow.
                (1) version (2) duplicate (3) model
                (4) copy (5) figurehead

5. Poems and paintings Poets and painters are artists who have much in common. Study each of the reproductions of paintings that follow. Examine the image carefully. Just what do you see? What feelings does the picture suggest? If a person or persons appear, try to flesh out in your mind their background and character. Is rhythm, metaphor, or symbol important in the picture? After you have studied each picture in this way, select the one that you associate most powerfully with one of the poems in this unit. Be ready to discuss or write about your choice and the reasons for it.

Optional: Select one picture that inspires you to write your own poem, and write the poem.

MAX SCHMITT IN A SINGLE SCULL
Thomas Eakins. *1871. The Metropolitan Museum of Art,*
Purchase, 1934 Alfred N. Punnett Fund and Gift of George D. Pratt.

STATE PARK Jared French. *1946. Whitney Museum, New York.*
Egg tempera on composition board. Sight: 23½ × 23½ in. Gift of Mr. and
Mrs. R. H. Donnelly Erdman 65.78.

HEAD OF JOAN
Richard Lahey. *1931.*
Whitney Museum,
New York.
Oil on composition
board.
23¾ × 19¾ in.
Purchase
31.273.

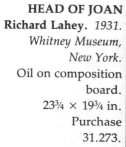

NORTHEASTER Winslow Homer. *1895. The Metropolitan Museum of Art,* Gift of George A. Hearn, 1910.

DEMPSEY AND FIRPO George Bellows. *1924. Whitney Museum, New York.* Oil on canvas. 51 × 63¼ in. Purchase, with funds from Gertrude Vanderbilt Whitney 31.95.

Freedom and Diversity

Movements celebrating freedom and cultural diversity in America have become quite prominent recently. Yet the quest for individual freedom and the acceptance of a multicultural society joined together by common bonds has long been the dream of many Americans. In an ideal, all-inclusive world, everyone works together to reach his or her potential.

It is, however, much easier to hold the dream than to shape it into reality. The stifling of freedom and diversity takes many forms, from economic, political, and social to educational and psychological. Inequality of opportunity, secrecy and deception in government, greed in business, and even the misguided teachings of a parent to a child can all act to create division and hatred rather than foster unity and acceptance. It must always be asked whether freedom and acceptance of diversity are societal issues or whether they lie primarily within an individual's own character and personality.

from *SONG OF MYSELF*
Walt Whitman

1

I celebrate myself, and sing myself,
And what I assume you shall assume,
For every atom belonging to me as good belongs to
    you.

I loafe and invite my soul,
I lean and loafe at my ease observing a spear of
    summer grass. . . .   5

6

A child said *What is the grass?* fetching it to me with
    full hands;
How could I answer the child? I do not know what it
    is any more than he.

I guess it must be the flag of my disposition, out of
    hopeful green stuff woven.

Or I guess it is the handkerchief of the Lord,
A scented gift and remembrancer designedly dropt,   10
Bearing the owner's name someway in the corners,
    that we may see and remark, and say *Whose?* . . .

And now it seems to me the beautiful uncut hair of
    graves.

Tenderly will I use you, curling grass.
It may be you transpire from the breasts of young
    men;
It may be if I had known them I would have loved
    them;   15

continued

Walt Whitman, thought by many critics to be the greatest American poet, is certainly foremost as a champion of the American dream of fostering individuality, freedom, and acceptance of diversity. An advocate for the ordinary man, Whitman, who served in the Civil War, believed that each person should be accepted on the basis of his merits and not on the basis of his ethnic background or sexual orientation. These excerpts from Whitman's long and most famous poem express his highly original thoughts about what it means to be a human being who is free and at one with the beauty of nature.

DEFINITIONS AND EXPLANATIONS

remembrancer (line 10)   Souvenir; keepsake.

transpire (line 14)   Pass through.

sprout (line 28)   The first shoot of growth from a seed or a branch.

Vivas (line 34)   Cheers.

engagements (line 37)   Battles.

curlacue (line 46)   A line of curves and curls (usually spelled ''curlicue'').

august (line 47)   Dignified and majestic.

vindicate (line 48)   Justify; prove right.

tenon'd and mortis'd (line 56)   Formed into a very strong joint, as in the joining of two pieces of wood.

dissolution (line 57)   Death; disintegration.

amplitude (line 58)   Great size or extent.

voluptuous (line 64)   Richly and fully satisfying to the senses.

vitreous (line 67)   Glasslike.

limpid (line 69)   Clear.

pismire (line 73)   Ant.

chef-d'oeuvre (line 74)   Masterpiece.

infidels (line 78)   Nonbelievers.

placid (line 79)   Calm.

demented (line 84)   Crazed.

barbaric (line 95)   Wild and unrestrained.

yawp (line 95)   A loud call or cry.

scud (line 96)   Clouds or spray driven by the wind.

1. In the first line of the poem, Whitman is optimistic, cheerful, and full of a sense of his own individual worth. Select three or four other examples of lines that express these characteristics and explain how they do so.

2. Whitman's sense of his individual worth is rooted in a global philosophy about humanity and nature which extends beyond the individual. Explain this philosophy in detail. How does each of the following passages help you to understand Whitman's philosophy?

Lines 8–10	Line 53
Lines 33–34	Lines 64–71
Line 39	Lines 75–78
Lines 44–46	Lines 86–87

3. Because the poem is written in **free verse** (without using a regular **rhythm** or **meter**) much of its poetic effect is gained through the use of other devices, examples of which are listed below. Read the list, then find a second example of each device and explain how it helps to make the poem effective.

alliteration
"A scented gift and remembrancer designedly dropt" (line 10)

repetition
"It may be you transpire from the breasts of young men;
It may be if I had known them I would have loved them;
It may be you are from old people, . . ." (lines 14–16)

emphatic rhythms
"With music strong I come, with my cornets and my drums" (line 30)

colorful diction
"Vivas to those who have fail'd!" (line 34)

imagery
". . .earth of the mountains misty-topt!" (line 66)

metaphor
"I guess it must be the flag of my disposition, out of hopeful green stuff woven." (line 8)

personification
"Press close bare-bosom'd night. . ." (line 61)

hyperbole
"And a mouse is miracle enough to stagger sextillions of infidels." (line 78)

4. Whitman deals with both his sense of his own importance and his death. How does Whitman view his death? How does the underlying philosophy of the poem explain the poet's interest in these two subjects?

5. Give three examples from the poem which prove that Whitman is an enthusiastic champion of free individuality. Explain why you chose each example.

WRITING

1. Select two freedoms that you consider essential in today's society. Write an essay explaining why those freedoms are important.

2. Select two freedoms that you consider important but are being challenged. Write an essay persuading a court to accept your point of view.

Whitman wrote that, for him, music was the omnipotent "combiner, nothing more spiritual, nothing more sensuous, a god, yet completely human." How is "Song of Myself" musical? Whitman's poem "When Lilacs Last in the Dooryard Bloom'd," written after the assassination of Abraham Lincoln, was set to music by the American composer Roger Sessions in 1971. Sessions dedicated his piece to the memory of Martin Luther King, Jr., and John F. Kennedy. Read the poem and listen to a recording of the music. How does the poem express views similar to those of "Song of Myself"? How does the music capture those views?

Song of Myself

It may be you are from old people, and from women,
    and from offspring taken soon out of their
    mothers' laps.
And here you are the mothers' laps.

This grass is very dark to be from the white heads of
    old mothers,
Darker than the colorless beards of old men,
Dark to come from under the faint red roofs of
    mouths.   20
O I perceive after all so many uttering tongues,
And I perceive they do not come from the roofs of
    mouths for nothing.

I wish I could translate the hints about the dead
    young men and women,
And the hints about old men and mothers, and the
    offspring taken soon out of their laps.

What do you think has become of the young and old
    men?   25
And what do you think has become of the women
    and children?

They are alive and well somewhere;
The smallest spout shows there is really no
    death, . . .

continued

51

All goes onward and outward—nothing collapses.

18

With music strong I come, with my cornets and my
    drums,   30
I play not marches for accepted victors only, I play
    marches for conquer'd and slain persons.

Have you heard that it was good to gain the day?
I also say it is good to fall, battles are lost in the same
    spirit in which they are won.

Vivas to those who have fail'd!
And to those whose war-vessels sank in the sea!   35
And to those themselves who sank in the sea!

And to all generals that lost engagements, and all
    overcome heroes!
And the numberless unknown heroes equal to the
    greatest heroes known!

20

In all people I see myself, none more and not one a
    barley-corn less,
And the good or bad I say of myself I say of them.   40

I know I am solid and sound,
To me the converging objects of the universe
    perpetually flow,
All are written to me, and I must get what the writing
    means.

I know I am deathless,
I know this orbit of mine cannot be swept by a
    carpenter's compass,   45
I know I shall not pass like a child's curlacue cut with
    a burnt stick at night.

I know I am august,
I do not trouble my spirit to vindicate itself or be
    understood,
I see that the elementary laws never apologize, . . .

I exist as I am, that is enough,   50
If no other in the world be aware I sit content,
And if each and all be aware I sit content.

One world is aware and by far the largest to me, and
    that is myself,
And whether I come to my own today or in ten
    thousand or ten million years,
I can cheerfully take it now, or with equal
    cheerfulness I can wait.   55

My foothold is tenon'd and mortis'd in granite,
I laugh at what you call dissolution,
And I know the amplitude of time.

21

I am he that walks with the tender and growing
    night,
I call to the earth and sea half-held by the night.   60

Press close bare-bosom'd night—press close magnetic
    nourishing night!
Night of south winds—night of the large few stars!
Still nodding night—mad naked summer night.

Smile O voluptuous cool-breath'd earth!
Earth of the slumbering and liquid trees!   65
Earth of departed sunset—earth of the mountains
    misty-topt!
Earth of the vitreous pour of the full moon just tinged
    with blue!
Earth of shine and dark mottling the tide of the river!
Earth of the limpid gray of clouds brighter and clearer
    for my sake!

continued

Far-swooping elbow'd earth—rich apple-blossom'd
        earth!   70
Smile, for your lover comes.

31

I believe a leaf of grass is no less than the
        journeywork of the stars,
And the pismire is equally perfect, and a grain of
        sand, and the egg of the wren,
And the tree-toad is a chef-d'oeuvre for the highest,
And the running blackberry would adorn the parlors
        of heaven,   75
And the narrowest hinge in my hand puts to scorn all
        machinery,
And the cow crunching with depress'd head
        surpasses any statue,
And a mouse is miracle enough to stagger sextillions
        of infidels.

32

I think I could turn and live with animals, they are so
        placid and self-contain'd,
I stand and look at them long and long.   80

They do not sweat and whine about their condition,
They do not lie awake in the dark and weep for their
        sins,
They do not make me sick discussing their duty to God,
Not one is dissatisfied, not one is demented with the
        mania of owning things, . . .
Not one is respectable or unhappy over the whole
        earth.   85

In the faces of men and women I see God, and in my
    own face in the glass,
I find letters from God dropt in the street, and every
    one is sign'd by God's name,
And I leave them where they are, for I know that
    wheresoe'er I go,
Others will punctually come for ever and ever.

51

Do I contradict myself?   90
Very well then I contradict myself,
(I am large, I contain multitudes.)

52

The spotted hawk swoops by and accuses me, he
    complains of my gab and my loitering.

I too am not a bit tamed, I too am untranslatable,
I sound my barbaric yawp over the roofs of the
    world.   95

The last scud of day holds back for me,
It flings my likeness after the rest and true as any on
    the shadow'd wilds,
It coaxes me to the vapor and the dusk. . . .

I bequeath myself to the dirt to grow from the grass I
    love;
If you want me again look for me under your boot-
    soles.   100

You will hardly know who I am or what I mean,
But I shall be good health to you nevertheless,
And filter and fibre your blood.

Failing to fetch me at first keep encouraged,
Missing me one place search another,   105
I stop somewhere waiting for you.

DREAM VARIATION

Langston Hughes

To fling my arms wide
In some place of the sun,
To whirl and to dance
Till the white day is done.
Then rest at cool evening   5
Beneath a tall tree
While night comes on gently,
    Dark like me—
That is my dream!

To fling my arms wide   10
In the face of the sun,
Dance! Whirl! Whirl!
Till the quick day is done.
Rest at pale evening. . .
A tall, slim tree. . .   15
Night coming tenderly
    Black like me.

What is it that some people find exciting about dancing? In some cases, dancing represents an escape from reality, an opportunity to lose oneself in music and physical expression. Many people dance on happy occasions to demonstrate their joy and delight. The dance in Langston Hughes's poem, however, takes on a deeper meaning.

STUDY QUESTIONS

1. How would you describe the mood created by the opening of this poem?

2. What is the speaker's dream?

3. What do the whirling and dancing represent?

4. How is the day different from the evening?

5. Why, in the second **stanza**, does the speaker want to fling his arms "In the face of the sun"?

6. Explain the last two lines of the poem.

WRITING

If you were writing music for this poet's dance, what would it sound like? What speeds would you use? How would the volume change? What instruments would you use? Answer the foregoing questions and explain your responses fully. If you can perform the music to your dance and/or the dance itself, do so for your class.

MUSIC

The wild, whirling dance that the poem speaks of is passionate and intense. It celebrates freedom. One piece of classical music that also reflects this uncontrolled emotion is the "Danse Sacrale" from Igor Stravinsky's *Rite of Spring*. Listen to this selection and explain how the tempo, the dynamics, and the orchestration help to create the piece's mood.

MUCH MADNESS IS DIVINEST SENSE

Emily Dickinson

Much Madness is divinest Sense—
To a discerning Eye—
Much Sense—the starkest Madness—
'Tis the Majority
In this, as All, prevail—   5
Assent—and you are sane—
Demur—you're straightway dangerous—
And handled with a Chain—

The right to exhibit individualism, to support diversity, to be a member of a minority group, to take a new or unpopular stand, is one of the most valuable components of the American dream. Yet, America is a land of contradictions, its practices not always in harmony with its ideals. America has not always been kind to those who have disagreed with the political and social mainstream—women suffragists, early labor organizers, Viet Nam veterans, and civil rights leaders, for example. This short, powerful poem sums up this American contradiction by implying that the majority opinion may often be ''Madness'' which, because it is held by most people, is accepted as ''Sense.''

DEFINITIONS AND EXPLANATIONS

Emily Dickinson had a fiercely independent mind and spirit. In her physical life, she seemed to express this independence in a negative way, for she withdrew from society, finally becoming almost a total recluse. In her mental life, she gave more positive expression to her independence. She championed the cause of abolition of slavery, for example. Above all, she expressed her devotion to the supreme value of individuality and to freedom in many hundreds of short, brilliant poems.

discerning (line 2)   Observing with understanding; clearly recognizing a difference.

starkest (line 3)   Most extreme; sheerest.

prevail (line 5)   Triumph; be victorious.

assent (line 6)   Agree.

demur (line 7)   Disagree; object.

1. How is the first line of the poem a **paradox**? How can madness be sense? What do you think the line is probably meant to convey?

2. The third line of the poem is the same **paradox** in reverse. How can sense be madness? What meanings does the poet intend ''sense'' and ''madness'' to have here?

3. How does ''Eye'' in line 2 refer to the individual?

4. In this context, what does the word ''Majority'' (line 4) connote? How is the **connotative** or figurative meaning different from the **denotative** or literal meaning of the word?

5. How is the word ''Chain'' in line 8 used **connotatively**? Name two or three other objects which could have been used to suggest the same thing that ''Chain'' suggests. Why did you choose them?

6. How does the poet feel about much of majority opinion? About much of minority opinion? About the treatment of the minority by the majority? Do you agree? Why or why not?

WRITING

1. This poem indirectly suggests that the unthinking acceptance of labels such as ''madness'' and ''sense'' can be dangerous. How can words and phrases commonly used today, such as ''progress,'' ''freedom-loving peoples,'' ''the welfare underclass,'' ''rights,'' and ''pro-life'' be used in misleading ways or as covers for other, more negative, meanings? Write a short essay dealing with this issue.

2. Write about an instance in which a majority group treated a minority unfairly. You might select the way Jews were treated by Nazi Germany, blacks were treated by conservative whites in the South before the civil rights era, or drinkers were treated by prohibitionists in the 1920's. How might you feel if you were a member of one of these minority groups?

1. Verdi's opera *Nabucco* contains a chorus, "Va, pensiero, sull'ali dorati" (Go, thoughts, on wings of gold), in which Hebrew slaves in Babylonian captivity sing of the freedom of their thoughts in contrast to their physical bondage. This chorus became, in the 1840's, a rallying cry for those fighting for Italian unification. The establishment banned its performance in public and required that it be cut from the opera. Listen to a recording of it. Explain why you think it had such a powerful effect on people. In your explanation, examine both lyrics and music.

2. Listen to songs that celebrate freedom and individuality such as those by Peter, Paul, and Mary ("Leavin' On a Jet Plane"), Bob Dylan ("Blowin' In the Wind"), or Simon and Garfunkel ("Homeward Bound"). How do these songs reflect nontraditional attitudes towards individuality and freedom? How are their lyrics symbolic?

FIRST LESSON
Phyllis McGinley

The thing to remember about fathers is, they're men.
A girl has to keep it in mind.
They are dragon-seekers, bent on improbable rescues.
Scratch any father, you find
Someone chock-full of qualms and romantic terrors, 5
Believing change is a threat—
Like your first shoes with heels on, like your first
    bicycle
It took such months to get.

Walk in strange woods, they warn you about the
    snakes there.
Climb, and they fear you'll fall. 10
Books, angular boys, or swimming in deep water—
Fathers mistrust them all.
Men are the worriers. It is difficult for them
To learn what they must learn:
How you have a journey to take and very likely, 15
For a while, will not return.

hough it certainly represents a double standard, fathers often raise their daughters differently from the way they raise their sons. How are the sons and daughters treated differently? This poem reveals a daughter's attitudes towards her father's protectiveness.

DEFINITIONS AND EXPLANATIONS

dragon-seekers (line 3)   During the Age of Chivalry, the fashion was for a knight to have a ladylove, a pure and helpless creature. It was the duty of the knight to devote himself to protecting his ladylove from the dangers and evils of the world. Dragons were mythical beasts—huge, fire-breathing, winged serpents. Besides being quite horrible, dragons were regarded as **symbols** of sin and evil. So, in the tales of those days, knights sought out and slew dragons to protect their ladyloves.

improbable (line 3)   Not likely to be true or real.

qualms (line 5)   Misgivings; fears.

romantic (line 5)   Not realistic.

STUDY QUESTIONS

1. According to the speaker, what are some of the things that fathers worry about in regard to their daughters? How justified are these fears? Why?

2. How does the opening line of the poem suggest the fathers' views about protecting their daughters? What meaning is the word "men" given in the rest of the poem?

3. What is the "journey" mentioned in line 15?

4. Do the fathers' worries reflect the natural concerns of a good parent or not? Why? What larger comment does the poem seem to make about the attitude of men towards women given the fathers' fears and concerns?

5. What is the "first lesson" that gives the poem its title?

6. Could a son write a similar poem to his mother? Why or why not?

WRITING

Write a journal entry explaining how you feel about your parents' concerns in regard to your dating and staying out late with friends. How have they tried to raise you? How have they changed as you've moved into adolescence?

STAR QUILT

Roberta Hill Whiteman

There are notes to lightning in my bedroom.
A star forged from linen thread and patches.
Purple, yellow, red like diamond suckers, children

of the star gleam on sweaty nights. The quilt unfolds
against sheets, moving, warm clouds of Chinook.   5
It covers my cuts, my red birch clusters under pine.

Under it your mouth begins a legend,
and wide as the plain, I hope Wisconsin marshes
promise your caress. The candle locks

us in forest smells, your cheek tattered   10
by shadow. Sweetened by wings, my mothlike heart
flies nightly among geraniums.

We know of land that looks lonely,
but isn't, of beef with hides of velveteen,
of sorrow, an eddy in blood.   15

Star quilt, sewn from dawn light by fingers
of flint, take away those touches
meant for noisier skins,

anoint us with grass and twilight air,
so we may embrace, two bitter roots   20
pushing back into the dust.

Roberta Hill Whiteman, a member of the Oneida tribe, grew up in Wisconsin. As an American Indian, she is acutely aware of how mainstream American culture can envelop and subsume the community oriented lifestyle of her forebears. In "Star Quilt," the poet and her husband vow to preserve the values of their culture.

DEFINITIONS AND EXPLANATIONS

forged (line 2)   Created, brought together.

Chinook (line 5)   In this case, a warm, moist southwest wind emanating from the coast of Oregon.

velveteen (line 14)   A fabric, usually cotton, woven to imitate the feeling and appearance of velvet.

eddy (line 15)   A small current of water (or, as here, blood) running against the main current.

STUDY QUESTIONS

1. From what was the quilt created? How does the connection with stars make the quilt more than just a fabric?

2. What is the effect of the candle? What mood is created by "your cheek tattered by shadow" (lines 10–11)?

3. Why does the speaker compare her heart to a moth? **Symbolically**, how has she gotten wings?

4. What do they know (lines 13–15)? Explain.

5. In lines 16–21, the speaker invokes the quilt. What does she want of it? What is meant by "sewn from dawn light by fingers of flint"?

6. Why are the speaker and her husband "two bitter roots pushing back into the dust"?

7. How is the quilt a **symbolic** refuge for the American Indian couple?

WRITING

Compare the theme in these final lines from "Dover Beach" by Matthew Arnold with the theme of "Star Quilt."

Ah, love, let us be true
To one another! for the world which seems
To lie before us like a land of dreams,
So various, so beautiful, so new,
Hath really neither joy, nor love, nor light,
Nor certitude, nor peace, nor help for pain;
And we are here as on a darkling plain
Swept with confused alarms of struggle and flight,
Where ignorant armies clash by night.

MY MOTHER PIECED QUILTS
Teresa Palomo Acosta

they were just meant as covers
in winters
as weapons
against pounding january winds

but it was just that every morning I awoke to these   5
october ripened canvases
passed my hand across their cloth faces
and began to wonder how you pieced
all these together
these strips of gentle communion cotton and flannel
      nightgowns   10
wedding organdies
dime store velvets

how you shaped patterns square and oblong and
     round
positioned
balanced   15
then cemented them
with your thread
a steel needle
a thimble

how the thread darted in and out   20
galloping along the frayed edges, tucking them in
as you did us at night
oh how you stretched and turned and rearranged
your michigan spring faded curtain pieces
my father's santa fe work shirt   25
the summer denims, the tweeds of fall

continued

Imagine the warm comfort of a fluffy quilt. How does it make you feel? Have you ever felt attached to a quilt or blanket because of special recollections from your childhood? Teresa Palomo Acosta remembers the homemade quilts her mother made. These homemade quilts were pieced together from many different fabrics that happened to be handy. The result was a series of works of art which also warmed and comforted those who used them.

DEFINITIONS AND EXPLANATIONS

communion cotton (line 10)   Cotton used in the communion service of the Catholic church.

organdies (line 11)   Very fine transparent linen.

corpus christi (line 34)   Literally, the body of Christ.

muslin (line 50)   A fine linen.

thrashings (line 51)   Beatings, wear and tear.

STUDY QUESTIONS

1. How does the poet describe the basic purpose of the quilts in the first **stanza**? What kind of language does she use?

2. What did the speaker think about as she awoke each morning?

3. How does line 21 suggest that the quilts were like children to the speaker's mother?

4. What did the mother use to make the quilts?

5. Why is the speaker's recollection of sitting with her mother while she made the quilts special?

6. How is the mother the "river current carrying the roaring notes" (lines 37–38)? How is she "the caravan master....driving...artillery" (lines 41–42)?

7. How does quiltmaking allow the mother to deliver "herself in separate testimonies" (line 43)?

8. How are the quilts recollections of the past?

9. Why are the quilts "armed/ready/ shouting/celebrating" (line 53)?

10. Overall, what is the mood of this poem? How does the **rhythm** help to create this mood? What effect does the poet's use of **imagery** have on the reader? Why does the last line of the poem have a powerful effect?

in the evening you sat at your canvas
—our cracked linoleum floor the drawing board
me lounging on your arm
and you staking out the plan: 30
whether to put the lilac purple of easter against the
    red plaid of winter-going-
into-spring
whether to mix a yellow with blue and white and
    paint the
corpus christi noon when my father held your hand
whether to shape a five-point star from the   35
somber black silk you wore to grandmother's funeral

you were the river current
carrying the roaring notes...forming them into
    pictures of a little boy reclining
a swallow flying   40
you were the caravan master at the reins
driving your threaded needle artillery across the
    mosaic cloth bridges
delivering yourself in separate testimonies

oh mother you plunged me sobbing and laughing
into our past   45
into the river crossing at five
into the spinach fields
into the plainview cotton rows
into tuberculosis wards
into braids and muslin dresses   50
sewn hard and taut to withstand the thrashings of
    twenty-five years

stretched out they lay
armed / ready / shouting / celebrating

knotted with love
the quilts sing on   55

Write a paragraph which describes an object to which you have an emotional attachment. Describe the object as vividly as you can. Explain why the object has such a strong significance to you.

THE UNKNOWN CITIZEN
W. H. Auden

To JS/07/M/378   This Marble Monument Is Erected
  by the State

He was found by the bureau of Statistics to be
One against whom there was no official complaint,
And all the reports on his conduct agree
That, in the modern sense of an old-fashioned word,
    he was a saint,
For in everything he did he served the Greater
    Community.   5
Except for the War till the day he retired
He worked in a factory and never got fired,
But satisfied his employers, Fudge Motors Inc.
Yet he wasn't a scab or odd in his views,
For his Union reports that he paid his dues,   10
(Our report on his Union shows it was sound)
And our Social Psychology workers found
That he was popular with his mates and liked a
    drink.
The Press are convinced that he bought a paper every
    day
And that his reactions to advertisements were normal
    in every way.   15
Policies taken out in his name prove that he was fully
    insured,
And his Health-card shows he was once in hospital
    but left it cured.
Both Producers Research and High-Grade Living
    declare

continued

In a dictatorship or totalitarian state, individuality, cultural diversity, and personal freedom are much less important than the interests of the government. In a democracy, the state is supposed to serve the interests of individuality, cultural diversity, and personal freedom. How often is this ideal achieved in American society? How free can people be allowed to be in a democracy? In this day and age of computerization and government awareness of everything that goes on, how much individuality can be maintained by the citizens of our society?

DEFINITIONS AND EXPLANATIONS

The Unknown Citizen (title) The Unknown Soldier is an unidentified soldier killed in World War I. He is honored by a marble monument in Arlington National Cemetery as a **symbol** and representative of all the American soldiers who died in that war and other wars. The title "The Unknown Citizen" is an **allusion** to the concept of The Unknown Soldier.

scab (line 9) A worker who refuses to join a union; a strikebreaker.

Installment Plan (line 19) This is a method of buying on credit. The buyer pays part of the price at the time of sale and the balance in regular installments until the bill is paid in full. The method has been criticized because poorer people are tempted to buy things they cannot afford and build up a heavy burden of debt. Some sellers using the plan reap unfairly large profits by charging a total amount far in excess of the normal price.

Eugenist (line 26) A specialist in the science of improving human beings by controlling heredity.

STUDY QUESTIONS

1. Who is speaking in this poem? What is the occasion for his words? Where has the speaker gotten his information about the Citizen? Why does he approve of the Citizen's life? What message does the speaker offer to other citizens?

2. How does the epigraph (the inscription above the poem) show the attitude of the state toward the Citizen? Read the whole inscription and find the **internal rhyme** that occurs in the line. Which word in the line rhymes with "state"? What is the emotional state created by this rhyme?

He was fully sensible to the advantages of the
    Installment Plan
And had everything necessary to the Modern Man,   20
A phonograph, a radio, a car and a frigidaire.
Our researchers into Public Opinion are content
That he held the proper opinions for the time of year;
When there was peace, he was for peace; when there
    was war, he went.
He was married and added five children to the
    population,   25
Which our Eugenist says was the right number for a
    parent of his generation,
And our teachers report that he never interfered with
    their education.
Was he free? Was he happy? The question is absurd:
Had anything been wrong, we should certainly have
    heard.

3. Read line 4 again. What is traditionally meant when someone is called a saint? What makes a modern "saint"? How is the Citizen a modern saint?

4. What would the speaker consider to be normal reactions to advertisements (line 14)? Why would he be pleased that the Citizen was "sensible to the advantages of the Installment Plan" (Line 19)?

5. What **ironic** aspect is present in the contrast between peacetime and wartime attitudes as it is suggested in line 24?

6. How do lines 22–23 provide information about public opinion in this society?

7. What is suggested by the use of "their" in line 27?

8. Why is the speaker sure that the Citizen felt free and happy? What does this suggest about the state?

9. Why is the title "The Unknown Citizen" **ironic** even though the speaker offers so much information about him? How may the citizen be "unknown" even though so many facts are known about him?

10. Why does Auden use straightforward, unpoetic **diction** throughout the poem? Why does he use simple mechanical **rhymes** such as Inc.—drink, day—way, plan—man? How does his choice of words add to the effect of the poem?

Write an essay explaining how it probably feels to live in the Citizen's society. Include specific details about the world in which he lives. Be imaginative.

EUROPE AND AMERICA
David Ignatow

My father brought the emigrant bundle
of desperation and worn threads,
that in anxiety as he stumbles
tumble out distractedly;
while I am bedded upon soft green money   5
that grows like grass. Thus,
between my father who lives on a bed of anguish
for his daily bread, and I who tear money
at leisure by the roots,
where I lie in sun or shade,   10
a vast continent of breezes, storms to him,
shadows, darkness to him, small lakes,
difficult channels to him, and hills,
mountains to him, lie between us.

My father comes of a hell   15
where bread and man have been kneaded
and baked together. You have heard the scream
as the knife fell; while I have slept
as guns pounded on the shore.

Millions of people left their native countries to come to America in search of a better way of life for themselves and their families. Poverty was common among immigrant families as the parents struggled to provide for the children. Often, because of hard work and dedication to the belief that education is the way out of poverty, the children of immigrants lived a far better life than did their parents. David Ignatow, a Jewish-American poet born in Brooklyn, New York in 1914, compares the difficult life of his immigrant father to his own.

DEFINITIONS AND EXPLANATIONS

emigrant (line 1) A person who leaves his or her country.

kneaded (line 16) Formed or shaped into a mass with the hands, as in kneading dough to bake bread.

STUDY QUESTIONS

1. What bundle does the father bring with him? How does it affect him? How is the son's life contrasted with the **image** of the father's?

2. How is the contrast made in the first sentence of the poem continued in the second? How do the phrases "soft green money," "money that grows like grass," and "tear money at leisure by the roots" reflect the son's life? Are these effective **metaphors**? Explain.

3. What lies between the father and the son? How is each of these things perceived differently by the two men? Why?

4. What kind of world did the father come from? How is this world different from the world in which the son was brought up? The poem was first published in 1948, after World War II. How, then, does the last sentence of the poem show the difference between living in Europe and living in the United States?

5. How do you think the son feels about his father and their differences?

WRITING

1. This poem uses metaphors to contrast the lifestyles of the father and son. Write a detailed analysis of the metaphors, and explain how they are used to create contrasting images.

2. Are you from or do you know someone who is originally from another country? Freewrite about your own experience or, after having spoken to other people, their experience. How is life in the two countries different? Which is better? Why?

THE NEGRO SPEAKS OF RIVERS
Langston Hughes

I've known rivers:
I've known rivers ancient as the world and older than
    the flow of human blood in human veins.

My soul has grown deep like the rivers.

I bathed in the Euphrates when dawns were young.
I built my hut near the Congo and it lulled me to sleep.   5
I looked upon the Nile and raised the pyramids above it.
I heard the singing of the Mississippi when Abe Lincoln
    went down to New Orleans, and I've seen its
    muddy bosom turn all golden in the sunset.

I've known rivers:
Ancient, dusky rivers.

My soul has grown deep like the rivers.   10

DEFINITIONS AND EXPLANATIONS

Rivers (title)   Rivers are important to civilization even today. In ancient times, they were absolutely essential to the growth of great civilizations.

Euphrates (line 4)   The Euphrates River rises in the mountains of Turkey, joins the Tigris River, and flows into the Persian Gulf. The ancient civilization of Mesopotamia flourished in the valley between the Tigris and Euphrates.

Congo (line 5)   The Congo River, in volume of water, is the greatest river of Africa. Ancient black civilizations flourished on its banks.

Nile (line 6)   The great Egyptian civilization grew up 5000 years ago along the fertile lands bordering the Nile.

raised the pyramids (line 6)   Egypt depended on slave labor to sustain its wealth and build its monuments. Many of these slaves were Nubians, blacks who dwelled to the south of Egypt.

Mississippi (line 7)   This great American river was intimately associated with the lives of the black slaves who worked on its levees and on the cotton plantations along its route.

Flowing rivers are often seen as symbols of eternity. By associating the black experience with rivers essential to the major civilizations of human history, Hughes establishes a link with a heritage extending back ten thousand years. The river is also a symbol of wisdom and experience. This too is attached to the black experience.

DEFINITIONS AND EXPLANATIONS *continued*

New Orleans (line 7)   This city was the capital of the cotton trade. When Abe Lincoln was a very young man, he was hired to take a flatboat loaded with produce from Indiana down the Mississippi to New Orleans. This was the first time that young Lincoln saw something of the world outside the wilderness where he had grown up. Among other things he saw in New Orleans was a slave auction with slaves in shackles and chains.

dusky (line 9)   Dark; shadowy.

STUDY QUESTIONS

1. Who is the speaker? Why would he be "the Negro"? How old is the speaker? To whom is he speaking?

2. Why did the speaker choose the four rivers mentioned in the poem?

3. How are the rivers **symbolic**?

4. Why is the phrase "I've known rivers" repeated at the beginning of the first two lines? What is the effect of other **repetitions** used in the poem?

5. How are the rivers "older than the flow of human blood in human veins"?

6. What is meant by "when dawns were young" in line 4?

7. How is the Mississippi described as if it were a person? Why? What does the speaker mean when he says that he has seen the Mississippi's "muddy bosom turn all golden in the sunset"?

WRITING

What two sides of black history does the poem suggest?
Does it express defeat or hope? Explain in a brief essay.

MUSIC

Listen to a recording of "Ol' Man River" from *Show Boat* by Jerome Kern. How does the music give the feeling of the flowing river? How do the lyrics convey a message similar to that conveyed in "The Negro Speaks of Rivers"?

WOMEN
Alice Walker

They were women then
My mama's generation
Husky of voice—Stout of
Step
With fists as well as   5
Hands
How they battered down
Doors
And ironed
Starched white   10
Shirts
How they led
Armies

Headragged Generals
Across mined   15
Fields
Booby-trapped
Ditches
To discover books
Desks   20
A place for us
How they knew what we
Must know
Without knowing a page
Of it   25
Themselves.

Often, women are seen as the binding strength which holds a family together, the force which impels the younger generation to reach greater heights and successes. Through hard work and determination, countless women have become the guiding forces of their families, using their emotional as well as physical strength to provide a better life for their children. Alice Walker here writes about African-American women who have endured the rigors of poverty and hard work in order to help the younger generation.

DEFINITIONS AND EXPLANATIONS

husky (line 3)   Here, meaning hoarse with emotion.

starched (line 10)   Stiffened without creases.

Headragged Generals (line 14)   When working as cleaning women, they wore kerchiefs on their heads (headrags) to protect their hair and scalps. The women are described as generals because of their emotional strength and the fact that they fought against poverty and discrimination.

STUDY QUESTIONS

1. How do the first five lines of the poem convey the strength of the women Alice Walker is writing about? What kind of strength is she referring to?

2. How does the poet suggest that the women were fighting a war? What was their role in the war? What was the reason for the war?

3. How does the poet suggest that the women faced many obstacles in attaining their goals?

4. Why does the poet italicize the word "must" in line 23?

5. This poem is only one sentence long. Nevertheless, the poet makes it clear where to pause and how to phrase the lines. How does she do this? How should the poem be read aloud?

6. How are lines 22–26 **ironic**? What do these lines demonstrate about the importance of obtaining a good education?

WRITING

1. Do you know anyone who has sacrificed so that his or her children could be successful? Write an essay describing the hardships and the results.

2. Imagine that you have a friend who wants to drop out of school. Write a letter to your friend arguing against it.

VICTORY IN DEFEAT

Edwin Markham

Defeat may serve as well as victory
To shake the soul and let the glory out.
When the great oak is straining in the wind,
The boughs drink in new beauty, and the trunk
Sends down a deeper root on the windward side.   5
Only the soul that knows the mighty grief
Can know the mighty rapture. Sorrows come
To stretch out spaces in the heart for joy.

Here is an entirely different comment on freedom and self-awareness, a comment that raises some interesting questions on the role of individual character in the quest for deep inner knowledge.

DEFINITIONS

windward (line 5)   The side from which the wind strikes.

rapture (line 7)   Great joy; ecstasy.

STUDY QUESTIONS

1. How does the use of **paradox** make the title intriguing?

2. How is the **analogy** of the oak "straining in the wind" used to explain the theme of victory in defeat?

3. What two **metaphors** are used to de-scribe the "mighty rapture" of personal fulfillment? Why were these metaphors chosen?

4. How, according to the poem, can we find victory in defeat? How does this poem echo the theme of "The Negro Speaks of Rivers"?

WRITING

Do you agree with the poem's message? Write an essay explaining your views.

GEORGE GRAY

Edgar Lee Masters

I have studied many times
The marble which was chiseled for me—
A boat with a furled sail at rest in a harbor.
In truth it pictures not my destination
But my life.   5
For love was offered me and I shrank from its
    disillusionment;
Sorrow knocked at my door, but I was afraid;
Ambition called to me, but I dreaded the chances.
Yet all the while I hungered for meaning in my life.
And now I know that we must lift the sail   10
And catch the winds of destiny
Wherever they drive the boat.
To put meaning in one's life may end in madness,
But life without meaning is the torture
Of restlessness and vague desire—   15
It is a boat longing for the sea and yet afraid.

The poem "Victory in Defeat" suggests that an individual can overcome adverse outward circumstances to achieve fulfillment. "George Gray" also suggests the importance of a person's character in shaping his or her own life.

DEFINITIONS AND EXPLANATIONS

George Gray (title)   This poem comes from a collection of short, interrelated poems called the *Spoon River Anthology*. Each poem deals with a particular person who lived in a typical small Midwestern town called Spoon River, located in western Illinois. In each poem, the person named in the title tells his or her own story. However, the story is told from an unusual perspective, for each person is dead and is speaking from the grave. All the poems together give the reader a realistic cross section of the people of heartland America. *Spoon River Anthology* is one of the great achievements of American literature.

marble (line 2)   Gravestone.

furled (line 3)   Rolled up and secured to the mast.

disillusionment (line 6)   Disappointment; disenchantment.

destiny (line 11)   Fate.

STUDY QUESTIONS

1. What was the "boat with a furled sail at rest in a harbor" carved on George Gray's tombstone intended to represent? In George Gray's view, why is this intention **ironic**?

2. How does the picture on the gravestone become a **metaphor** that is extended throughout the poem? Which lines carry the metaphor?

3. What inferences can you make from the poem about George Gray's life? What seems to have been his main character weakness? What has he learned from his life?

4. How are sorrow and ambition **personified** in lines 7 and 8? How do these personifications strengthen the force of the poem?

5. Explain the last three lines of the poem as fully as you can.

WRITING

The poet Alfred Tennyson wrote, in *In Memoriam*, "'Tis better to have loved and lost than never to have loved at all." He also wrote, in "Ulysses," that, though people are "made weak by time and fate," they are still "strong in will to strive, to seek, to find, and not to yield." Write an essay explaining how Edgar Lee Masters would probably feel about Tennyson's remarks.

Freedom and Diversity

1. Memorable lines Continue to add to your collection of memorable or quotable lines. From the poems in this unit, select two passages of one line or several lines. The basis of your selection may be strength of image, music of line, depth of emotion, appeal of theme, or any combination of these. Write the passages in your notebook with title and author. Memorizing the lines will give you added pleasure.

2. Briefly review the poems in this unit. Then, answer the following questions:

   a. How does "First Lesson" deal with the theme of liberation as it specifically concerns women?

   b. How does "The Negro Speaks of Rivers" deal with the theme of liberation as it specifically concerns African Americans?

   c. How does "Europe and America" contrast the struggles people face when they are poor with those they might face when they are prosperous? How does "Women" treat the striving for the education of one's children?

   d. How does "Song of Myself" offer praise for the supreme value of individuality?

   e. How do "George Gray" and "Victory in Defeat" emphasize the importance of character in the pursuit of personal freedom?

   f. How are "Star Quilt" and "My Mother Pieced Quilts" similar in theme?

3. Show your knowledge of terms in poetry. Here are five short passages from poems in this unit. Choosing from the list of terms that follows, name the term applicable to each passage and explain why the passage is an example of the term you selected.

> **personification**   **irony**
> **paradox**   **metaphor**
> **alliteration**

   a. "The spotted hawk swoops by and accuses me, he complains of my gab and my loitering."
   —Walt Whitman: "Song of Myself"

b. "so we may embrace, two bitter roots pushing back into the
dust."
—Roberta Hill Whiteman: "Star Quilt"

c. "Much Madness . . .
Much Sense—the starkest Madness—"
—Emily Dickinson: "Much Madness is divinest Sense"

d. "Only the soul that knows the mighty grief
Can know the mighty rapture. . . ."
—Edwin Markham: "Victory in Defeat"

e. "Believing change is a threat—
Like your first shoes with heels on, like your first bicycle"
—Phyllis McGinley: "First Lesson"

4. Review your knowledge of vocabulary by choosing the numbered
word or phrase whose meaning is closest to the underlined word.

a. forged   (1) separated   (2) immersed   (3) created
                  (4) developed   (5) inserted

b. august   (1) miserable   (2) dignified   (3) little
                  (4) rotund   (5) mildewed

c. kneaded   (1) wanted   (2) assisted   (3) inquired
                  (4) shaped   (5) terminated

d. discerning   (1) observing with understanding
                  (2) attacking with great speed
                  (3) finishing with efficiency
                  (4) building with creativity
                  (5) learning with assistance

e. disillusionment   (1) intelligence   (2) proportionment
                     (3) enforcement   (4) defilement
                     (5) disappointment

f. "With the proper effort," Allison said, "we will prevail over the
obstacles."
        (1) be delirious   (2) be frightened   (3) be enthused
        (4) be treated   (5) be victorious

g. The dishonest student had no qualms about cheating on the test.
        (1) misgivings   (2) objections   (3) attitudes
        (4) notions   (5) responses

h. All four of Joseph's grandparents were in rapture over his beauty
and cuteness when he was born.
        (1) despair   (2) ecstasy   (3) anguish
        (4) surprise   (5) misery

i. Bob and Marilyn found the performance of the opera to be
   <u>voluptuous</u>.
   > (1) quietly appealing and soothing
   > (2) significantly disturbing   (3) superbly rewarding
   > (4) fascinatingly awful   (5) richly appealing to the senses

j. Marge and Lester were able to <u>vindicate</u> their behavior with sub-
   stantive proof of its causes.
   > (1) diminish   (2) increase   (3) finish
   > (4) justify   (5) enhance

5. Poems and paintings   Poets and painters are artists who have much
in common. Study each of the reproductions of paintings that follow.
Examine the image carefully. Just what do you see? What feelings does
the image arouse in you? What mood or idea does the picture suggest?
If a person or persons appear, try to flesh out in your mind their back-
ground and character. Is rhythm, metaphor, or symbol important in
the picture? After you have studied each picture in this way, select the
one that you associate most powerfully with one of the poems in this
unit. Be ready to discuss or write about your choice and the reasons
for it.

Optional: Select one picture that inspires you to write your own
poem and write the poem.

TORMENTED MAN   Leonard Baskin.
1956. Whitney Museum, New York.
Ink on paper. 39½ × 26½ in. Purchase, with
funds from the Living Arts Foundation Fund
57.52.

THE SUBWAY   George Tooker. *1950. Whitney Museum, New York.*
Egg tempera on composition board. Sight: 18⅛ × 36⅛ in. Purchase, with funds from the
Juliana Force Purchase Award 50.23.

MIRAGE LE TEMPS   Yves Tanguy. *1954. The Metropolitan*
Museum of Art, George A. Hearn Fund, 1955.

GOVERNMENT BUREAU George Tooker. *The Metropolitan Museum of Art,*
George A. Hearn Fund, 1956.

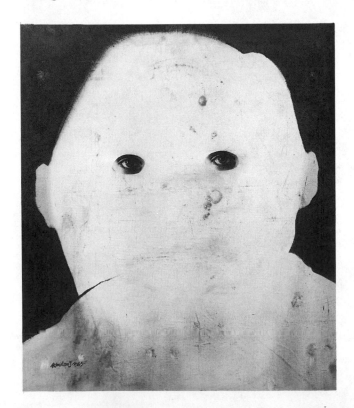

GAZER Hiram Williams.
1965. Whitney Museum, New York.
Oil and collage on canvas. 80 × 68
in. Gift of Mr. and Mrs. Leonard
Bancour. 66.119.

Visions of Humanity

"Love thy neighbor as thyself."
Old Testament

"Therefore all things whatsoever ye would that men should do to you, do you even so to them."
New Testament

"No man is an Island, entire of itself.
Every man is a piece of the continent."
John Donne

"It's coming yet for a' that,
That man to man the world o'er,
Shall brothers be for a' that."
Robert Burns

These well-known quotations, and many more, all express in different words the same great ideal of love and cooperation. The ideal vision of humanity is as old as civilization. The prophets, philosophers, and poets of ancient times recognized the interdependence and common lot of all people and incorporated this ideal into the great religions, philosophies, and poems.

The ideal is also as new as American democracy. One side of the ideal is the recognition of individuality, of the right of every person to have the opportunity for the fullest realization of his or her potential. The other side of that ideal is the vision of humanity—the recognition of the interdependence, the oneness, the unifying qualities of all members of the human race.

This unit presents a number of poems which share ideas about this vision.

from *THE PEOPLE, YES*
Carl Sandburg

The copperfaces, the red men, handed us tobacco,
the weed for the pipe of friendship,
also the bah-tah-to, the potato, the spud.
Sunflowers came from Peruvians in ponchos.
Early Italians taught us of chestnuts,   5
walnuts and peaches being Persian mementos,
Siberians finding for us what rye might do,
Hindus coming through with the cucumber,
Egyptians giving us the onion, the pea,
Arabians handing advice with one gift: 10
"Some like it, some say it's just spinach."
    To the Chinese we have given
    kerosene, bullets, Bibles
and they have given us radishes, soy beans, silk,
poems, paintings, proverbs, porcelain, egg foo yong,   15
gunpowder, Fourth of July firecrackers, fireworks,
and labor gangs for the first Pacific railways.
    Now we may thank these people
    or reserve our thanks
    and speak of them as outsiders   20
    and imply the request,
"Would you just as soon get off the earth?"
holding ourselves aloof in pride of distinction

continued

In the poem "The Tuft of Flowers," Robert Frost wrote:

" 'Men work together,' I told him from the heart,
'Whether they work together or apart.' "

How can people work together even when they are apart? After exploring and developing your own answer to this question, discover what Carl Sandburg has to say in *The People, Yes*.

DEFINITIONS AND EXPLANATIONS

bah-tah-to (line 3)   *Batata* is the Spanish word from which our word "potato" is derived. Sandburg's spelling is intended to show the pronunciation.

ponchos (line 4)   A poncho is a colorful cloak. It is similar to a blanket with a hole in the middle for the head, the two halves hanging down over shoulders and torso. Ponchos are worn in Latin American countries.

aloof (line 23)   Holding oneself apart; cold and distant in manner.

pride of distinction (line 23)   Sense of being different and superior.

commodious (line 29)   Roomy; spacious.

STUDY QUESTIONS

1. In lines 1–4, what does the speaker suggest about our relationship with other peoples of the earth? How does the mention of food serve his purpose well? How does he show a sense of humor in lines 1–11?

2. How does Carl Sandburg work two instances of **irony** into lines 12–17 where he tells us what we have given to the Chinese and what they have given to us?

3. What are the two possible attitudes toward other peoples as described in lines 18–30? Which attitude does the speaker favor? How do you know?

4. Why does the speaker describe people as "fellow creepers" (line 29)? Why does the speaker use the word "commodious" to describe the earth?

5. Sandburg writes in **free verse,** mixing slang and colloquialisms with formal

saying to ourselves this costs us nothing
as though hate has no cost   25
as though hate ever grew anything worth growing.
Yes we may say this trash is beneath our notice
or we may hold them in respect and affection
as fellow creepers on a commodious planet
saying, "Yes you too you too are people."   30

language. Give an example of such a mixture. What is the effect of this **diction?** Why does he use two different words for American Indians and three different words for potato? Give an example of Sandburg's use of the inventory list. What is the effect of such long lists of items?

WRITING

The title of the book-length poem from which this excerpt is taken is *The People, Yes*. What do you think the title means? Write a brief essay stating Sandburg's message, and explain why the message is important to us today.

MUSIC

Leonard Bernstein's musical *Candide* is about finding happiness in truth. One song from the musical, ''Make Our Garden Grow,'' examines the metaphoric relationship between a well-tended garden with many kinds of plants and a well-integrated community with many kinds of people. Explain how the song does this, and then compare its message with that of the poem you have just studied.

A BLACK MAN TALKS OF REAPING
Arna Bontemps

I have sown beside all waters in my day.
I planted deep, within my heart the fear
That wind or fowl would take the grain away.
I planted safe against this stark, lean year.

I scattered seed enough to plant the land   5
In rows from Canada to Mexico
But for my reaping only what the hand
Can hold at once is all that I can show.

Yet what I sowed and what the orchard yields
My brother's sons are gathering stalk and root,   10
Small wonder then my children glean in fields
They have not sown, and feed on bitter fruit.

The Bible says, in "Galatians 6:7," "whatsoever a man soweth, that shall he also reap." On a figurative level, this quotation can serve eloquently as the model for the work ethic: the more effort one puts into something, the more one will receive from it. This is, of course, generally true today, with serious effort and education the key means of improving one's situation. Unfortunately, the quotation did not always prove true for everyone. Arna Bontemps, an important African-American writer of the Harlem Renaissance, writes here of a farmer who sows many fields but rarely benefits from their fruit. As you read this poem about the unfortunate farmer, think about what symbolic explanations can be made.

DEFINITIONS AND EXPLANATIONS

sown (line 1)   Planted seeds deeply in the ground so that they take root and grow.

reaping (line 7)   The process of harvesting grain with a sickle, scythe (special curved knives used for the process) or, in modern times, a reaping machine.

glean (line 11)   To walk behind the reapers and gather up the leftover grain that has fallen from their hands.

STUDY QUESTIONS

1. According to lines 1–6, what has the speaker of the poem done? How is it appropriate?

2. According to lines 7–8, what has been the result, for him, of the sowing? Is this fair? Why or why not?

3. How does the speaker's experience differ from the biblical quotation on which this poem is based?

4. What has happened to the fruits of what the speaker has sown? Whom does he mean **figuratively** when he refers to his "brother's sons"?

5. What do the last two lines mean? Why is the fruit bitter? Why is gleaning less favorable than reaping?

6. Literally, the poem is about a sower who apparently reaps less than he should. Given the title, what **symbolic** meaning does the poem have? How does this relate to modern times?

WRITING

Have you ever put a great deal of effort into something only to receive less than you felt you should? Write a narrative of the occasion, telling what happened, how you felt, and what you did about it.

THE PEDIGREE OF HONEY

Emily Dickinson

The Pedigree of Honey
Does not concern the Bee—
A Clover, any time, to him,
Is Aristocracy—

While scientists study the laws of nature, poets study nature's universal wisdom and truths. Here, Emily Dickinson uses nature imagery to make an important statement about human society. Her simple, unadorned language carries with it a deep, complex meaning.

DEFINITIONS AND EXPLANATIONS

Pedigree (line 1)   A written record of ancestry, usually used to prove superiority of breeding and background.

Clover (line 3)   The clover is one of the most common of all flowers, growing in practically every meadow, pasture, and lawn. It is not generally considered to be a particularly beautiful or distinguished flower.

Aristocracy (line 4)   A privileged or ruling class.

STUDY QUESTIONS

1. Why did the poet choose the clover rather than some other flower as her **symbol?** How is the clover symbolic?

2. Why does the bee value the clover? Why is the clover "Aristocracy" to the bee?

3. How does the reader know that the poem is not to be taken literally but is intended **symbolically?** What is the underlying idea suggested by the **metaphor?**

4. Why might the poet **rhyme** the long, bookish word "Aristocracy" with the short common word "Bee"?

WRITING

In a carefully planned paragraph or two, tell exactly how the poem is an extended metaphor. How can Dickinson's beliefs be applied to today's world?

WHEN IN ROME
Mari Evans

Mattie dear
the box is full
take
whatever you like
to eat   5
       (an egg
       or soup
       ...there ain't no meat)

there's endive there
and   10
cottage cheese
       (whew! if I had some
       black-eyed peas...)

there's sardines
on the shelves   15
and such
but
don't
get my anchovies
they cost   20
too much!
       (me get the
       anchovies indeed!
       what she think, she got—
       a bird to feed?)   25

there's plenty in there
to fill you up.
       (yes'm. just the
       sight's
       enough!   30
       Hope I lives till I get
       home
       I'm tired of eatin'
       what they eats in Rome...)

One role the black woman has often held in American society is that of maid in a white household. In "When in Rome," Mari Evans, a black poet, examines the relationship between one maid and her employer in this comic dialogue.

DEFINITION AND EXPLANATION

When in Rome (title)   The expression "When in Rome do as the Romans do" is generally used to mean that visitors or travelers should follow the ways and customs of those around them. In addi-tion, the connotation of "Rome" is of an ancient, superior civilization.

box (line 2)   Refrigerator.

STUDY QUESTIONS

1. Identify the two speakers. What is the occasion for the "conversation?" Who is the main speaker? Whose words are in parentheses? Why? Why is this fact significant?

2. Judging from her own words, how does the first speaker view her own attitude toward the other speaker? Is that view accurate? Explain.

3. How do the maid's words reveal her personality? Tell everything you can infer about her from her remarks.

4. How is the contrast between the two speakers shown in the way the thoughts of each are expressed, the attitude held by each, and the **diction** used by each? How are the words of the two speakers tied together?

WRITING

This poem reflects a stereotypical relationship between a pseudo-enlightened white "lady" and a proud black maid. Keeping in mind that this does not by any means represent all or even most relationships, describe it in detail. Explain why it is stereotypical and what is wrong with it. Tell what you would consider to be the ideal relationship between an employer and her maid.

NANI
Alberto Ríos

Sitting at her table, she serves
the sopa de arroz to me
instinctively, and I watch her,
the absolute *mamá*, and eat words
I might have had to say more   5
out of embarrassment. To speak,
now-foreign words I used to speak,
too, dribble down her mouth as she serves
me albóndigas. No more
than a third are easy to me.   10
By the stove she does something with words
and looks at me only with her
back. I am full. I tell her
I taste the mint, and watch her speak
smiles at the stove. All my words   15
make her smile. Nani never serves
herself, she only watches me
with her skin, her hair. I ask for more.

I watch the *mamá* warming more
tortillas for me. I watch her   20
fingers in the flame for me.
Near her mouth, I see a wrinkle speak
of a man whose body serves
the ants like she serves me, then more words
from more wrinkles about children, words   25
about this and that, flowing more
easily from these other mouths. Each serves
as a tremendous string around her,

continued

Often, second- and third-generation Americans have become assimilated into American culture to the point where their grandparents' customs become unfamiliar to them and their fluency in their original culture's native tongue becomes minimal. In this poem, Alberto Ríos speaks of a young man who is enjoying a hearty meal served by his immigrant grandmother, his Nani. Though she emanates great expressiveness, he is troubled by the fact that he can understand perhaps only one-third of what she is saying to him because he knows so little Spanish.

DEFINITIONS AND EXPLANATIONS

Nani (title)   An affectionate way of referring to a grandmother; the American Spanish form of "granny."

sopa de arroz (line 2)   Rice soup.

mamá (line 4)   Mother.

dribble (line 8)   To drip down in streaks from the mouth.

albóndigas (line 9)   Spiced meatballs, a tasty Spanish dish.

tortillas (line 20)   A round, thin, flat cake of cornmeal, which is usually wrapped around chicken, ground beef, or some other hot filling.

STUDY QUESTIONS

1. What do the words "instinctively" and "absolute *mamá*" in lines 2 and 4 reveal about the nani?

2. Why is the speaker embarrassed? How does he feel about his inability to speak his grandmother's language? Why does he say that his nani's words "dribble down her mouth"? What image is created by this?

3. How does the grandmother react to the speaker?

4. What do the wrinkles speak about? How are they "a tremendous string"..."holding her together"?

5. What does the speaker wonder? Why? What is the effect of the wrinkles on the old woman?

6. What is the grandmother serving?

holding her together. They speak
nani was this and that to me   30
and I wonder just how much of me
will die with her, what were the words
I could have been, was. Her insides speak
through a hundred wrinkles, now, more
than she can bear, steel around her,   35
shouting, then, What is this thing she serves?

She asks me if I want more.
I own no words to stop her.
Even before I speak, she serves.

WRITING

What kind of relationship does the speaker have with his grandmother? Write a description of the relationship you have (or can imagine having) with your grandparents. Include a story which shows the relationship.

MUSIC

Aaron Copland's "El Salon Mexico" uses Mexican dance music and popular themes to portray joy and delight in day-to-day living. Write a description of this piece which explains how the composer expresses the love of life he perceived on his visit to Mexico.

CHINATOWN #1

Laureen Mar

She boards the bus at Chinatown,
holding the brown paper shopping bag
with twine handles that comes from
San Francisco or Vancouver.
It is worn thin with creases.   5
An oil spot darkens one side
where juice dripped from a warm
roast duck, another shopping trip.
Today there is fresh bok choy
wrapped in Chinese newspapers.   10
Grasping the rail with her right hand,
she climbs the steps carefully,
smiling at the driver, looking down
to check her footing, glancing
at him again. She sways down the aisle   15
as if she still carried wood buckets
on a bamboo pole through the village,
from the well to her house.
Her gray silk pajamas are loose,
better than ''pantsuits.''   20
Sometimes there are two or three women,
chattering with the quick, sharp tongue
of the wren: dried mushrooms too
expensive, thirteen dollars a pound now.
She sits down and sets the bag between her knees.   25
Her shoulder is close to mine.
I want to touch it, tell her I can understand
Chinese. Instead, I stare at the silver
bar crossing her back, and hope she knows
this is an Express; it does not stop before Genesee.   30

Chinatowns in big cities like New York or San Francisco teem with restaurants, garment factories, and the apartments of immigrants who speak little English. These people, often poor, live in a community which is isolated by language from the rest of the city, though many Americans visit to frequent the restaurants. Consequently, a gap may exist between Chinese immigrants and Chinese-Americans who have escaped the ghetto of a Chinatown.

DEFINITIONS AND EXPLANATIONS

bok choy (line 9)   A Chinese vegetable in the cabbage family.

wood buckets on a bamboo pole (lines 16–17)   In China, people would use a bamboo pole balanced on the back of the neck with a bucket attached to either end as a means of carrying water, and other things.

gray silk pajamas (line 19)   Chinese women traditionally wore silk outfits which resembled American pajamas.

dried mushrooms (line 23)   Meaty, thick black mushrooms, preserved by drying, are a Chinese delicacy.

STUDY QUESTIONS

1. Why is the woman referred to as "she"? Why does her bag come from either San Francisco or Vancouver?

2. How is the bag described? What feeling is created by this description? How is the bag a **metaphor?**

3. How does she board the bus? What link does the poet make here with China? Why are her gray silk pajamas better than pantsuits?

4. How is the conversation between the women described? What do they talk about? Why is this a "universal conversation"?

5. How do we know that the speaker feels an emotional bond with the woman? Why does she want to touch her shoulder? Why doesn't she?

6. What does the silver bar of the seat's back **symbolize?**

WRITING

Imagine that the immigrant woman sees the Americanized Chinese woman who is the speaker in this poem. Write your own poem from the point of view of the immigrant woman describing and reacting to the Americanized woman. In addition to or instead of writing a poem, write your description/reaction in the form of a letter from the immigrant woman to someone in China.

LOSSES
Randall Jarrell

It was not dying: everybody died.
It was not dying: we had died before
In the routine crashes—and our fields
Called up the papers, wrote home to our folks,
And the rates rose, all because of us.   5
We died on the wrong page of the almanac,
Scattered on mountains fifty miles away;
Diving on haystacks, fighting with a friend,
We blazed up on the lines we never saw.
We died like aunts or pets or foreigners.   10
(When we left high school nothing else had died
For us to figure we had died like.)

In our new planes, with our new crews, we bombed
The ranges by the desert or the shore,
Fired at towed targets, waited for our scores—   15
And turned into replacements and woke up
One morning, over England, operational.
It wasn't different: but if we died
It was not an accident but a mistake
(But an easy one for anyone to make).   20
We read our mail and counted up our missions—
In bombers named for girls, we burned
The cities we had learned about in school—
Till our lives wore out; our bodies lay among
The people we had killed and never seen.   25
When we lasted long enough they gave us medals;
When we died they said, "Our casualties were low."
They said, "Here are the maps"; we burned the
        cities.

It was not dying—no, not ever dying;
But the night I died I dreamed that I was dead,   30
And the cities said to me: "Why are you dying?
We are satisfied, if you are; but why did I die?"

Of the various ways we fail to reach ideal realizations of humanity, none shocks us so much as the killing and destruction of war. This poem by Randall Jarrell creates a vivid picture of aerial warfare during World War II and its horrible tragedy. Jarrell served as a pilot in the Air Corps during World War II and writes with hair-raising accuracy.

DEFINITIONS AND EXPLANATIONS

almanac (line 6)   A book published yearly with a calendar of various kinds of data, information, and events.

operational (line 17)   Ready to be used for actual combat.

casualties (line 27)   The number of persons wounded, killed, and captured.

STUDY QUESTIONS

1. Who is the "we" referred to in line 2 and throughout the poem?

2. How did they die while still in training? How did they die "on the wrong page of the almanac" (line 6)? Why do you think the poet says it this way?

3. What other details of the training are given? Why?

4. The three comparisons in the **simile** on line 10 represent three ways the young airmen felt about the death of a comrade during training operations. Describe the feeling represented by each of the three comparisons. How do lines 11–12 explain the feelings?

5. Explain the change described in lines 16–17. How does Jarrell's choice of words suggest the dramatic suddenness of the change?

6. Explain the **ironic** contrasts in lines 22–23.

7. What does the title of the poem mean? Why is it a powerful title?

WRITING

By repeating the phrase "It was not dying," the speaker suggests that the idea of dying is acceptable. In the final four lines, however, he suggests that the destruction of the cities, the purpose for which the airman risked his life, is not acceptable. Why should this be the case? How did the speaker "die" the night that he dreamed he was dead and the cities spoke to him?

plato told
e e cummings

plato told
him:he couldn't
believe it(jesus

told him; he
wouldn't believe   5
it)lao

tsze
certainly told
him,and general
(yes   10

mam)
sherman;
and even
(believe it
or   15

not)you
told him:i told
him; we told him
(he didn't believe it,no

sir)it took   20
a nipponized bit of
the old sixth

avenue
el;in the top of his head:to tell

him   25

Using no capitals, ending lines in surprising places, and applying his own rules for punctuation, Edward Estlin (always called e e) cummings developed a unique free verse style. His verse achieves startling effects of humor, emphasis, and lyricism. This poem will look strange to you at first. When reading it, however, ignore its weird appearance and read the poem naturally.

EXPLANATIONS

plato (line 1)   Plato (427?–347 B.C.) was one of the great Greek philosophers. In *The Republic*, Plato outlines plans for an ideal society in which human beings live together in perfect harmony.

lao tsze (lines 6–7)   Lao Tsze was a philosopher who founded Taoism, one of the great religions of China. Taoism teaches kindness and love, even the returning of injury with kindness.

general...sherman (lines 9 and 12)

William Tecumseh Sherman is recognized as one of the great Union generals of the Civil War. However, he is said to have summed up his feelings about war in the famous phrase "War is hell."

nipponized bit of...sixth avenue el (lines 21–24)   Before World War II, an elevated train ran on Sixth Avenue in New York City. When it was torn down to be replaced by the subway, the scrap iron was sold to Japan (Nippon). This metal was used by Japan for armaments to fight World War II.

STUDY QUESTIONS

1. What is it that Plato, Jesus, Lao Tsze, and General Sherman told? Who are the "you," "I," and "we" who told the same thing? How is this true?

2. Who is the "he" who was told but "wouldn't" believe?

3. What makes "him" finally believe?

What actual event does the "nipponized bit of the old sixth avenue el; in the top of his head" probably **symbolize?** Why does cummings use this **image?**

4. e e cummings deals with a serious subject by using a light touch rather than a moralizing tone. How does he accomplish this? Give examples.

WRITING

This poem deals with the same theme as "Losses." In a comparative essay, tell which poem you prefer and why. You may wish to deal with imagery, diction, and so on.

ATOMIC

Louis Ginsberg

The splitting apart
    Of man from man
Dooms more than splitting
    The atom can.

In one blaze, will   5
    All things be gone:
The Empire State
    And the Parthenon?

And must the sudden
    Atom's flash   10
Turn cities, statues,
    And poems to ash?

Quick! The foe
    In us is curled,
More fearsome than any   15
    Foe in the world!

The splitting of the atom resulted in a weapon that is viewed as a threat to all humanity. However, this poem points out that the threat does not come from atom-splitting but from another source.

EXPLANATIONS

Empire State (line 7) This building in New York City was for a long time the tallest building in the world.

Parthenon (line 8) The ancient Greeks built the Parthenon, a temple dedicated to their goddess Athena. Many regard it as the most beautiful structure of all time.

STUDY QUESTIONS

1. According to the first **quatrain,** where does the true threat lie? How true is this? How has the invention of nuclear weapons made the threat even more frightening?

2. Why does the poet refer to the destruction of only two buildings, the Empire State and the Parthenon?

3. Why did the poet choose to refer to the destruction of cities, statues, and poems? How can poems be destroyed?

4. Who or what is the "foe" referred to in the final **quatrain?** What is the **connotation** of the word "curled"?

5. How does the use of the word "quick" in the final **stanza** suggest an emergency? How does Ginsberg use **alliteration, rhythm,** and line length to add to this sense?

WRITING

What perspective on war does this poem convey? How does the poem compare to "Losses" and "plato told" in terms of message, poetic form, and language?

ANY HUMAN TO ANOTHER
Countee Cullen

The ills I sorrow at
Not me alone
Like an arrow,
Pierce to the marrow,
Through the fat   5
And past the bone.

Your grief and mine
Must intertwine
Like sea and river,
Be fused and mingle,   10
Diverse yet single,
Forever and forever.

Let no man be so proud
And confident,
To think he is allowed   15
A little tent
Pitched in a meadow
Of sun and shadow
All his little own.

Joy may be shy, unique,   20
Friendly to a few,
Sorrow never scorned to speak
To any who
Were false or true.

Your every grief   25
Like a blade
Shining and unsheathed
Must strike me down.
Of bitter aloes wreathed,
My sorrow must be laid   30
On your head like a crown.

Countee Cullen, a black poet of the Harlem Renaissance, writes in this poem about the connection between human suffering and the human family ideal. In addition to writing poetry, Cullen spent many years as a high-school teacher in New York City.

DEFINITIONS AND EXPLANATIONS

marrow (line 4)   The innermost part of the bone.

diverse (line 11)   Separate; different.

aloes (line 29)   The aloe is a spiny-leaved plant with a bitter juice.

STUDY QUESTIONS

1. According to the poem, what bonds all humans? Why?

2. How does Cullen use a **simile** in lines 1–6 to describe the effect of the ills?

3. How are "Your grief and mine" (line 7) compared to the sea and the river?

4. What mistaken picture of themselves do "proud" and "confident" people have? Why?

5. How are joy and sorrow contrasted in the fourth **stanza?**

6. According to the last **stanza,** what must happen to "my sorrow"? What is the crown made of?

7. What plea does the poem make?

WRITING

Despite surface differences, the problems humans face are often quite similar. Describe at some length, several common problems that people face. Offer possible solutions to show that more can be accomplished when people stick together than when they remain at odds.

MUSIC

This poem suggests the need for brotherhood, tolerance, and an end to divisiveness because all people must live together. The song "Somewhere" from Leonard Bernstein's *West Side Story* (lyrics by Stephen Sondheim) also explores this need. Listen to the words and the music of the song. What exactly is the theme of the lyrics? How does the music convey the yearning for peace and harmony?

IT WAS A LONG TIME BEFORE

Leslie Marmon Silko

It was a long time before
I learned that my Grandma A'mooh's
real name was Marie Anaya Marmon.
I thought her name really was "A'mooh."
I realize now it had happened when I was a baby   5
and she cared for me while my mother worked.
I had been hearing her say
      "a'moo'ooh"
which is the Laguna expression of endearment
for a young child   10
spoken with great feeling and love.

Her house was next to ours
and as I grew up
I spent a lot of time with her
because she was in her eighties   15
and they worried about her falling.
So I would go check up on her—which was really
an excuse to visit her.
After I had to go to school
I went to carry in the coal bucket   20
which she still insisted on filling.
I slept with her
in case she fell getting up in the night.

She still washed her hair with yucca roots
or "soap weed" as she called it. She said   25
it kept white hair like hers from yellowing.
She kept these yucca roots on her windowsill

continued

Think about what makes people thrive. Naturally, the interaction with other human beings is one of the first things that comes to mind. In this poem, Leslie Marmon Silko, an American Indian born in Albuquerque, New Mexico, recalls her relationship with her great-grandmother and how the older woman changed when she no longer had people to talk to. Like many grandparents of the "old world," Leslie Marmon Silko's great-grandmother preserved traditional customs.

DEFINITIONS AND EXPLANATIONS

Marie Anaya Marmon (line 3) The poet's great-grandmother, she was an American Indian of the Laguna Pueblo. She was married to a white American. Their child was the poet's grandfather.

Laguna (line 9) The Laguna Indians lived on the Laguna Pueblo in west central New Mexico. A pueblo is an Indian village. This particular village was known to willingly accept mixed marriages between whites and American Indians and the children from these marriages.

yucca root (line 24) The root of a tree-like plant of the lily family. American Indians believed that the root had medicinal powers.

red chili (line 30) An extremely hot pepper.

juniper ash (line 35) Burned bark of the juniper tree, a member of the pine family.

Albuquerque (line 38) The capital of New Mexico.

morning glories (line 44) A plant with elaborate flowers shaped like trumpets.

STUDY QUESTIONS

1. Why did the poet think that Marie's name was Grandma "A'mooh"? What does "a'moo'ooh" mean in English? How does the first **stanza** establish the nature of the relationship between the poet and her great-grandmother?

2. Why did the poet spend a great deal of time with her great-grandmother? How do lines 17–18 suggest that she enjoyed spending time with the older woman? How does the poem capture some of the traditional daily life of the Laguna people?

and I remember I was afraid of them for a long time
because they looked like hairy twisted claws.

I watched her make red chili on the grinding stone   30
the old way, even though it had gotten difficult for her
to get down on her knees.
She used to tell me and my sisters
about the old days when they didn't have toothpaste
and cleaned their teeth with juniper ash,   35
and how, instead of corn flakes, in the old days they ate
''*maaht'zini*'' crushed up with milk poured over it.

Her last years they took her away to Albuquerque
to live with her daughter, Aunt Bessie.
But there was no fire to start in the morning   40
and nobody dropping by.
She didn't have anyone to talk to all day
because Bessie worked.
She might have lived without watering morning glories
and without kids running through her kitchen   45
but she did not last long
without someone to talk to.

3. What recollections does the poet have about her great-grandmother? Why might the poet have included her fear of the yucca roots? How does this add to the poem's effect? How do these recollections reflect the continuation of the oral tradition of American Indians? How is the poem a combination of the American Indian oral and European written traditions?

4. What happened to the great-grandmother when she became very old? Why did she die, according to the poet? What point is the poet making about people's need for human contact?

5. When this poem is read, it sounds like a story rather than a poem. Nevertheless, it is a poem. Why?

WRITING

1. One problem society faces today is what to do with elderly people who cannot take care of themselves any longer. Write an essay of approximately 250 words in which you offer three possible solutions for this problem.

2. Write for ten minutes in your journal about a grandparent (or some other adult) who was (or is) very dear to you. Tell about some special feelings and recollections you have about that person. Explain why the person was (or is) so important to you. Afterwards, you might want to transform your journal entry into a poem.

I SEE A STAR

Alonzo Lopez

I see a star
   yet it is day.
The hands of my mother
   make it grow.
It is a black star   5
   set against a white sky.

How gentle that star,
Now that she weaves
devil's claws
Together to make   10
   a basket.

The culture and traditions of American Indians are based on a bond with nature. The rhythms of their lives were related directly to the changes of the seasons. Their food, clothing, and shelter came from nature. Above all, the spiritual life of the American Indian people came from their interplay with nature, nurturing their sense of reality and identity. This way of life, though certainly not without its difficulties, has been increasingly threatened by the materialism and industrialization of America. What is the place of the American Indian in today's vision for humanity? Alonzo Lopez, a Papago Indian from Arizona, offers one view.

EXPLANATION

devil's claws (line 9) A shrub of the Southwest whose fibers are used in basket-making.

STUDY QUESTIONS

1. What is the speaker's mother doing? How do you picture her in this activity?

2. How do you picture the speaker? What do you imagine are his thoughts and feelings as he watches his mother?

3. What does the first line mean? How are the star and the basket used as **symbols?**

4. Why do you think the poet made the star black and the sky white in lines 5–6?

5. Why is the word "gentle" used to describe the star in line 7?

6. Why does Lopez isolate the words "a basket" in the climactic final line?

7. What role do you foresee for the speaker in today's world?

WRITING

The cultural traditions of this speaker play a key role in his life. What role have cultural traditions played in your life? Do you feel they have been a help or a handicap? Explain why.

MUSIC

The traditional life of the American Indian has been captured in a musical vision by the composer Samuel Coleridge Taylor. Listen to "Hiawatha's Wedding Feast" from *Hiawatha*, based on Longfellow's poem. How does this view of the American Indian differ from that of Lopez?

MENDING WALL
Robert Frost

Something there is that doesn't love a wall,
That sends the frozen-ground-swell under it
And spills the upper boulders in the sun;
And makes gaps even two can pass abreast.
The work of hunters is another thing: 5
I have come after them and made repair
Where they have left not one stone on a stone,
But they would have the rabbit out of hiding,
To please the yelping dogs. The gaps I mean,
No one has seen them made or heard them made,   10
But at spring mending-time we find them there.
I let my neighbor know beyond the hill;
And on a day we meet to walk the line
And set the wall between us once again.
We keep the wall between us as we go.   15
To each the boulders that have fallen to each.
And some are loaves and some so nearly balls
We have to use a spell to make them balance:
"Stay where you are until our backs are turned!"
We wear our fingers rough with handling them.   20
Oh, just another kind of outdoor game,
One on a side. It comes to little more:
There where it is we do not need the wall:
He is all pine and I am apple orchard.
My apple trees will never get across   25
And eat the cones under his pines, I tell him
He only says, "Good fences make good neighbors."
Spring is the mischief in me, and I wonder
If I could put a notion in his head:
"*Why* do they make good neighbors? Isn't it   30

continued

What sort of relationship with neighbors do you favor? Do you prefer to be close and mutually helpful when the need arises, or do you prefer to keep a safe distance to protect yourself from involvement? How close do people have to live to one another to be neighbors? Are people who live in the same town or city neighbors in any way? in the same state? in the same nation? anywhere on the planet earth? This poem, one of the most widely read of all American poems, is about two neighbors. Or is it?

DEFINITIONS AND EXPLANATIONS

Mending Wall (title)   New England is crisscrossed with low stone walls. The walls, or fences, are built out of stones of all sizes and shapes that are fitted roughly on top of one another. These walls usually are used to mark the boundaries between properties.

frozen-ground-swell (line 2)   Water expands when it freezes. In the winter, the frozen water in the ground causes the ground to swell and heave upward.

spell (line 18)   Magic formula.

give offense (line 34)   Insult or displease.

old-stone savage (line 40)   A primitive person of the Stone Age.

go behind (line 43)   Look into; think critically about.

STUDY QUESTIONS

1. Who is the speaker? Who is the other person? Give a few details of their work as described by the speaker. What do they say to each other in the course of their work?

2. Which lines show that the speaker has a sense of humor? Which lines show that he likes to think about things and not just accept them because they are customary? Which lines show that the speaker doesn't like to force his thinking on someone else?

3. How does the speaker feel about walls between neighbors? What does the speaker imply about his point of view in lines 1 and 35–36?

Where there are cows? But here there are no cows.
Before I built a wall I'd ask to know
What I was walling in or walling out,
And to whom I was like to give offense.
Something there is that doesn't love a wall,   35
That wants it down." I could say "Elves" to him,
But it's not elves exactly, and I'd rather
He said it for himself. I see him there
Bringing a stone grasped firmly by the top
In each hand, like an old-stone savage armed.   40
He moves in darkness as it seems to me,
Not of woods only and the shade of trees
He will not go behind his father's saying,
And he likes having thought of it so well
He says again, "Good fences make good neighbors."   45

4. What is the other person's point of view? How did he arrive at that point of view? What is the meaning of "old-stone savage armed" in line 40 and of "darkness" in line 41?

5. Give examples of "walling in" and "walling out" (line 33). How can walls "give offense"?

6. What larger ideal about human relationships does the poem seem to be suggesting?

7. How is the natural, easygoing conversational tone achieved even though the poem is written in **iambic pentameter**?

WRITING

Explain, in an analytical essay, how the wall is a metaphor for divisiveness and separation among people. How have the geopolitical events of recent times proven that good fences (don't) make good neighbors?

MUSIC

Listen to Simon and Garfunkel's song "I Am a Rock." What point of view or position does the song present? How do the lyricists use irony in this song? Compare its message to that of "Mending Wall."

Visions of Humanity

1. **Memorable lines** Continue to add to your collection of memorable or quotable lines. From the poems in this unit, select two passages of one line or several lines. The basis of your selection may be strength of image, music of line, depth of emotion, appeal of theme, or any combination of these. Write the passages in your notebook with title and author. Memorizing the lines will give you added pleasure.

2. Briefly review the poems in this unit. Then, answer the following questions:
   a. How does ''The Pedigree of Honey'' find in nature a lesson for the ideal human family?
   b. How does *The People, Yes* emphasize the contributions of various ethnic groups to American culture?
   c. Why does ''Losses'' see the destruction of great cities as the most serious loss that comes with war?
   d. According to ''Mending Wall,'' how does nature respond to the ''walls'' that people construct?
   e. How does ''plato told'' espouse the idea that love and peace are the best ways of overcoming obstacles to harmony among the peoples of the world?

3. Show your knowledge of terms in poetry. Here are five short passages from the poems in this unit. Choosing from the list of terms that follows, name the term applicable to the passage and explain why the passage is an example of the term you selected.

alliteration	quatrain
iambic pentameter	simile
free verse	

   a. ''I have come after them and made repair
      Where they have left not one stone on a stone,''
      —Robert Frost: ''Mending Wall''

b. "sir)it took
   a nipponized bit of
   the old sixth"
   —e. e. cummings: "plato told"

c. "poems, paintings, proverbs, porcelain, egg foo yong,"
   —Carl Sandburg: *The People, Yes*

d. "Your grief and mine
   Must intertwine
   Like sea and river,"
   —Countee Cullen: "Any Human to Another"

e. "In one blaze, will
     All things be gone:
   The Empire State
     And the Parthenon?"
   —Louis Ginsberg: "Atomic"

4. Review your knowledge of vocabulary by choosing the numbered word or phrase whose meaning is closest to the underlined word.

a. <u>almanac</u>   (1) kind of necktie (2) book of data
                (3) a shade of green (4) donations to the poor
                (5) something for all males

b. <u>casualties</u>   (1) causes (2) easygoing activities
                (3) solemn promises (4) losses in battle
                (5) attacks on enemies

c. <u>commodious</u> (1) spacious (2) intellectual (3) cramped
                (4) narrow (5) sharp-edged

d. <u>diverse</u>   (1) similar (2) unusual (3) monochromatic
                (4) intense (5) different

e. <u>aristocracy</u> (1) privileged class (2) wrist motions
                (3) haughtiness (4) criticism (5) support

f. The Mexican woman was wearing an attractive <u>poncho</u>.

       (1) wig (2) skirt (3) cloak (4) earring (5) braid

g. Many workers were <u>gleaning</u> in the fields.

       (1) lounging (2) working hard (3) searching
       (4) praying (5) gathering leftovers

h. The singing was so wonderful that it cast a <u>spell</u> over the audience.
       (1) mist (2) magical formula (3) modest happiness
       (4) intense delight (5) sour mood

i. The athlete who didn't like his fans preferred to remain <u>aloof</u>.
(1) cold and distant (2) hateful and angry
(3) close and warm (4) soft and cuddly
(5) quiet and reserved

j. We tried hard not to <u>give offense</u> when we were with people

whose customs were unfamiliar to us.
(1) crack jokes (2) arouse suspicion (3) display anger
(4) create displeasure (5) divide and conquer

5. Poems and Paintings Poets and painters are artists who have much in common. Study each of the reproductions of paintings that follow. Examine the image carefully. Just what do you see? What feelings does the image arouse in you? What mood or idea does the picture suggest? If a person or persons appear, try to flesh out in your mind their background and character. Is rhythm, metaphor, or symbol important in the picture? After you have studied each picture in this way, select the one that you associate most powerfully with one of the poems in this unit. Be ready to discuss or write about your choice and the reasons for it.

Optional: Select one picture that inspires you to write your own poem and write the poem.

PREACHER Charles White. *1952. Whitney Museum, New York.* Ink on cardboard. Sight: 21⅜ × 29⅜ in. Purchase 52.25.

TO THE LYNCHING!
Paul Cadmus. *1935.*
Whitney Museum, New York.
Graphite and watercolor on paper.
Sight: 20½ × 15¾ in. Purchase 36.32.

WAVING THE FLAG
George Grosz. *1947–48.*
Whitney Museum, New York.
Watercolor on paper. Sight: 25 ×
18 in. Purchase and exchange 54.9.

THE EMPEROR
Abraham Rattner. *1944.*
Whitney Museum, New York.
Oil on canvas. 28¾ × 23¾ in.
Purchase 45.6.

MOONLIGHT
Joseph Hirsch. *1937.*
Whitney Museum, New York.
Oil on canvas. 24¾ × 17¾ in. Purchase
43.2.

128

Nature and Our Environment

Americans, feeling extraordinarily proud of our technological progress, have glorified science, technology, and industry. We have reshaped the natural environment for the sake of greater comfort and convenience. Today, we take for granted our abundance of food, our cars, our planes, our medical techniques, our televisions, video cameras, and compact disc players, skyscrapers, and highways.

Recently, however, we have discovered that by tinkering with nature, we are tampering with something far more complex and fragile than we realized. We are now faced with an appalling ecological crisis. Our natural resources are fast dwindling. Our land, our waters, and the very air we breathe are becoming more polluted with each passing hour. The delicate balance of plant and animal life is threatened.

In this life, however, nothing is clear-cut. Though nature is beautiful, harmonious, and complex, it is also ruthless and cruel. Nature includes plagues, famines, droughts, floods, volcanic eruptions, and earthquakes. Nature includes disease and death. Nature is ruled, in part, by the brutal law of survival of the fittest. Though science and technology have caused damage, few of us would want to return to humanity's primitive state with its endless privations and hardships.

In their love for the order and beauty of nature, poets have been among the first ecologists. They have long recognized the damage industrialization, science, and technology have wrought. On the other hand, they have also seen the multitude of blessings brought by creative human intelligence as it is expressed through science and technology.

GOD'S WORLD
Edna St. Vincent Millay

O world, I cannot hold thee close enough!
    Thy winds, thy wide grey skies!
    Thy mists, that roll and rise!
Thy woods, this autumn day, that ache and sag
And all but cry with color! That gaunt crag   5
To crush! To lift the lean of that black bluff!
World, World, I cannot get thee close enough!

Long have I known a glory in it all,
    But never knew I this:
    Here such a passion is   10
As stretcheth me apart,—Lord, I do fear
Thou'st made the world too beautiful this year;
My soul is all but out of me,—let fall
No burning leaf; prithee, let no bird call.

DEFINITIONS AND EXPLANATIONS

world (line 1) The world of nature.

gaunt (line 5) Bare; grim.

crag (line 5) A steep, rugged rock mass.

lean (line 6) Angle; slant.

bluff (line 6) A cliff.

prithee (line 14) An archaic word meaning "please" or "I pray thee."

Humans have deep feelings about nature. We get pleasure and inspiration from its harmony and beauty. When we can, we go to mountains, to seashores, to lakesides, and even to the desert to be close to nature's beauty. We try to protect and conserve that beauty in our parks, but much more needs to be done to ensure the survival of our natural resources. This poem expresses Edna St. Vincent Millay's intense feelings about the beauty she observes in nature.

STUDY QUESTIONS

1. How does the poet suggest the idea of the fall season?

2. The poet uses the device of **apostrophe** in each **stanza.** To whom or what is each stanza addressed?

3. Observing the world around her, the speaker says that she wants to hold it very close, to crush, to lift, and again, to hold it close. She refers to the woods as aching, almost crying. What **image** does she seem to be suggesting by this use of **personification?** What is the emotional effect of this image?

4. How does the speaker's emotional state change in the second **stanza?** Why does she beg that no burning leaf fall or bird call? How is the phrase "burning leaf" used as a **metaphor?** How is this image appropriate to the meaning of the poem?

5. How is **alliteration** used in the poem to reinforce the emotional force of the words?

6. In each of the **stanzas,** two lines are shorter than the others. What is the effect of the shorter lines?

WRITING

If you were to write a similar poem, what season of the year would you choose? Where would you set your poem? Why? Having answered the above in a clear manner, write the poem.

MUSIC

Listen to "Autumn" from Vivaldi's *The Four Seasons.* How does the composer create a musical mood which reflects the generally accepted characteristics of the fall? Listen to the other movements. How do they reflect the moods of the seasons they represent?

THE MORNS ARE MEEKER
THAN THEY WERE

Emily Dickinson

The morns are meeker than they were—
The nuts are getting brown—
The berry's cheek is plumper—
The Rose is out of town.

The Maple wears a gayer scarf—   5
The field a scarlet gown—
Lest I should be old fashioned
I'll put a trinket on.

Edna St. Vincent Millay responded to the beauty of autumn with almost unbearably intense passion. In this poem, Emily Dickinson writes about exactly the same subject. Her personality was different from Millay's, and her poem makes an interesting contrast with ''God's World.''

STUDY QUESTIONS

1. Why are ''The morns . . . meeker than they were'' (line 1)? Why is ''The Rose . . . out of town'' (line 4)?

2. How is **personification** used throughout this poem to describe autumn? Give four examples. What is the general mood conveyed by these descriptions?

3. How are these **personifications** used both to describe and to establish a psychological relationship between the speaker and the autumn scene? What is that relationship? How does the relationship affect the speaker?

4. Emily Dickinson lived much of her life as a recluse, physically isolated from people and society. What does this poem show about the state of mind of the poet in her solitary life?

WRITING

Write an essay comparing this poem to ''God's World.'' How are the two poems alike? How are they different? Which of the poems do you prefer? Explain why and support your view with specific details.

THE RHODORA
Ralph Waldo Emerson

On Being Asked, Whence Is the Flower?

In May, when sea-winds pierced our solitudes,
I found the fresh Rhodora in the woods,
Spreading its leafless blooms in a damp nook,
To please the desert and the sluggish brook.
The purple petals, fallen in the pool,   5
Made the black water with their beauty gay;
Here might the red-bird come his plumes to cool,
And court the flower that cheapens his array.
Rhodora! if the sages ask thee why
This charm is wasted on the earth and sky,   10
Tell them, dear, that if eyes were made for seeing,
Then Beauty is its own excuse for being:
Why thou were there, O rival of the rose!
I never thought to ask, I never knew:
But, in my simple ignorance, suppose   15
The self-same Power that brought me there brought
    you.

It is commonly accepted that nature is capable of moving us with its beauty. Why it does so is a matter for philosophers. Indeed, the question "What is beauty?" has stimulated thinkers for many generations. In "The Rhodora," Ralph Waldo Emerson, one of the giants of American literature, ponders these two questions.

DEFINITIONS AND EXPLANATIONS

Rhodora (title)   A small wild shrub with beautiful purple flowers that bloom in May before the leaves of the plant come out.

nook (line 3)   A half-hidden, sheltered spot.

court (line 8)   Seek closeness to or the affection of.

sages (line 9)   Wise persons.

STUDY QUESTIONS

1. How has the speaker been spending his time?

2. Describe the rhodora and the setting in which it is growing, providing as many visual details as you can. Include examples of sounds, smells, and the feel of the air.

3. How does the rhodora cheapen the array of the red-bird (line 8)?

4. How is the charm of the rhodora wasted, according to the sages (lines 9–10)?

5. How does the speaker answer the question that the sages ask?

6. What is the link that brought the speaker and the rhodora together? How is this link related to nature and our environment?

WRITING

The introduction to this poem stated that Emerson grapples with the questions of what beauty is and how nature moves us with its beauty. Describe how Emerson deals with these two important questions. What are his conclusions? How valid do they seem to be? Explain.

OREAD
H. D. (Hilda Doolittle)

Whirl up, sea—
whirl your pointed pines,
splash your great pines
on our rocks,
hurl your green over us,   5
cover us with your pools of fir.

Our world can be seen as having three major divisions. They are the land, the sea, and the sky. In the poems by Millay, Dickinson, and Emerson, you read about the land. Hilda Doolittle (who always went by her initials, H. D.) writes here about the sea. She paints a picture of the wild sea crashing against a rocky, mountainous shoreline. Her vision, however, is not one seen by the ordinary eye, but by her own original mind.

DEFINITION AND EXPLANATION

Oread (title)   In Greek mythology, the realms of nature were guarded by minor goddesses called nymphs. The Oreads were the nymphs who watched over the mountains. Other nymphs were the Nereids, who protected the Mediterra-nean sea, the Naiads, who guarded the rivers and streams, and the Dryads, who looked after the trees and forests.

fir (line 6)   An evergreen tree similar to a pine.

STUDY QUESTIONS

1. The speaker in this poem is an Oread, a nymph of the mountain against which the stormy sea is raging. How do the great waves appear to her? How do the pools of seawater among the rocks appear?

2. What feelings about the stormy sea does this poem evoke? What underlying principle of nature does the poem seem to suggest?

3. The poem is notable for its concise, strong **imagery.** Read aloud the first words of each line. How do you react to the **connotation, imagery,** and **sound effects** of these words?

WRITING AND MUSIC

''The Sea and Sinbad's Ship'' and ''The Ship Goes to Pieces Against a Rock'' from Rimsky-Korsakov's *Sche-herazade* both portray a storm. Compare the musical presentation of the storm to the poetic one.

137

STARS
Sara Teasdale

Alone in the night
  On a dark hill
With pines around me
  Spicy and still,

And a heaven full of stars   5
  Over my head,
White and topaz
  And misty red;

Myriads with beating
  Hearts of fire   10
That aeons
  Cannot vex or tire;

Up the dome of heaven
  Like a great hill,
I watch them marching   15
  Stately and still,

And I know that I
  Am honored to be
Witness
  Of so much majesty.   20

DEFINITIONS AND EXPLANATIONS

topaz (line 7) A gem of brilliant yellow color.
myriads (line 9) Countless numbers.
aeons (line 11) A period of thousands and thousands of years.
vex (line 12) Annoy; irritate.
stately (line 16) Dignified.

As mentioned in the previous lesson, the great divisions of our world are the land, the sea, and the sky. This poem is about the sky. Some people feel the pale blue sky of day with its bright sun and white clouds or the multicolored brilliant sky of sunrise and sunset is most beautiful. Others feel that the dark sky of night with its millions of shining stars is more exquisite.

STUDY QUESTIONS

1. Usually, daylight is associated with better vision. How is this reversed in the case of the stars? What does this reversal suggest? What quality of the stars is suggested in lines 11 and 12? How does the poet use language to suggest this?

2. Where is the speaker standing? What does she see directly around her? What is the quality of the air? Why is the location important? How long does the speaker stand there?

3. List several words and phrases that **personify** the stars. What qualities are given to these "persons" in such words as "Stately" and "majesty" as well as the others you've selected?

4. Why does the speaker say that she is "honored" to witness the stars? In what position does it place the speaker in relation to the entire scene? What is the speaker's state of mind? How do you account for this?

5. Why are the short **stanzas** and lines, the simple **rhythms**, and the **alliteration** in lines 4 and 16 appropriate to the mood of the poem? When reading the poem aloud, what voice quality would you use?

6. Grammatically, the entire poem is a single sentence. What is the first main verb in the poem? Where does it occur? Why is this an effective arrangement?

WRITING

Stars are so far away that it takes many years for their light to reach us. When we look at the stars, we are bridging the gap of time because we may be seeing something that occurred hundreds of years before we were born. How does this make you feel? Write an essay or a journal entry describing and explaining your emotions.

MUSIC

Mozart's *Eine Kleine Nachtmusik* (*A Little Night Music*) is often described as music for a starry night and music to soothe the soul. Why do you think this is the case? Which part might make ideal background music for an oral reading of "Stars"? Why? What makes Mozart's music so beautiful and so enjoyable?

STARFISH
Lorna Dee Cervantes

They were lovely in the quartz and jasper sand
As if they had created terrariums with their bodies
On purpose; adding sprigs of seaweed, seashells,
White feathers, eel bones, miniature
Mussels, a fish jaw. Hundreds; no—   5
Thousands of baby stars. We touched them,
Surprised to find them soft, pliant, almost
Living in their attitudes. We would dry them, arrange
    them,
Form seascapes, geodesics ... We gathered what we
    could
In the approaching darkness. Then we left hundreds of   10
Thousands of flawless five-fingered specimens
    sprawled
Along the beach as far as we could see, all massed
Together: little martyrs, soldiers, artless suicides
In lifelong liberation from the sea. So many
Splayed hands, the tide shoveled in.   15

Have you ever seen a starfish? This poem is a reflection on the poet's days at the beach when many starfish were washed up on the sand. Often, people would take the starfish, dry them, and save them. The poet views them in an unusual way.

DEFINITIONS AND EXPLANATIONS

quartz and jasper (line 1)   Minerals which make up sand.

terrariums (line 2)   Enclosures, like fishtanks, with soil, plants and so on for studying animals.

sprigs (line 3)   Small pieces of a plant.

geodesics (line 9)   Here, patterns created by straight lines.

splayed (line 15)   Spread wide open and outward.

STUDY QUESTIONS

1. How are the starfish on the beach like terrariums?

2. What are the starfish terrariums encasing?

3. What mood is created when the poet refers to the starfish as, simply, "stars" spread out across the beach?

4. Why are the starfish "almost living in their attitudes"?

5. What would the people referred to as "we" do with the starfish? Why?

6. Why are the starfish "little martyrs, soldiers, artless suicides"?

7. How is the phrase "in lifelong liberation from the sea" **paradoxical?**

8. What final **image** is the reader left with?

WRITING

1. Write a recollection of a time when you were in a quiet place. Be as descriptive as possible, telling about the sounds, setting, mood, colors, people (if any) and so on.

2. Write a short story about an occurrence in a quiet place. Be as detailed and descriptive as possible.

EARTH AND RAIN,
THE PLANTS & SUN
Simon J. Ortiz

Once near San Ysidro
on the way to Colorado,
I stopped and looked.

The sound of a meadowlark
through smell of fresh cut alfalfa.   5

Raho would say,
"Look, Dad." A hawk

sweeping
          its wings

clear through   10
          the blue
of whole and pure
          the wind
                    the sky.

It is writhing   15
overhead.
Hear. The Bringer.
          The Thunderer.

Sunlight falls
through cloud curtains,   20
a straight bright shaft.

continued

Sometimes, looking out at the distant horizon from a high vantage point can produce a feeling of excitement and exhilaration. Simon Ortiz, an American Indian poet, expresses the overwhelming emotion he feels when he looks out across the open sky. In this poem, Ortiz expresses the joy of nature's beauty and its continuous regenerative process.

DEFINITIONS AND EXPLANATIONS

alfalfa (line 5)   A plant generally grown for hay.

Katzina (line 27)   Southwest Indian dancers who wear elaborate masks that represent ancestral spirits.

STUDY QUESTIONS

1. What did the speaker hear and smell when he stopped on the road? What did his son see? What mood is created?

2. Why are lines 7–14 set up the way they are?

3. To what do the words "The Bringer" and "The Thunderer" refer?

4. What **images** are created by the description of sunlight in lines 19–26? Why are they effective?

5. What is the role of the Katzina in this poem?

6. What love is being talked about in lines 30–33? Why is this love important to the speaker?

7. How is the earth made new again? Who is coming?

8. How would you describe the final message of the poem?

It falls,
    it falls,
down
    to earth,   25
a green plant.

Today, the Katzina come.
The dancing prayers.
Many times, the Katzina.
The dancing prayers.   30
It shall not end,
son, it will not end,
this love.

Again and again,
the earth is new again.   35
They come, listen, listen.
Hold on to your mother's hand.
They come

O great joy, they come.
The plants with bells.   40
The stones with voices.
Listen, son, hold my hand.

1. If you were a parent, what advice would you give your child about preserving nature? Why? Be specific. How would you reinforce the ideas you discuss? What kinds of examples would you give your child an opportunity to see and experience?

2. How might the traditional view of nature held by American Indians have influenced this poet? Explain.

FUELED
Marcie Hans

Fueled
by a million
man-made
wings of fire—
the rocket tore a tunnel   5
through the sky—
and everybody cheered.
Fueled
only by a thought from God—
the seedling   10
urged its way
through the thicknesses of black—
and as it pierced
the heavy ceiling of the soil—
and launched itself   15
up into outer space—
no
one
even
clapped.   20

The machines of human science and technology as well as the "machines" of nature are a fertile subject for the poet's imagination. This poem contrasts the excitement attached to a technological achievement and the short shrift often given to natural "miracles."

STUDY QUESTIONS

1. What is the first machine described in the poem? How is it fueled? How does it act?

2. What is the second "machine"? How is it fueled? How does it act?

3. What is everybody's reaction to the first machine? to the second? Why?

4. Nowhere does the speaker directly give her own reaction to the two machines or to everybody else's reactions to them. What are her reactions? How do you know?

5. How are the appearance of the poem on the printed page and the subject matter of the poem connected?

6. Why do you think the poem is called "Fueled"? Why is this a good title?

7. This poem is based on a contrast between a human-made machine and a **metaphoric** "machine" of nature. What other pairs of such machines might make a suitable subject for a poem? Why?

WRITING

Choose one of the pairs of "machines" you listed in question seven and write a poem contrasting the pair.

AUTO WRECK
Karl Shapiro

Its quick soft silver bell beating, beating,
And down the dark one ruby flare
Pulsing out red light like an artery,
The ambulance at top speed floating down
Past beacons and illuminated clocks   5
Wings in a heavy curve, dips down,
And brakes speed, entering the crowd.
The doors leap open, emptying light;
Stretchers are laid out, the mangled lifted
And stowed into the little hospital.   10
Then the bell, breaking the hush, tolls once,
And the ambulance with its terrible cargo
Rocking, slightly rocking, moves away,
As the doors, an afterthought, are closed.

We are deranged, walking among the cops   15
Who sweep glass and are large and composed.
One is still making notes under the light.
One with a bucket douches ponds of blood
Into the street and gutter.
One hangs lanterns on the wrecks that cling,   20
Empty husks of locusts, to iron poles.

Our throats were tight as tourniquets,
Our feet were bound with splints, but now,
Like convalescents intimate and gauche,
We speak through sickly smiles and warn   25

continued

The automobile, certainly one of the technological marvels of the modern age, is also one of its great dangers. There is something ironically tragic and unacceptable about the death and injury caused by auto accidents. When there is an automobile accident on the open road, a long line of slowed traffic is created merely by the rubber-necking of other drivers who are stunned and mesmerized by the sight. In the street, a crowd will quickly gather around the scene of any dreadful accident. The twisted metal and broken glass, the blood and torn flesh will rivet the attention and haunt the consciousness of the beholder in a way different from that of any other disaster. This poem is about just such an accident.

DEFINITIONS AND EXPLANATIONS

beacons (line 5)   Lights.

deranged (line 15)   Made insane.

douches (line 18)   Washes.

husks (line 21)   Dry, rough, useless outside coverings, as husks of corn.

convalescents (line 24)   People gradually recovering health after an illness.

intimate (line 24)   Close and friendly.

gauche (line 24)   Awkward; lacking poise.

saw (line 26)   Saying; proverb.

banal (line 27)   Commonplace; hackneyed.

resolution (line 27)   A decision to do something.

stillbirth (line 34)   A birth in which the baby is born dead.

occult (line 36)   Beyond understanding; mysterious.

denouement (line 38)   Outcome or solution of the problem of a story.

expedient (line 39)   Convenient; suitable to the circumstances.

With the stubborn saw of common sense,
The grim joke and the banal resolution.
The traffic moves around with care,
But we remain, touching a wound
That opens to our richest horror.   30
Already old, the question Who shall die?
Becomes unspoken Who is innocent?
For death in war is done by hands;
Suicide has cause and stillbirth, logic;
And cancer, simple as a flower, blooms.   35
But this invites the occult mind,
Cancels our physics with a sneer,
And spatters all we knew of denouement
Across the expedient and wicked stones.

1. Who are the speakers (the ''we'') in this poem?

2. Briefly describe each step in the ambulance's approach as seen by the crowd. Why does its bell sound ''quick'' and ''soft''? What makes the crowd see the ambulance ''Pulsing out red light like an artery'' (line 3)? Why does the poet use this **image?**

3. Who are the ''mangled''? How has the scene affected the crowd mentally? In contrast, how do the police behave? Why?

4. Why are the wrecked automobiles described as ''Empty husks of locusts'' in line 21?

5. How has the scene made the spectators feel physically? How can this be explained? What kind of remarks do they make as they begin to recover? Give an example.

6. How do the last seven lines suggest the differences between death in an auto accident and other ways of dying? How does the poet use ''spatter'' as a **metaphor** in the last two lines? What has **figuratively** been spattered? What has literally been spattered?

WRITING

Have you ever been a close witness to a terrible auto accident? In a well-developed paragraph, describe your reactions as clearly as possible. How long did they last? Why is the scene so vivid in your mind? If you have never witnessed such an accident, use your imagination to help you write the paragraph.

SURGEONS MUST BE VERY CAREFUL

Emily Dickinson

Surgeons must be very careful
When they take the knife!
Underneath their fine incisions
Stirs the Culprit—Life!

It has become increasingly clear that for many of the benefits of modern medicine, we pay the price of serious side effects. Consequently, we are becoming aware that we must weigh the advantages of such benefits against the serious damage they can do. In recent years, society has recognized that many surgeons are often too ready to perform operations that are unnecessary. More broadly, we are learning that when we treat illness, we are at the same time tampering with the underlying processes of life, which are more complicated than we have recognized. In this short poem, Emily Dickinson shows she recognized all this a long time ago.

DEFINITIONS

incisions (line 3)   Cuts made by a surgeon into tissues and organs.

culprit (line 4)   Guilty person.

STUDY QUESTIONS

1. Read the whole poem aloud and then close your eyes. What **image** do you see? Describe the picture in every detail. What single line in the poem has played the greatest part in suggesting to you the image you have described?

2. A key word in the meaning of this poem is "Culprit." How is "Life" the culprit in this case?

3. How does the speaker really feel about the surgeon's "fine incisions"?

4. What relationship between "Life" and illness is the speaker pointing out? What warning does she give to the surgeons and, by implication, to doctors in general? Do you agree with her? Why? Why not?

WRITING

A major issue in medical practice today is whether or not doctors should take extraordinary measures to save a life even when the chances for a return to a normal life are virtually nonexistent. How do you feel about this? Take a stand and write a persuasive essay expressing your point of view.

EIGHT-CYLINDER MAN
Florence Ripley Mastin

He grinds the clover at its root
with a creaking and enormous foot.
In his circumference vast and dim
no small life has a place for him.
The needlepoint of curious moss   5
where delicate footprints cross,
the brook composing mountain blues,
the bereaved and cynical yews,
columbines dancing on a wall—
these he has never seen at all.   10

Speed is the only register
within his mind, and in that blur
of gas and gleaming chromium
he adds the swiftly mounting sum
of miles, a purely abstract space,   15
and passes summer face to face.

On our vast system of highways and in our powerful cars, we can travel with amazing speed and comfort. Many people become attached to their cars and the speed with which they can travel. Suddenly, the speed of the car and the frenetic rush to get somewhere have become terribly important, and the car has become like a part of the body.

DEFINITIONS AND EXPLANATIONS

needlepoint (line 5) Skillfully worked embroidery.

bereaved (line 8) Suffering from a serious loss as of love, hope, or happiness.

cynical (line 8) Questioning; pessimistic.

yews (line 8) A variety of evergreen trees.

columbines (line 9) A variety of especially lovely flowers.

abstract (line 15) Thought of in a general way apart from anything concrete, specific, or particular.

STUDY QUESTIONS

1. How have the human and the car become like one creature?

2. What is the "creaking and enormous foot" (line 2) that crushes the clover? In what sense is it "enormous"?

3. What are some of the delicate sights and sounds that the driver misses as the car speeds down the highway? Which sights can you add that are not mentioned in the poem? Why is the moss compared to needlepoint? Why is this an appropriate **metaphor**? How is **personification** used to describe the brook? Why are the yews described as "bereaved"?

4. What is the rich, intricate, and lovely world around the driver reduced to? What is the only impression that registers on the driver's mind? Why is space abstract to the driver?

5. According to the speaker, how have cars affected the people who drive them?

WRITING

In some ways, this poem is a commentary on the natural beauty that is lost to those who rush through life. Write an essay explaining how we can recapture and appreciate some of nature's beauty despite the hectic life of today's world.

A WAY OF LIFE

Howard Nemerov

It's been going on a long time.
For instance, these two guys, not saying much, who
    slog
Through sun and sand, fleeing the scene of their
    crime,
Till one turns, without a word, and smacks
His buddy flat with the flat of an axe,   5
Which cuts down on the dialogue
Some, but is viewed rather as normal than sad
By me, as I wait for the next ad.

It seems to me it's been quite a while
Since the last vision of blonde loveliness   10
Vanished, her shampoo and shower and general style
Replaced by this lean young lunk-
head parading along with a gun in his back to confess
How yestereve, being drunk
And in a state of existential despair,   15
He beat up his grandma and pawned her invalid
    chair.

But here at last is a pale beauty
Smoking a filter beside a mountain stream,
Brief interlude, before the conflict of love and duty
Gets moving again, as sheriff and posse expound,   20
Between jail and saloon, the American Dream
Where Justice, after considerable horsing around,
Turns out to be Mercy; when the villain is knocked
    off,
A kindly uncle offers syrup for my cough.

continued

The problem of pollution takes many different forms, some less obvious than others. More and more attention is being given to the problem of mind pollution, particularly as caused by television pouring its programs and commercials into virtually every American home. There is good reason to believe that television is one of our most powerful educational forces, playing a far more important role than our schools in shaping the mind and character of the American people. Some experts believe that commercial television tends to reduce the regular viewer to a robot-like creature whose capacity for feeling and thinking creatively has been weakened significantly. Practically everybody recognizes the ways in which commercials influence viewers. The programs themselves influence viewers in less obvious ways that are alarming more and more people. Howard Nemerov writes about the programs, the commercials, and one television viewer.

DEFINITIONS AND EXPLANATIONS

existential (line 15)   Living without purpose or meaning.

expound (line 20)   Explain; interpret.

global hats (line 26)   Space helmets.

depilatory (line 38)   A commercial product, used by women mainly, for removing unwanted hair from such areas as legs and upper lips.

STUDY QUESTIONS

1. What episode from a television program is described in the first **stanza?** Why does the viewer see the incident "rather as normal than sad" (line 7)? How does the viewer react to the violent smacking down of the "buddy"? How does the viewer react to the entire scene? Why is this **anticlimactic?**

2. What scene, following the commercial, is described in the second **stanza?** What commercial then follows in the third stanza? How does the viewer feel about the commercial?

3. What scene is described in the third **stanza?** What commercial follows?

And now these clean-cut athletic types   25
In global hats are having a nervous debate
As they stand between their individual rocket ships
Which have landed, appropriately, on some rocks
Somewhere in Space, in an atmosphere of hate
Where one tells the other to pull up his socks   30
And get going, he doesn't say where; they fade,
And an angel food cake flutters in the void.

I used to leave now and again;
No more. A lot of violence in American life
These days, mobsters and cops all over the scene.   35
But there's a lot of love, too, mixed with the strife,
And kitchen-kindness, like a bedtime story
With rich food and a more kissable depilatory.
Still, I keep my weapons handy, sitting here
Smoking and shaving and drinking the dry beer.   40

4. What scene is described in the fourth **stanza?** What popular kind of program is this scene from? How does the line "Somewhere in Space, in an atmosphere of hate" tie together and bring to a strong climax all the scenes described? What commercial follows?

5. How are the last five lines of the poem **ironic?** What meaning is given to "love" (line 36) and to the activities of the viewer?

6. Why are the title and the first line of the poem **ironic?**

WRITING

Choose a program and a commercial which you think are ridiculous. Explain why. Tell how they manipulate the viewer's intelligence and emotions.

WHEN I HEARD THE LEARN'D ASTRONOMER

Walt Whitman

When I heard the learn'd astronomer,
When the proofs, the figures, were ranged in
    columns before me,
When I was shown the charts and diagrams, to add,
    divide, and measure them,
When I, sitting, heard the astronomer where he
    lectured with much applause in the lecture room,
How soon unaccountable I became tired and sick,   5
Till rising and gliding out I wandered off by myself,
In the mystical moist night air, and from time to time,
Looked up in perfect silence at the stars.

In order to understand nature better and to reshape it for human benefit, scientists analyze it. By observing and measuring the universe, science aims to understand it more completely. Walt Whitman thinks that something valuable may be lost by scientific analysis. Do you agree?

DEFINITION

unaccountable (line 5)   Not explainable.

STUDY QUESTIONS

1. Who is the speaker of this poem? Where is the speaker when the poem opens (lines 1–5)? What is the speaker listening to and what is he shown? What does the speaker do? How does this action affect his mood? How does the **alliterative** phrase "mystical moist night air" reflect the speaker's changed mood?

2. How does the lecture affect the others in the audience? How does it affect the speaker? How does the poet use **repetition** to reflect the speaker's mood?

3. How does the poem suggest that something in nature is lost through scientific analysis?

WRITING

Do you agree or disagree with the point of view expressed in the poem? Take a stand and explain it in a paragraph or two.

MUSIC

This poem concludes with a peaceful, meditative mood. A work of music which expresses the same mood is Samuel Barber's "Adagio for Strings." How would you describe this selection? How does it develop? Why is it peaceful and evocative?

MR. ATTILA
Carl Sandburg

They made a myth of you, professor,
    you of the gentle voice,
    the books, the specs,
    the furtive rabbit manners
    in the mortar-board cap   5
    and the medieval gown.

They didn't think it, eh professor?
On account of you're so absent-minded,
you bumping into the tree and saying,
"Excuse me, I thought you were a tree,"   10
passing on again blank and absent-minded.

Now it's "Mr. Attila, *how* do you do?"
Do you pack wallops of wholesale death?
Are you the practical dynamic son-of-a-gun?
Have you come through with a few abstractions?   15
Is it you Mr. Attila we hear saying,
"I beg your pardon but we believe we have made
    some degree of progress on the residual qualities
    of the atom"?

DEFINITIONS AND EXPLANATIONS

Attila (title)   Attila was a king of an ancient tribe of barbarians, the Huns. Called the Scourge of God, Attila attacked central Europe and Rome.

myth (line 1)   Imaginary picture of a person.

specs (line 3)   Eyeglasses; spectacles.

furtive (line 4)   Secretive.

mortar-board cap (line 5)   The academic cap worn by college professors and students on ceremonious occasions.

medieval gown (line 6)   The black gown is worn along with the mortar-board cap. The cap and gown as a costume are a symbol of learning and of the highest achievements of civilized society.

abstractions (line 15)   Principles; concepts.

residual (line 18)   Describing what is left after a process is completed, as ash after a fire or fallout after an atomic explosion.

In the modern world, the scientist is a giant who has created vast changes at an ever-accelerating pace. For a long time, the scientist was worshipped as a hero. Then, as the result of brilliant work in mathematics and physics, came nuclear weapons. The destructiveness of these weapons is terrible to contemplate. Even worse are the long-term residual effects of fallout and contamination.

STUDY QUESTIONS

1. The mythical Professor Attila is described in the first two **stanzas** of the poem. How are the professor's appearance, personal mannerisms, and behavior described? What kind of person, in general, was this Professor Attila imagined to be?

2. In line 7, who are "they"? What is it, exactly, that "they" think?

3. How is the new Professor Attila described in the third **stanza?** How do the professor's words, quoted in lines 17–18, add to this real picture of him? How does the **allusion** in the Professor's name add to the real picture of him?

4. Sandburg often gives his poetry a special flavor by mixing colorful slang with formal literary language and by introducing humor in a very serious context. How does he accomplish this in this poem? How effective is this technique? Why?

WRITING

1. Does the work of the scientists who created the atomic bomb deserve the rebuke it receives in this poem? Justify your answer. How has the work of other scientists posed similar problems?

2. Some people have argued that nuclear weapons are blessings in disguise because they provide a deterrent for world leaders who might otherwise wage war. How do you feel? Explain. How do you think Sandburg would react?

NIGHT JOURNEY
Theodore Roethke

Now as the train bears west,
Its rhythm rocks the earth,
And from my Pullman berth
I stare into the night
While others take their rest.   5
Bridges of iron lace,
A suddenness of trees,
A lap of mountain mist
All cross my line of sight,
Then a bleak wasted place,   10
And a lake below my knees.
Full on my neck I feel
The straining at a curve;
My muscles move with steel,
I wake in every nerve.   15
I watch a beacon swing
From dark to blazing bright;
We thunder through ravines
And gullies washed with light.
Beyond the mountain pass   20
Mist deepens on the pane;
We rush into a rain
That rattles double glass.
Wheels shake the roadbed stone,
The pistons jerk and shove,   25
I stay up half the night
To see the land I love.

In this poem, the speaker is on a train traveling at high speed at night. The experience itself has many similarities to that of the driver in "Eight-Cylinder Man." However, people react to similar experiences in different ways.

DEFINITIONS AND EXPLANATIONS

Pullman (line 3)   A railroad car with sleeping berths for overnight journeys.

bleak (line 10)   Bare and desolate.

ravines (line 18)   Long deep hollows in the earth's surface.

gullies (line 19)   Channels; narrow ravines.

STUDY QUESTIONS

1. In which part of the United States is the train traveling? Why is this significant?

2. How does the poet use **imagery** to make the poem come alive? Give examples of visual imagery (things seen), auditory imagery (things heard) and kinesthetic imagery (things felt in the muscles and nerves of the body).

3. How do many of the lines suggest the high speed of the train? Give several examples.

4. How does the speaker seem to feel? How are those feelings created?

5. "Eight-Cylinder Man" and other poems suggest that science and technology are often in conflict with nature. How does Roethke seem to feel about this issue?

WRITING

Write an essay or a poem in which other aspects of science and technology (or their products) create the same attitudes as does "Night Journey."

THE WHEEL TURNS
from *THE PEOPLE, YES*
Carl Sandburg

The wheel turns.
The wheel comes to a standstill.
The wheel waits.
The wheel turns.

"Something began me   5
and it had no beginning:
something will end me
and it has no end."

The people is a long shadow
trembling around the earth,   10
stepping out of fog gray into smoke red
and back from smoke red into fog gray
and lost on parallels and meridians
learning by shock and wrangling,
by heartbreak so often and loneliness so raw   15
the laugh comes at least half true,
"My heart was made to be broken."

"Man will never write,"
they said before the alphabet came
and man at last began to write.   20
"Man will never fly,"
they said before the planes and blimps
zoomed and purred in arcs
winding their circles around the globe.

continued

hat is the final estimate that we should make of "progress," of the changes created by science and technology, of the resulting ecological problems? Looking at the whole picture, should we be optimistic or pessimistic? Carl Sandburg looked at one part of this complex picture in "Mr. Attila" and gave us his reaction. This excerpt from *The People, Yes* tells us how Sandburg feels about the whole story of the workings of human intelligence.

DEFINITIONS AND EXPLANATIONS

parallels (line 13)   The imaginary lines, parallel to the equator, drawn on a map to show distance from the equator (degrees of latitude).

meridians (line 13)   The imaginary lines drawn around the earth, running through the North and South Poles, that show degrees of longitude.

wrangling (line 14)   Quarreling angrily.

reciprocals (line 47)   Interacting parts; things having corresponding but reversed actions.

STUDY QUESTIONS

1. How is the "wheel" mentioned in the opening four lines used as a **metaphor?**

2. Who is the speaker of the quoted statement in lines 5–8? How does that speaker feel about the human race?

3. In the third **stanza** (lines 9–17), what is suggested about "the people" and their story by such **images** as "fog gray" and "smoke red" and "lost on parallels and meridians"? Why are the words "My heart was made to be broken" (line 17) spoken with a laugh?

4. Who are the speakers of the quoted words in the fourth **stanza** (line 18 and line 21)? How are they shown to be wrong?

5. Why is the literal mention of the wheel in lines 34–36 important? How does Sandburg describe the creative process of invention in these lines and in lines 37–40?

6. How would you describe the combined effect of the series of **images** and **rhythms** of lines 44–47?

7. What kind of answer does the whole poem suggest to the last two questions—"Where to? what next?" Explain.

167

"Man will never make the United States of Europe   25
nor later yet the United States of the World,
"No, you are going too far when you talk about one
    world flag for the great Family of Nations,"
    they say that now.

And man the stumbler and finder, goes on,   30
    man the dreamer of deep dreams,
    man the shaper and maker,
    man the answerer.
The first wheel maker saw a wheel, carried
in his head a wheel, and one day found his   35
hands shaping a wheel, the first wheel.
The first wagon makers saw a wagon, joined
their hands and out of air, out of what
had lived in their minds, made the first
wagon.   40
One by one man alone and man joined
has made things with his hands
beginning in the fog wisp of a dim imagining
resulting in a tool, a plan, a working model,
    bones joined to breath being alive   45
in wheels within wheels, ignition, power,
transmission, reciprocals, beyond man alone,
alive only with man joined.
        Where to? what next?

WRITING

Some people find it easy to arrive at answers to difficult problems because they are not realistic. They oversimplify and see what they wish to see in order to arrive at the answer they want. In the poem, Sandburg has tackled the difficult question of human destiny. Write a paragraph explaining whether or not you believe he was realistic in arriving at this answer.

MUSIC

"The Wheel Turns" is about the glory and progress of mankind in all its complex simplicity. Listen to Aaron Copland's *Fanfare for the Common Man*. How does this selection capture the view of humanity held by Sandburg?

Nature and Our Environment

1. Memorable lines Continue to add to your collection of memorable or quotable lines. From the poems in this unit, select two passages of one line or several lines. The basis of your selection may be strength of image, music of line, depth of emotion, appeal of theme, or any combination of these. Write the passages in your notebook with title and author. Memorizing the lines will give you added pleasure.

2. Briefly review the poems in this unit. Then, answer the following questions:

a. How does ''God's World'' celebrate the beauty of nature in autumn?

b. How does ''Oread'' suggest unity in the natural beauty of land and sea?

c. How does ''When I Heard the Learn'd Astronomer'' express the contrast between scientific analysis and the grandeur of nature?

d. Why would ''A Way of Life'' appeal to the supporters of public television?

e. How does ''The Wheel Turns'' demonstrate that humanity has overcome some of the negative qualities ascribed to it?

3. Show your knowledge of terms in poetry. Here are five short passages from the poems in this unit. Choosing from the list of terms that follows, name the term applicable to the passage and explain why the passage is an example of the term you selected.

metaphor	**anticlimax**
apostrophe	**personification**
kinesthetic imagery	

a. ''Thy winds, thy wide grey skies!
   Thy mists that roll and rise!''
   —Edna St. Vincent Millay: ''God's World''

b. "The Maple wears a gayer scarf—"
   —Emily Dickinson: "The morns are meeker than they were"

c. "One hangs lanterns on the wrecks that cling,
   Empty husks of locusts to iron poles."
   —Karl Shapiro: "Auto Wreck"

d. "Till one turns, without a word, and smacks
   His buddy flat with the flat of an axe,
   Which cuts down on the dialogue
   Some, but is viewed rather as normal than sad
   By me, as I wait for the next ad."
   —Howard Nemerov: "A Way of Life"

e. "Full on my neck I feel
   The straining at a curve;
   My muscles move with steel,
   I wake in every nerve."
   —Theodore Roethke: "Night Journey"

4. Review your knowledge of vocabulary by choosing the numbered word or phrase whose meaning is closest to the underlined word.

a. sages   (1) money earned (2) wise persons
             (3) elderly men (4) young girls (5) pieces

b. myriads   (1) small amounts (2) pyramids (3) mirror-like
             (4) countless numbers (5) totals

c. depilatory (1) hair remover (2) negative (3) stain remover
             (4) talkative (5) abusive

d. culprit   (1) wool gatherer (2) attacker (3) guilty person
             (4) day laborer (5) dilettante

e. bleak   (1) bare and desolate (2) bluish in color
             (3) quiet and withdrawn (4) different
             (5) cheerful

f. Under tremendous pressure, the woman had become deranged.
        (1) locked up (2) manipulated (3) sold
        (4) insane (5) removed from the ranch

g. "Do not be gauche at the dinner table," she exclaimed.
        (1) Mexican sandwich (2) awkward (3) old
        (4) materialistic (5) heavily involved

h. The matter ought to be handled in the most expedient manner possible.
        (1) explained (2) malevolent (3) deficient
        (4) experienced (5) convenient

i. The professor liked to <u>expound</u> upon his favorite theories regarding the possibility of life in outer space.
    (1) explain   (2) facilitate   (3) prove
    (4) evaluate   (5) analyze

j. The suspect moved around in a <u>furtive</u> manner.
    (1) frightened   (2) cruel   (3) secretive
    (4) incarcerated   (5) adept

5. Poems and paintings   Poets and painters are artists who have much in common. Study each of the reproductions of paintings that follow. Examine the image carefully. Just what do you see? What feelings does the image arouse in you? What mood or idea does the picture suggest? If a person or persons appear, try to flesh out in your mind their background and character. Is rhythm, metaphor, or symbol important in the picture? After you have studied each picture in this way, select the one that you associate most powerfully with one of the poems in this unit. Be ready to discuss or write about your choice and the reasons for it.

Optional: Select one picture that inspires you to write your own poem and write the poem.

EXPRESS TRAIN   Thomas Hart Benton. *ca. 1927. Whitney Museum, New York.*
Variation: **GOING WEST** Lithograph. Sheet: 18½ × 29½ in. Image: 12¼ × 23⅜ in. Purchase
31.604.

BLAST FURNACE—NUMBER 2
Thomas Hart Benton. *1929.*
Whitney Museum, New York.
Variation: **STUDY FOR MURAL,**
STEEL INK ON PAPER. Sight: 12⅞
× 9¼ in. 31.487.

THE GREAT WAVE AT KANAGAWA **Katsushika Hokusai.** *1823–29.*
The Metropolitan Museum of Art, The Howard Mansfield Collection,
Rogers Fund, 1936.

THE BEACH **William Baziotes.** *1955. Whitney Museum, New York.*
Oil on canvas. 36 × 48 in. Purchase 56.12.

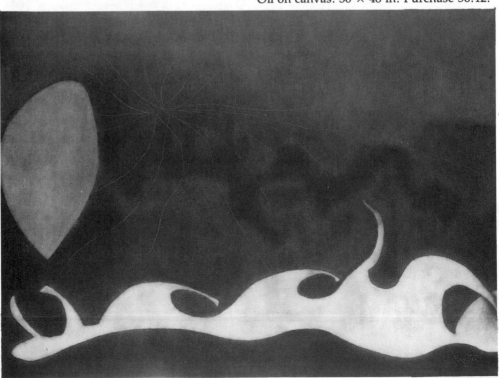

174

Values

*"It is easier for a camel to go through
the eye of a needle, than for a rich man
to enter into the kingdom of God."*

New Testament

*"And now abideth faith, hope, charity, these three:
but the greatest of these is charity."*

New Testament

*"A crowd is not company, and faces are
but a gallery of pictures, and talk but a
tinkling cymbal, where there is no love."*

Francis Bacon

*"Beauty is truth, truth beauty,—that is all
Ye know on earth, and all ye need to know."*

John Keats

As the foregoing quotations show, there is a universal
need for belief in the great and basic laws of life that dates back
to ancient times. Human beings need values—moral, ethical,
and spiritual convictions, to guide us through our daily lives.

In recent years, a subtle dissatisfaction has worked its way
into the American conscience. Among writers, thinkers, and
ordinary people, there has been an emptiness, a sense of
something missing in life, a yearning for a new and better set
of values. This unit will show us what our poets have said
about the pressing need for values and the predominance of
materialism.

TRUTH
Gwendolyn Brooks

And if sun comes
How shall we greet him?
Shall we not dread him,
Shall we not fear him
After so lengthy a   5
Session with shade?

Though we have wept for him,
Though we have prayed
All through the night-years—
What if we wake one shimmering morning to   10
Hear the fierce hammering
Of his firm knuckles
Hard on the door?

Shall we not shudder?—
Shall we not flee   15
Into the shelter, the dear thick shelter
Of the familiar
Propitious haze?

Sweet is it, sweet is it
To sleep in the coolness   20
Of snug unawareness.

The dark hangs heavily
Over the eyes.

In humanity's value system, truth ranks at the top. Though everybody will say that truth is good and right, how many people will act accordingly? There are other issues involved as well. For example, do people really want truth, or do they prefer to be comfortable? On the other hand, is truth *always* good and right? And, finally, do we really know what truth is?

STUDY QUESTIONS

1. In the first **stanza,** how are truth and untruth represented by **symbols?**

2. According to lines 7–8, how have people felt about the truth? What are the ''night-years'' (line 9)?

3. How is **personification** used to characterize truth in the second **stanza?**

4. How does the poet use language to sketch a contrasting picture of the absence of truth in lines 16–21?

5. In the last two lines of the poem, what does the speaker finally seem to be suggesting about the choice between truth and untruth?

6. How does the poet use the music of **repetition** to give emotional intensity to her words?

WRITING

Gwendolyn Brooks is a distinguished African-American poet. What comment might she be making in this poem about racial problems in America? Explain in detail.

ON THE PULSE OF MORNING

Maya Angelou

A Rock, A River, A Tree
Hosts to species long since departed,
Marked the mastodon,
The dinosaur, who left dried tokens
Of their sojourn here   5
On our planet floor,
Any broad alarm of their hastening doom
Is lost in the gloom of dust and ages.

But today, the Rock cries out to us, clearly, forcefully,
Come, you may stand upon my   10
Back and face your distant destiny,

But seek no haven in my shadow.
I will give you no hiding place down here.

You, created only a little lower than
The angels, have crouched too long in   15
The bruising darkness
Have lain too long
Face down in ignorance.
Your mouths spilling words

Armed for slaughter.   20
The Rock cries out to us today, you may stand upon
    me,
But do not hide your face.

Across the wall of the world,
A River sings a beautiful song. It says,
Come, rest here by my side.   25

continued

What does the inauguration of a new president of the United States signify? What do people expect in a new administration? It is very likely that some time during your high-school years, a president will be inaugurated. Think of the dreams people have. Think of their needs and hopes. Think about how the country places its faith in a president to lead it and to bring it good fortune. This poem was written by the esteemed writer Maya Angelou especially for the inauguration ceremony of President William Jefferson (Bill) Clinton in January 1993. It is a poem of inspiration and hope, one which combines the knowledge of the past with a vision for the future. As you finish reading the poem ask yourself how it expresses the hopes and dreams people have for the coming years for themselves and their children and their children's children.

DEFINITIONS AND EXPLANATIONS

mastodon (line 3)   An extinct predecessor of the modern elephant.

sojourn (line 5)   a temporary stay or visit to a place.

cynicism (line 38)   contemptuous distrust.

sear (line 38)   a scar which was burned in by intense heat.

Pawnee, Apache, Seneca, you Cherokee Nation (lines 58–59)   American Indian tribes.

Ashanti, the Yoruba, the Kru (line 65)   African tribes.

Midas (line 99)   A legendary ancient Greek king who asked the gods to turn all he touched to gold. He was granted his wish.

mendicant (line 99)   A beggar.

1. Why does the poet choose the Rock, the River, and the Tree as the three universal objects for this poem? How does the first **stanza** reinforce her choice?

2. What purpose does the Rock serve? What does it want from humanity? How does it describe humanity?

3. What song does the River sing? How have countries with their arbitrary boundaries, responded to the River's song? What does the River seem to want most of all?

4. Describe the time when the Tree, the Rock and the River were one.

5. Who wishes to respond to the singing River and the wise Rock? What do they hear? What does the Tree say?

6. Why does the Tree describe the horrible recollections of humanity's abuse of itself? Why are the lines ''History, despite its wrenching pain,/Cannot be unlived, but if faced/With courage, need not be lived again.'' so significant?

7. Why is the **stanza** ''Lift up your eyes. . .'' so short? What point is being emphasized by its separation from the rest of the poem?

8. How should people treat the dream? Why?

9. The last two **stanzas** appear to be building to a climax. How does the poet create this effect? What is the climax of this poem? Why is the simple phrase ''Good morning'' so effective a conclusion?

10. How are we, according to the poet, ''On the Pulse of Morning''?

WRITING

This is a poem of hope, a poem which asks the readers to recognize the faults of the past and build upon them to create a better world. Which faults of the past would you like to see rectified? Write a plan for creating a piece of a better world which keeps in mind Maya Angelou's vision of humanity.

Each of you, a bordered country,
Delicate and strangely made proud,
Yet thrusting perpetually under siege.
Your armed struggles for profit
Have left collars of waste upon   30
My shore, currents of debris upon my breast.
Yet today I call you to my riverside,
If you will study war no more.

Come, clad in peace,
And I will sing the songs   35
The Creator gave to me when I and the
Tree and the rock were one.
Before cynicism was a bloody sear across your
Brow and when you yet knew you still
Knew nothing.   40
The River sang and sings on.

There is a true yearning to respond to
The singing River and the wise Rock.
So say the Asian, the Hispanic, the Jew
The African, the Native American, the Sioux,   45
The Catholic, the Muslim, the French, the Greek

The Irish, the Rabbi, the Priest, the Sheik,
The Gay, the Straight, the Preacher,
The privileged, the homeless, the Teacher.
They hear. They all hear   50
The speaking of the Tree.

They hear the first and last of every Tree
Speak to humankind today. Come to me, here beside
     the River.
Plant yourself beside the River.

Each of you, descendant of some passed   55
On traveller, has been paid for.

You, who gave me my first name, you,
Pawnee, Apache, Seneca, you
Cherokee Nation, who rested with me, then
Forced on bloody feet,   60
Left me to the employment of
Other seekers—desperate for gain,
Starving for gold.

You, the Turk, the Arab, the Swede, the German, the
     Eskimo, the Scot,
You the Ashanti, the Yoruba, the Kru, bought,   65
Sold, stolen, arriving on the nightmare
Praying for a dream.

Here, root yourselves beside me.
I am that Tree planted by the River,
Which will not be moved.   70
I, the Rock, I, the River, I, the Tree
I am yours—your passages have been paid.
Lift up your faces, you have a piercing need
For this bright morning dawning for you.
History, despite its wrenching pain,   75
Cannot be unlived, but if faced
With courage, need not be lived again.

Lift up your eyes upon
This day breaking for you.
Give birth again   80
To the dream.

Women, children, men,
Take it into the palms of your hands,
Mold it into the shape of your most

Private need. Sculpt it into 85
The image of your most public self.
Lift up your hearts
Each new hour holds new chances
For a new beginning.
Do not be wedded forever 90
To fear, yoked eternally
To brutishness.

The horizon leans forward,
Offering you space to place new steps of change.
Here, on the pulse of this fine day 95
You may have the courage
To look up and out and upon me, the
Rock, the River, the Tree, your country.
No less to Midas than the mendicant.
No less to you now than the mastodon then. 100

Here, on the pulse of this new day
You may have the grace to look up and out
And into your sister's eyes, and into
Your brother's face, your country
And say simply 105
Very simply
With hope—
Good morning.

RICHARD CORY
Edwin Arlington Robinson

Whenever Richard Cory went down town,
We people on the pavement looked at him:
He was a gentleman from sole to crown,
Clean favored, and imperially slim.

And he was always quietly arrayed,   5
And he was always human when he talked;
But still he fluttered pulses when he said,
"Good-morning," and he glittered when he walked.

And he was rich—yes, richer than a king—
And admirably schooled in every grace: 10
In fine, we thought that he was everything
To make us wish that we were in his place.

So on we worked, and waited for the light,
And went without the meat, and cursed the bread;
And Richard Cory, one calm summer night,   15
Went home and put a bullet through his head.

DEFINITIONS AND EXPLANATIONS

sole to crown (line 3)   Foot to head.

Clean favored (line 4)   Having fine, handsome features.

imperially (line 4)   Majestically; aristocratically.

arrayed (line 5)   Dressed in fine clothing.

grace (line 10)   A sense of what is right and proper; charming and pleasing behavior.

in fine (line 11)   In conclusion.

Among the most widely read and best known of all American poems, "Richard Cory" tells a dramatic story with a shocking surprise ending. Stated in carefully chosen language, the poem is mind-boggling in that it puzzles and makes the reader think and probe in the darkest corners of his or her mind.

STUDY QUESTIONS

1. According to lines 2, 13, and 14, who are the speakers of the poem? How would you describe their condition of life? Why do they curse the bread? What is the light they are waiting for?

2. How did Richard Cory act towards the people when he "went down town"? How do they feel about him?

3. Which phrases tell you something about Richard Cory's personality, background, and appearance? Why are they effective in creating a picture of Cory?

4. Robinson uses words like "crown," "imperially," "arrayed," "glittered," "king," "grace," and so on when writing about Richard Cory. How do words such as these contribute to our impression about the title character? What is their **connotation?**

5. The last line shocks the reader because it contrasts with everything that has preceded it about Richard Cory. How is the force of the last line's shock added to by the **image,** the **diction,** the **rhythms,** and the **rhyme** of the line?

WRITING

1. The irony of the poem is that the ordinary people worked hard and waited for an improvement in their condition. On the other hand, Richard Cory, a man who seemed to have everything he could possibly want or need, chose to end his life by suicide. In a paragraph, explain what comment on values the poem may be making. How do you feel about the irony of the poem?

2. In your journal, write an entry discussing how you feel about material wealth vs. spiritual wealth. Which is more important? Why? How can we be happy without material possessions?

3. The speaker of "Richard Cory" delivers the eulogy at Richard's funeral. Write the eulogy.

MUSIC

Study the lyrics to Simon and Garfunkel's song "Richard Cory" which are different from the words of the poem. From what point of view is the song written? Compare and contrast the lyrics with the words of the poem in terms of theme and message.

LUCINDA MATLOCK

Edgar Lee Masters

I went to the dances at Chandlerville,
And played snap-out at Winchester.
One time we changed partners,
Driving home in the moonlight of middle June,
And then I found Davis.   5
We were married and lived together for seventy
    years,
Enjoying, working, raising the twelve children,
Eight of whom we lost
Ere I had reached the age of sixty.
I spun, I wove, I kept the house, I nursed the sick,   10
I made the garden, and for holiday
Rambled over the fields where sang the larks,
And by Spoon River gathering many a shell,
And many a flower and medicinal weed—
Shouting to the wooded hills, singing to the green
    valleys.   15
At ninety-six I had lived enough, that is all,
And passed to a sweet repose.
What is this I hear of sorrow and weariness,
Anger, discontent and drooping hopes?
Degenerate sons and daughters,   20
Life is too strong for you—
It takes life to love Life.

In each generation of young people, there are those who react against the values of the older generation. In recent years, some people have sought more satisfying values in the form of a simpler, more natural way of life. That lifestyle and the values that govern it are not new, of course, as this poem about a member of a much older generation shows.

DEFINITIONS AND EXPLANATIONS

Lucinda Matlock (title) This is another poem from *Spoon River Anthology*. Remember that the speaker has died and is looking back on and evaluating her life.

Chandlerville (line 1) and **Winchester** (line 2) These are towns in western Illinois, the region in which *Spoon River Anthology* is set.

snap-out (line 2) Dancers formed two circles, an inner and an outer. They skipped by each other in opposite directions. At a signal, a young man would claim the girl of his choice by snapping her through the circle. The purpose of such rural folk dances was courting.

medicinal weed (line 14) Most folk remedies are based on the use of herbs and plants that have medicinal properties.

repose (line 17) Rest.

degenerate (line 20) Sunk to a lower level; deteriorated.

STUDY QUESTIONS

1. What are the two memories of her youth that stand out in Lucinda's mind? What do these show about her? How did she meet her future husband?

2. How does the poem show that Lucinda lived a simple and self-reliant life? What losses did she face? How did she react to them?

3. How do you explain Lucinda's "shouting" and "singing" (line 15)? Why does she say "that is all" (line 16)?

4. How do you account for the younger generation's having feelings of "anger, discontent, drooping hopes" (line 19)?

5. What does the last line of the poem, "It takes life to love Life" mean?

WRITING

Have you ever felt that the older generation had values different from your own? Write about a situation in which you felt that to be the case.

KINDLY UNHITCH THAT STAR, BUDDY
Ogden Nash

I hardly suppose I know anybody who wouldn't
    rather be a success than a failure,
Just as I suppose every piece of crabgrass in the
    garden would much rather be an azalea,
And in celestial circles all the run-of-the-mill angels
    would rather be archangels or at least cherubim
    and seraphim,
And in the legal world all the little process-servers
    hope to grow up into great big bailiffim and
    sheriffim.
Indeed, everybody wants to be a wow,   5
But not everybody knows exactly how.
Some people think they will eventually wear
    diamonds instead of rhinestones
Only by everlastingly keeping their noses to their
    grhinestones,
And other people think they will be able to put in
    more time at Palm Beach and the Ritz
By not paying too much attention to attendance at the
    office but rather in being brilliant by starts and
    fits.   10
Some people after a full day's work sit up all night
    getting a college education by correspondence,
While others seem to think they'll get just as far by
    devoting their evenings to the study of the
    difference in temperament between brunettance
    and blondance.
Some stake their all on luck,
And others put their faith in their ability to pass the
    buck.

continued

In many ways, Lucinda Matlock was a typical American. In one major way, however, she was quite unusual. Americans characteristically value success by material things, by power, fame, money, and the status symbols that go with them. In the admiring picture he sketched of Lucinda Matlock, Edgar Lee Masters was speaking out against the American ethic of financial achievement. In this poem, Ogden Nash speaks out against the same thing, but with his own unique comic voice.

DEFINITIONS AND EXPLANATIONS

Kindly Unhitch That Star, Buddy (title) In one of his essays, Emerson wrote, "Hitch your wagon to a star." The statement has become widely known and is used as a proverb. It is often interpreted to mean "Be ambitious for great success," though that was not quite what Emerson had in mind.

azalea (line 2)   A beautiful flowering shrub.

celestial (line 3)   Heavenly.

archangels (line 3)   Angels of the chief rank.

cherubim (line 3)   An order of angels of high rank. Note that the word is of Hebrew origin. The singular is "cherub" and the plural is formed by adding the suffix "im."

seraphim (line 3)   An order of angels of high rank. Note that the singular is "seraph" and the plural is formed as in the case of "cherub."

process-servers (line 4)   Low-level officers of a judicial court, who deliver summonses or other court orders.

bailiffim (line 4)   A bailiff is an officer of the court, assistant to the sheriff. The actual plural of the word is "bailiffs."

sheriffim (line 4)   The sheriff is the chief law enforcement officer of a county. The plural is "sheriffs."

Palm Beach (line 9)   A Florida resort for the super rich.

Ritz (line 9)   A Parisian hotel, long known as one of the most elegant and expensive in the world.

In short, the world is filled with people trying to
     achieve success,   15
And half of them think they'll get it by saying No and
     half of them by saying Yes,
And if all the ones who say No said Yes, and vice
     versa, such is the fate of humanity that ninety-
     nine per cent of them still wouldn't be any better
     off than they were before,
Which perhaps is just as well because if everybody
     was a success nobody could be contemptuous of
     anybody else and everybody would start in all
     over again trying to be a bigger success than
     everybody else so they would have somebody to
     be contemptuous of and so on forevermore,
Because when people start hitching their wagons to a
     star,
That's the way they are.   20

1. Identify two lines that show that Nash is writing about material success.

2. Which line of the poem sums up most clearly what the poet thinks of success and the effects of success? In your own words, what does the line say?

3. According to the first line, how are the successes and the failures really the same people? What alternative is there?

4. How is the second line humorous?

5. Why is the phrase "run-of-the-mill angels" in line 3 humorous?

6. Through examples, show how the poem illustrates Nash's genius for finding startling **rhymes** in existing words and for fashioning rhymes out of nonexistent word forms and spellings.

7. Give one example from the poem of those who seek success by saying "yes" and one example of those who seek success by saying "no."

WRITING

Do you think Lucinda Matlock would have enjoyed reading this poem? Why or why not?

I TASTE A LIQUOR NEVER BREWED

Emily Dickinson

I taste a liquor never brewed,
From tankards scooped in pearl;
Not all the vats upon the Rhine
Yield such an alcohol!

Inebriate of air am I,   5
And debauchee of dew,
Reeling, through endless summer
    days,
From inns of molten blue.

When landlords turn the drunken bee
Out of the foxglove's door,   10
When butterflies renounce their drams,
I shall but drink the more!

Till seraphs swing their snowy hats,
And saints to windows run,
To see the little tippler   15
Leaning against the sun!

A sense of joy in being alive and a sense of being delighted to be one's self are states of mind that practically everybody seeks but all too few achieve. What may lead to that state of mind? One thing that might help is an appreciation of beauty in one of the many forms that it takes. Here, Emily Dickinson tells of the effect on her mind of nature's beauty during a glorious summer day and suggests to us the importance of nature's beauty in her value system.

DEFINITIONS AND EXPLANATIONS

tankards (line 2)   Large drinking cups with handles.

inebriate (line 5)   Made drunk; feeling exhilarated.

debauchee (line 6)   A person who indulges the appetite for sensual pleasure to an extreme.

foxglove's (line 10)   Of a plant that bears many thimble-shaped flowers on long stalks.

renounce (line 11)   Give up; swear off.

drams (line 11)   Small drinks of alcohol.

tippler (line 15)   Drunkard.

STUDY QUESTIONS

1. This poem is an extended **metaphor** in which the speaker speaks of herself as though she were finding joy on a drunken spree. Which words or phrases help to build the metaphorical **image** of a drunk on a spree? Who are some of the speaker's "drinking" companions? How does mention of these companions add to the effect of the image?

2. Why does the speaker really feel so "high"?

3. Why is the extended **metaphor** of this poem unusual and joyously comic?

4. The "spree" comes to its climax in the last **stanza.** What audience gathers to see the "drunkard"? Why is this audience humorously unrelated to the **figurative** meaning of the poem but appropriate to the literal meaning? Just how "high" does the drunkard finally feel?

5. Refer back to "Lucinda Matlock." Which lines tell you of a time Lucinda was feeling a "high" similar to that of the speaker in this poem? Was she "drunk" on the same "beverage"?

6. Do you think the words of this poem could readily be used as the lyrics of a song? Why?

WRITING

Is this poem real to you? Have you ever felt intoxicated or exalted by any contact you have had with natural beauty? If so, when? Has some other form of beauty ever had this kind of effect on you? When?

ON HEARING A SYMPHONY OF BEETHOVEN

Edna St. Vincent Millay

Sweet sounds, oh, beautiful music, do not cease!
Reject me not into the world again.
With you alone is excellence and peace,
Mankind made plausible, his purpose plain.
Enchanted in your air benign and shrewd, 5
With limbs a-sprawl and empty faces pale,
The spiteful and the stingy and the rude
Sleep like the scullions in the fairy-tale.

This moment is the best the world can give:
The tranquil blossom on the tortured stem. 10
Reject me not, sweet sounds! oh, let me live,
Till Doom espy my towers and scatter them,
A city spell-bound under the aging sun.
Music my rampart, and my only one.

DEFINITIONS AND EXPLANATIONS

Beethoven (title) Ludwig van Beethoven is regarded by many as the greatest of all composers of classical music, and his symphonies are among the supreme works of art of the world.

plausible (line 4) Acceptable; trustworthy.

benign (line 5) Kindly.

scullions (line 8) The lowest servants in the medieval castle, who did the rough work in the kitchen.

tranquil (line 10) Serene; placid.

tortured (line 10) Twisted; distorted.

rampart (line 14) Protective wall of a castle or fort.

As a basic part of human experience, beauty affects us in several ways. Often, beauty serves people as an intense expression of their own feelings. It is the high point of all the richness and joy that life has to offer. However, most of us have moments when we are feeling down, depressed, and unhappy. At such times, beauty can be a welcome escape, a relief from the pain, sadness, or worry we are feeling. The beauty of music has probably provided you with such escape and relief, as it does for the speaker of this poem.

STUDY QUESTIONS

1. In the **apostrophe** in the opening lines, to whom or what does the speaker address herself? What is her request?

2. The speaker suggests that there are two worlds, the world of real life and the world created by the music. How does she feel about each of these worlds? Give two or three words or phrases from the poem that show her feelings about each world.

3. In the fairy tale "The Sleeping Beauty," a castle is enchanted so that there is no aging or death for the people within. All is harmonious and peaceful. Which lines and phrases in the poem suggest that the poet is comparing her experience with the music to the atmosphere of the enchanted castle in "The Sleeping Beauty"? Which line tells you that the escape to the enchanted world cannot last?

4. How is a **metaphor** used in lines 9 and 10? Which flower best fits the **image?** Why?

5. How do we know that the poem is an English **sonnet?**

WRITING

For Emily Dickinson, beauty is the expression of life. For Millay, in this poem, beauty is an escape from life. Which vision of beauty appeals to you more? Why?

MUSIC

Listen to any of Beethoven's most intense symphonies while studying or thinking about the poem. The Third (*Eroica*), Fifth, Sixth (*Pastorale*) or Ninth (*Choral*) make for ideal starting points. How could the music have inspired the poem? How is the poem's intensity a reflection of the music's passion and exquisite beauty?

BARTER

Sara Teasdale

Life has loveliness to sell,
  All beautiful and splendid things,
Blue waves whitened on a cliff,
  Soaring fire that sways and sings,
And children's faces looking up   5
Holding wonder like a cup.

Life has loveliness to sell,
  Music like a curve of gold,
Scent of pine trees in the rain,
  Eyes that love you, arms that hold,   10
And for your spirit's still delight,
Holy thoughts that star the night.

Spend all you have for loveliness,
  Buy it and never count the cost;
For one white singing hour of peace   15
  Count many a year of strife well lost,
And for a breath of ecstasy
Give all you have been, or could be.

What makes life worthwhile? What values bring a sense of fulfillment and peace, a sense of deep and satisfying meaning to life despite the pain, hardship, and struggle we all experience? Richard Cory found no answer to these questions and could not go on living. Lucinda Matlock found meaning in the everyday struggle itself. Emily Dickinson saw beauty all around her and found her answer in the sense of ecstasy inspired by this beauty. Edna St. Vincent Millay saw everyday life as a painful experience from which beauty and music provided temporary escape and forgetfulness. The speaker in this poem sees both the hard, painful struggle and the joy of uplifting beauty. She sees life, as suggested by the title "Barter," as an exchange, a trade. One pays the price of pain for the ecstasy of beauty. Does the speaker profit from this barter? Does she get the better of the bargain?

STUDY QUESTIONS

1. Which three lines of the poem repeat the "barter" theme of the title, almost as a **refrain?** What is the "barter" or "trade" the speaker is proposing? How does the poet tell you that the speaker is satisfied that she has gotten the better of the trade?

2. Emily Dickinson reveled in the beauty of nature and Edna St. Vincent Millay in the beauty of music. How does Teasdale use these two forms of beauty in this poem? Which lines from this poem cite three other forms of beauty?

3. In line 8, a **simile** is used to express the beauty of music. The **image** created contains a shape (a curve) and a substance (gold). Why is the shape appropriate? Why is the substance?

4. What is the **rhyme** scheme of the three **stanzas?** How does this rhyme scheme fit the mood of the poem?

WRITING

Of the forms of beauty mentioned in this poem, which has the most appeal for you personally? Why? Can you give two other forms of beauty which you prefer that are not mentioned in this poem? Supply actual examples.

O TASTE AND SEE

Denise Levertov

The world is
not with us enough.
O taste and see

the subway Bible poster said,
meaning *The Lord*, meaning   5
if anything all that lives
to the imagination's tongue,

grief, mercy, language,
tangerine, weather, to
breathe them, bite,   10
savor, chew, swallow, transform

into our flesh our
deaths, crossing the street, plum, quince,
living in the orchard and being

hungry, and plucking   15
the fruit.

The British poet William Wordsworth wrote "The world is too much with us," suggesting, as have other poets in this volume, that we have become too involved in the technology of the world and its effects on us. Denise Levertov here suggests that we are not involved enough in the world. While one might think that she is referring to technology, she is, in fact, referring to the need for people to appreciate all of the natural things in life that we may tend to ignore.

DEFINITIONS AND EXPLANATIONS

"The world is not with us enough" (lines 1–2)   A reversal of the first line of a sonnet by the famous British poet William Wordsworth (1770–1850), which begins "The world is too much with us."

O taste and see (line 3)   A quotation from the Bible "Psalm 34," line 8. In context, the quotation is exhorting the people to taste of the Lord and see that He is good.

quince (line 13)   An apple-like fruit.

STUDY QUESTIONS

1. Why does the speaker think the world is not with us enough?

2. Why does the speaker say "O taste and see?" What does she want us to "taste and see"?

3. What verbs does the speaker use to express the power of her desire that we "taste and see?" Why does she choose those verbs?

4. What biblical **image** is recalled by the image of plucking the fruit? How are we living in an orchard? What point is the speaker making?

WRITING

1. The poet believes that "the world is not with us enough" and that we should "taste and see." Do you agree with her or not? Explain in a carefully supported essay.

2. Read Wordsworth's sonnet and compare his view with Levertov's.

EATING TOGETHER

Li-Young Lee

In the steamer is the trout
seasoned with slivers of ginger,
two sprigs of green onion, and sesame oil.
We shall eat it with rice for lunch,
brothers, sister, my mother who will   5
taste the sweetest meat of the head,
holding it between her fingers
deftly, the way my father did
weeks ago. Then he lay down
to sleep like a snow-covered road   10
winding through pines older than him,
without any travelers, and lonely for no one.

In many cultures, mealtime is an opportunity for a family to be together, to bond, to share the events of a day. It is also a time in which family members can gather strength from each other during a difficult period. In this poem, a Chinese family eats dinner together soon after the death of the father.

DEFINITIONS AND EXPLANATIONS

steamer   A bamboo cooking basket placed above boiling water. The food to be steamed, along with its seasonings, is placed in the basket and cooked. The steaming process allows food to remain moist and to retain its flavor. Trout steamed with ginger and scallions (green onion) is a popular traditional Chinese dish; a whole trout is usually served to a group of people.

deftly (line 8)   With agility; smoothly.

STUDY QUESTIONS

1. How complex is the description of the trout? Why?

2. Who will eat the trout? Why will the mother have the "sweetest meat of the head"? How does the speaker's description of the mother serve as a link to the father?

3. How is the death of the father described? What mood is captured in this description?

4. How does the description of the father contrast with that of the family?

5. Why might this meal be important for the unity of the family? How might it relate to the father?

WRITING

This poem is about keeping a family together after a tragic event by recalling an ethnic tradition. Write a description of an ethnic or religious tradition that helps to bind families together. The circumstances under which the traditional activity takes place can be either joyous or tragic.

POEM IN PROSE
Archibald MacLeish

This poem is for my wife.
I have made it plainly and honestly:
The mark is on it
Like the burl on the knife.

I have not made it for praise.   5
She has no more need for praise
Than summer has
Or the bright days.

In all that becomes a woman
Her words and her ways are beautiful: 10
Love's lovely duty,
The well-swept room.

Wherever she is there is sun
And time and a sweet air:
Peace is there,   15
Work done.

There are always curtains and flowers
And candles and baked bread
And a cloth spread
And a clean house.   20

Her voice when she sings is a voice
At dawn by a freshening sea
Where the wave leaps in the
Wind and rejoices.

Wherever she is it is now.   25
It is here where the apples are:
Here in the stars,
In the quick hour.

The greatest and richest good,
My own life to live in,   30
This she has given me—

If giver could.

$\mathbf{A}$ woodcarver aims to bring out the natural beauty in a piece of wood—the grain, the texture, the shape. In this poem about his wife, the poet has a similar aim. He wants to pay tribute to the natural qualities of his wife without adornment, addition, or exaggeration. That is why he calls it, paradoxically, "Poem in Prose." But the poet is not just writing about his wife. He is making a statement about love as a value for living.

DEFINITIONS AND EXPLANATION

"Like the burl on the knife" (line 4) A burl is a knot in a piece of wood. The line refers to the wooden handle on the knife.

freshening (line 22)   Invigorating.

STUDY QUESTIONS

1. What "mark" (line 3) is on the poem? How is it like the burl on the knife (line 4)?

2. When the speaker mentions "The well-swept room," "curtains and flowers," "candles and baked bread," "a cloth spread," and "a clean house," is he simply appreciating the fact that his wife is a good housekeeper? How does line 11, "Love's lovely duty" help to answer the question?

3. How are **metaphor** and **personification** used in lines 21–24? What mood is created by these **images?**

4. What does the word "now" mean in line 25? How does this line help to explain lines 30–31?

5. In the last line, the poet suggests that a person cannot *give* what his wife "has given" him. Why not?

WRITING

The woodcarver must use tools skillfully to bring out the natural beauty of the wood, to help the wood make its own statement. How has the poet used the tools of diction, imagery, rhythm, and rhyme effectively to make his poem "plainly and honestly"?

SINCE FEELING IS FIRST

e e cummings

since feeling is first
who pays any attention
to the syntax of things
will never wholly kiss you;

wholly to be a fool   5
while Spring is in the world

my blood approves,
and kisses are a better fate
than wisdom
lady i swear by all flowers. Don't cry   10
—the best gesture of my brain is less than
your eyelids' flutter which says

we are for each other: then
laugh, leaning back in my arms
for life's not a paragraph   15

And death i think is no parenthesis

Is love the chief and best of values? If so, how do we know this? Are we told by our brain, our logic, or our reason? Or, are we told by our heart, our feelings, and our instinct?

DEFINITION

syntax (line 3)   The rules of sentence structure.

STUDY QUESTIONS

1. What comparisons does the speaker make between language and life which suggest that mechanical or logical rules don't help us to understand either one?

2. What is really meant by the words "fool," "Spring," "blood," and "wisdom" in the second and third **stanzas?**

3. Why does the speaker choose flowers to swear by? What is a "gesture of my brain"? Why does the speaker con-

sider it less than the "eyelids' flutter" (lines 11–12)?

4. Why does the speaker say "laugh" to his beloved (line 14)?

5. In his own language style, as well as in his interpretation of life and love, e e cummings ignores conventional rules as he sees fit. Does his style seem to you to help or hinder the force of this poem? Why?

WRITING

How is the theme of this poem similar to that of "Poem in Prose"? How is its emphasis different? Which appeals to you more? Why?

THE TELEPHONE
Robert Frost

''When I was just as far as I could walk
From here today,
There was an hour
All still
When leaning with my head against a flower   5
I heard you talk.
Don't say I didn't, for I heard you say—
You spoke from that flower on the window sill—
Do you remember what it was you said?''

''First tell me what it was you thought you heard.''   10

''Having found the flower and driven a bee away,
I leaned my head,
And holding by the stalk,
I listened and I thought I caught the word—
What was it? Did you call me by my name?   15
Or did you say—
Someone said 'Come'—I heard it as I bowed.''

''I may have thought as much, but not aloud.''

''Well, so I came.''

One of the great things about love is the almost magical powers of communication that love gives to lovers. An exchange of glances or a touch of the hand can express worlds of meaning. Even when two lovers are far apart, the bonds of love can act like invisible telephone wires permitting them to hold conversations impossible for others. This poem is a dialogue between two lovers about a conversation they had on a "lovers' telephone."

STUDY QUESTIONS

1. Let us call the two lovers in the poem lover 1 and lover 2. Assuming that the first speaker is lover 1, which lines belong to lover 1 and which belong to lover 2?

2. What physical objects act as the two ends of the "telephone"? Why are they an appropriate **symbol**?

3. Where was lover 1 during the telephone conversation? Where was lover 2?

4. What testing and teasing about the "telephone" conversation takes place during the actual conversation recorded in the poem? How would you explain the teasing? What was actually said on the "telephone"?

5. What does the last line really say?

WRITING

Write a dialogue between two lovers expressing their emotions for each other. Try to make the conversation as natural as possible.

MUSIC

Listen to a recording of your favorite love songs. How do they capture the excitement of true love and the emotions that go with it?

LOVE IS NOT ALL
Edna St. Vincent Millay

Love is not all: it is not meat nor drink
Nor slumber nor a roof against the rain;
Nor yet a floating spar to men that sink
And rise and sink and rise and sink again;
Love can not fill the thickened lung with breath,   5
Nor clean the blood, nor set the fractured bone;
Yet many a man is making friends with death
Even as I speak, for lack of love alone.
It well may be that in a difficult hour,
Pinned down by pain and moaning for release,   10
Or nagged by want past resolution's power,
I might be driven to sell your love for peace,
Or trade the memory of this night for food.
It well may be. I do not think I would.

The poems about love you have just read by Archibald Mac-Leish, Robert Frost, and e e cummings suggest that love is everything. The title of this poem suggests that Edna St. Vincent Millay is going to disagree with them. What approach can she have in mind?

EXPLANATION

nagged by want past resolution's power (line 11) An acceptable paraphrase of this difficult line is: "frustrated by a need that cannot be filled despite strong determination."

STUDY QUESTIONS

1. According to the speaker, what are some of the practical needs that love does not satisfy? In which lines does the speaker enumerate these things?

2. At what two lines does the speaker's view change? How do these two lines remind you of Richard Cory?

3. What circumstances does the speaker mention which might drive her to exchange her love or its memory? Why?

4. After reviewing all the practicalities and possibilities, the speaker reveals her true feelings. What are they?

5. In view of the entire poem, does the speaker mean her opening statement literally? Why? In the context of the entire poem, why does the last line have an especially strong impact?

6. What is the **verse form** of this poem? Explain.

WRITING

Does the poem suggest anything to you about the probable future of the love relationship? Do enduring happiness and fulfillment in this relationship seem to be ahead, or are there heartbreak and tears in the future? Explain in a brief essay.

STOPPING BY WOODS ON A SNOWY EVENING

Robert Frost

Whose woods these are I think I know.
His house is in the village, though;
He will not see me stopping here
To watch his woods fill up with snow.

My little horse must think it queer   5
To stop without a farmhouse near
Between the woods and frozen lake
The darkest evening of the year.

He gives his harness bells a shake
To ask if there is some mistake.   10
The only other sound's the sweep
Of easy wind and downy flake.

The woods are lovely, dark, and deep,
But I have promises to keep,
And miles to go before I sleep,   15
And miles to go before I sleep.

The values we treasure help steer us through life. They shape our everyday decisions and choices and give meaning and direction to all the little things we do. Sometimes, though, a person may be faced with a conflict in values. Then, that person has to make the difficult decision of choosing one value over another.

STUDY QUESTIONS

1. On the surface, this poem narrates a simple incident. Why does the speaker stop? How does the horse react? What does the speaker see? What sounds does the speaker hear? How does the speaker feel about what he sees? Why does the speaker go on?

2. What does the secluded serenity of the woods, the frozen lake, the soft sounds, and the falling snow probably **symbolize** for the speaker? What parallel might be drawn between the meaning of this setting for this speaker and the meaning of Beethoven's symphony for the speaker of Edna St. Vincent Millay's poem? Why does the owner of the woods come into the speaker's mind?

3. How might lines 14 and 15 be **symbolic?** What are the "promises" and to whom might they have been made? What are the "miles to go" and the "sleep"?

4. An **image** that dominates this poem is captured in the words of lines 11–12. That image is reflected in the sounds of the **rhyme scheme** that moves through the poem. What is the rhyme scheme? How is the rhyme scheme used to create an "easy" sweep from each **stanza** to the one that follows? What change is made in the last stanza to bring the flowing pattern to a gentle end? How is the ending neatly reinforced?

WRITING

In reading the poem aloud, would you read the last two lines in the same way or would you read each line differently? Explain your point of view.

THE BLADES OF GRASS

Stephen Crane

In heaven,
Some little blades of grass
Stood before God.
"What did you do?"
Then all save one of the little blades   5
Began eagerly to relate
The merits of their lives.
This one stayed a small way behind,
Ashamed.
Presently, God said,   10
"And what did you do?"
The little blade answered, "Oh, my lord,
Memory is bitter to me,
For, if I did good deeds,
I know not of them."   15
Then God, in all His splendor,
Arose from His throne.
"Ah, best little blade of grass!" He said.

$\mathbf{W}$hy do most of us not like a person who brags and boasts, while most of us like a person who is modest and humble? Is it just a matter of psychology or personality, or is there some basic value involved? Is it somehow important for each of us to recognize how small and inconsequential we are in the scope of the universe? Is humility one of the laws of "the good life"? Is it true, as the Bible says, that the meek will inherit the earth?

STUDY QUESTIONS

1. Why has the poet chosen to write about blades of grass, not people, standing before God? What point does he want to drive home by the choice of this particular **image**?

2. Why does the one blade of grass say "Memory is bitter to me" (line 13)?

3. Why does God feel that the humble blade of grass is the best one?

WRITING

The humble blade of grass is, in the poem, rewarded in heaven for its value. What rewards are there for the humble person on earth? What rewards or benefits are there for human society at large in practicing humility? Explain in a detailed essay.

IN GOYA'S GREATEST SCENES
Lawrence Ferlinghetti

In Goya's greatest scenes we seem to see
                    the people of the world
        exactly at the moment when
        they first attained the title of
                    'suffering humanity'   5

    They writhe upon the page
                in a veritable rage
                of adversity
        Heaped up
                groaning with babies and bayonets   10
                    under cement skies
        in an abstract landscape of blasted trees
            bent statues bats wings and beaks
                slippery gibbets
        cadavers and carnivorous cocks   15
        and all the final hollering monsters
            of the
                'imagination of disaster'
        they are so bloody real
                it is as if they really still existed   20

    And they do

    Only the landscape is changed

continued

Great painters can often capture the horrors of war and human suffering through their art as graphically as poets can through their words. The painter Goya was able to do this exceptionally well. In this poem, Lawrence Ferlinghetti compares the physical violence of Goya's time to the intellectual violence of modern days where technology controls free thought and sets the tone for many Americans.

DEFINITIONS AND EXPLANATIONS

Goya (title)   Francisco Goya (1746–1828) was a Spanish painter and etcher. His series of etchings, "Disasters of War" (1810–1813), expresses the brutality and horror of the invasion of Spain by France led by Napoleon.

writhe (line 6)   To squirm or to twist.

gibbets (line 14)   A gallows, that is, the structure from which an individual is hanged during that form of execution.

cadavers (line 15)   Corpses; dead bodies.

carnivorous cocks (line 15)   Flesh-eating roosters.

false windmills (line 25)   Futile, misleading quests. In Cervantes's *Don Quixote* the title character duels with windmills. The duel with the windmill itself represents the unreachable dream. To duel with a false windmill is to search for what seems to be an ideal but is in fact something corrupt or evil.

tumbrils (line 32)   Two-wheeled carts that farmers use to carry loads from one place to another; these carts were also used during the French Revolution to carry prisoners to the guillotine.

STUDY QUESTIONS

1. What do Goya's "greatest scenes" show?

2. Why does the poet use the phrase "suffering humanity"?

3. How would you describe the **image** created by lines 6–8?

4. How does imagined disaster compare to real disaster?

5. What does the first **stanza** describe?

6. Why is line 22, "Only the landscape is changed" the turning point of the poem?

They still are ranged along the roads
    plagued by legionaires
        false windmills and demented roosters   25

They are the same people
        only further from home
  on freeways fifty lanes wide
    on a concrete continent
       spaced with bland billboards   30
    illustrating imbecile illusions of happiness

The scene shows fewer tumbrils
    but more maimed citizens
       in painted cars
    and they have strange license plates   35
  and engines
    that devour America

7. How does the poet prove that though things change they are still the same in many ways?

8. How would you describe the attitude Ferlinghetti has towards modern times?

WRITING

1. Compare this poem with "Eight-Cylinder Man."

2. Study several of Goya's paintings. How well does Ferlinghetti's description in the first stanza reflect the paintings' tone?

TO A WATERFOWL
William Cullen Bryant

Whither, 'midst falling dew,
While glow the heavens with the last steps of day,
Far, through their rosy depths, dost thou pursue
    Thy solitary way?

Vainly the fowler's eye   5
Might mark thy distant flight, to do thee wrong,
As, darkly seen against the crimson sky,
    Thy figure floats along.

Seek'st thou the plashy brink
Of weedy lake, or marge of river wide,   10
Or where the rocking billows rise and sink
    On the chafed ocean-side?

There is a Power, whose care
Teaches thy way along that pathless coast—
The desert and illimitable air,   15
    Lone wandering, but not lost.

All day thy wings have fanned,
At that far height, the cold, thin atmosphere;
Yet stoop not, weary, to the welcome land,
    Though the dark night is near.   20

And soon that toil shall end,
Soon shalt thou find a summer home, and rest,
And scream among thy fellows; reeds shall bend,
    Soon, o'er thy sheltered nest.

Thou'rt gone, the abyss of heaven   25
Hath swallowed up thy form, yet, on my heart
Deeply has sunk the lesson thou hast given,
    And shall not soon depart.

He who, from zone to zone,
Guides through the boundless sky thy certain flight,   30
In the long way that I must tread alone,
    Will lead my steps aright.

Despite our advanced knowledge, much of the universe and the place of the human race within it remains a mystery. What lies behind that mystery? The speaker in the poem observes one of the wonders of nature—the autumn flight of migratory birds from northern to southern climates. The speaker observes one of these birds flying through the sky as though it were following signposts. The speaker feels that in the bird's flight he sees God's hand at work.

DEFINITIONS AND EXPLANATIONS

Whither (line 1) Where.

fowler's eye (line 5) The eye of the hunter of wild fowl.

plashy brink (line 9) Water-splashed edge.

marge (line 10) Edge; bank.

billows (line 11) Great waves.

chafed ocean-side (line 12) The shore worn by the action of the waves.

STUDY QUESTIONS

1. What does the speaker first see?

2. Why is the air described as "desert" in line 15?

3. What does the bird do as night comes?

4. What is the bird's destination? What will happen there?

5. What parallel does the speaker feel between himself and the bird on its flight? Why? What comforting faith is inspired in the speaker?

6. What is the **rhyme scheme** of the poem? What is the **rhythm?** Why is the strong and regular rhythm appropriate to the statement the poem makes?

WRITING

Often, poets choose a particular style of language to create a mood and tone for their poetry. How does Bryant use biblical language in this poem? Why is this type of diction appropriate to the statement the poem makes? Explain your view using examples from the text to support it.

THE CREATION
James Weldon Johnson

And God stepped out on space,
And he looked around and said:
I'm lonely—
I'll make me a world.

And far as the eye of God could see   5
Darkness covered everything,
Blacker than a hundred midnights
Down in a cypress swamp.

Then God smiled,
And the light broke,   10
And the darkness rolled up on one side,
And the light stood shining on the other,
And God said, That's good!

Then God reached out and took the light in his hands,
And God rolled the light around in his hands   15
Until he made the sun;
And he set that sun a-blazing in the heavens.
And the light that was left from making the sun
God gathered it up in a shining ball
And flung it against the darkness,   20
Spangling the night with the moon and stars.
Then down between
The darkness and the light
He hurled the world;
And God said: That's good!   25

Then God himself stepped down—
And the sun was on his right hand,
And the moon was on his left;
The stars were clustered about his head,
And the earth was under his feet.   30
And God walked, and where he trod

continued

Many people wish for the support and sustenance of a deep and simple faith. For some, that yearning is richly satisfied by the accounts and tales of the Bible, perhaps above all by the account of the Creation. James Weldon Johnson here retells that tale in the form of a sermon to a Southern congregation by a black minister. In its simplicity, in its fireworks, and its tenderness, this is a retelling to stir every heart.

EXPLANATION

cypress swamp (line 8)   A variety of cypress tree known as the bald cypress grows liberally in Southern swamplands. Its widespreading roots can live under water. The roots produce knobs that extend above the water and supply them with air.

STUDY QUESTIONS

1. How does the first **stanza** immediately establish a bond with the human audience?

2. Why is a cypress swamp used in the comparison made in lines 5–8?

3. What three exciting actions are described in the fourth **stanza?** How are the mountains then made?

4. How is there a sharp contrast in **images** and mood between the sixth **stanza** (lines 34–41) and the seventh stanza (lines 42–50)?

5. Why is line 69 dramatic and appealing? What anticipation does the line evoke in the audience?

6. Why does line 85, ''Like a mammy bending over her baby,'' have enormous emotional force in the poem?

7. How is man created?

8. Why is the last line powerful?

9. How does the ''sermon'' humanize religious faith?

10. How does the language of this poem contrast with that of ''To A Waterfowl''? How effective are the two poems in expressing admiration for God's power?

WRITING

Compare this retelling of the Judeo-Christian creation story with the original version in the Bible. Which is more dramatically expressed for you as a reader? How are language and word choice responsible for the reader's reaction to each version?

His footsteps hollowed the valleys out
And bulged the mountains up.

Then he stopped and looked and saw
That the earth was hot and barren.   35
So God stepped over to the edge of the world
And he spat out the seven seas—
He batted his eyes and the lightnings flashed—
He clapped his hands, and the thunders rolled—
And the waters above the earth came down,   40
The cooling waters came down.

Then the green grass sprouted,
And the little red flowers blossomed,
The pine tree pointed his finger to the sky,
And the oak spread out his arms,   45
The lakes cuddled down in the hollows of the ground,
And the rivers ran down to the sea;
And God smiled again,
And the rainbow appeared,
And curled itself around his shoulder.   50

Then God raised his arm and he waved his hand
Over the sea and over the land,
And he said: Bring forth! Bring forth!
And quicker than God could drop his hand,
Fishes and fowls   55
And beasts and birds
Swam the rivers and the seas,
Roamed the forests and the woods,
And split the air with their wings.
And God said, That's good!   60

Then God walked around,
And God looked around
On all that he had made.
He looked at his sun,
And he looked at his moon,   65
And he looked at his little stars;

He looked on his world
With all its living things,
And God said: I'm lonely still.

Then God sat down— 70
On the side of a hill where he could think;
By a deep, wide river he sat down;
With his head in his hands,
God thought and thought,
Till he thought: I'll make me a man! 75

Up from the bed of the river
God scooped the clay;
And by the bank of the river
He kneeled him down;
And there the great God Almighty 80
Who lit the sun and fixed it in the sky,
Who flung the stars to the most far corner of the night,
Who rounded the earth in the middle of his hand;
This Great God,
Like a mammy bending over her baby, 85
Kneeled down in the dust
Toiling over a lump of clay
Till he shaped it in his own image;

Then into it he blew the breath of life,
And man became a living soul. 90
Amen. Amen.

MUSIC

Joseph Haydn wrote an oratorio called *The Creation* (*Die Schopfung*). Listen to several arias from this work and describe how they capture in music the admiration for God's role in the creation process in the same way that Johnson and others capture it in language. Haydn's "The Creation" uses material from Milton's *Paradise Lost*. You may also wish to note how effectively Milton's words are set to music.

A FATHER SEES A SON NEARING MANHOOD
from *THE PEOPLE, YES*
Carl Sandburg

A father sees a son nearing manhood.
What shall he tell that son?
"Life is hard; be steel; be a rock."
And this might stand him for the storms
and serve him for humdrum and monotony   5
and guide him amid sudden betrayals
and tighten him for slack moments.
"Life is a soft loam; be gentle; go easy."
And this too might serve him.
Brutes have been gentled where lashes failed.   10
The growth of a frail flower in a path up
has sometimes shattered and split a rock.
A tough will counts. So does desire.
So does a rich soft wanting.
Without rich wanting nothing arrives.   15
Tell him too much money has killed men
and left them dead years before burial:
the quest of lucre beyond a few easy needs
has twisted good enough men
sometimes into dry thwarted worms.   20
Tell him time as a stuff can be wasted.
Tell him to be a fool every so often
and to have no shame over having been a fool
yet learning something out of every folly
hoping to repeat none of the cheap follies   25
thus arriving at intimate understanding
of a world numbering many fools.
Tell him to be alone often and get at himself

continued

In this poem, a father advises his young son, giving him a set of guidelines and values to help him steer through the problems, pains, uncertainties, and complexities of life. The father knows that there is no easy or simple formula for living, but he wants to suggest values that will help his son lead a meaningful, satisfying existence. Of these suggestions, the one the father feels is most important is to be true and honest to oneself.

DEFINITIONS AND EXPLANATIONS

loam (line 8)   A rich soil.

lucre (line 18)   Money.

thwarted (line 20)   Frustrated; defeated.

Pavlov (line 39)   The great Russian scientist who discovered the "conditioned response." In his most famous experiment, he trained a dog to expect food whenever a bell rang. He showed that the dog would salivate whenever the bell rang even when food no longer came with the ringing of the bell.

Michael Faraday (line 40)   A great British scientist who discovered electromagnetism. He showed that when a wire passed through a magnetic field, electricity flowed in the wire.

STUDY QUESTIONS

1. In which lines does the father tell the son that courage or inner strength is important? What examples can you give of "storms" (line 4) and "sudden betrayals" (line 6)?

2. In which lines does the father tell the son that gentleness, or compassion, is important? How is the flower used as a **metaphor?** How does this advice relate to the advice to "be steel; be a rock" in line 3? Explain.

3. In which lines does the father tell the son that it is important to have strong personal goals? What warning, however, does the father give right after this advice? What goals are suggested by the words "rich soft wanting" in line 14?

4. In which lines does the father tell the son that humility is important, that no one should think of himself or herself as perfect? Why does the father believe that humility is important?

225

and above all tell himself no lies about himself
whatever the white lies and protective fronts   30
he may use amongst other people.
Tell him solitude is creative if he is strong
and the final decisions are made in silent rooms.
Tell him to be different from other people
if it comes natural and easy being different.   35
Let him have lazy days seeking his deeper motives.
Let him seek deep for where he is a born natural.
    Then he may understand Shakespeare
    and the Wright brothers, Pasteur, Pavlov,
    Michael Faraday and free imaginations   40
bringing changes into a world resenting change.
    He will be lonely enough
    to have time for the work
    he knows as his own.

5. In which lines does the father tell his son to be true to himself? What are the "white lies" and "protective fronts" (line 30)? What does mentioning these show about the father? In which lines does the father tell the son to cultivate his own personal individuality? his own natural talents and abilities?

6. Why does the father mention Shakespeare, the Wright Brothers, Pasteur, Pavlov, and Michael Faraday? Does he expect the son to achieve greatness like these men?

7. In what sense will the son be "lonely" (line 42)?

WRITING

1. Has this parent left out any advice that you think is important? What is it? Has this parent included any advice that you would prefer to omit? Explain.

2. Suppose this were advice to a daughter instead of a son. Would you change it in any way? Explain.

THE FORTRESS
Anne Sexton

while taking a nap with Linda

Under the pink quilted covers
I hold the pulse that counts your blood.
I think the woods outdoors
are half asleep,
left over from summer   5
like a stack of books after a flood,
left over like those promises I never keep.
On the right, the scrub pine tree
waits like a fruit store
holding up bunches of tufted broccoli.   10

We watch the wind from our square bed.
I press down my index finger—
half in jest, half in dread—
on the brown mole
under your left eye, inherited   15
from my right cheek: a spot of danger
where a bewitched worm ate its way through our soul
in search of beauty. My child, since July
the leaves have been fed
secretly from a pool of beet-red dye.   20

And sometimes they are battle green
with trunks as wet as hunters' boots,
smacked hard by the wind, clean
as oilskins. No,
the wind's not off the ocean.   25
Yes, it cried in your room like a wolf
and your pony tail hurt you. That was a long time ago.
The wind rolled the tide like a dying
woman. She wouldn't sleep,
she rolled there all night, grunting and sighing.   30

continued

When we speak of love, we sometimes speak of it as though it were one thing, but it comes in many forms. There is the love between sweethearts, between husband and wife, between brothers and sisters, between parent and child, between close friends. This poem is about a mother and her little daughter. It is the end of summer. They live in a house in a woodland setting near the ocean shore and have gone to bed for an afternoon nap. The mother's head is full of half-drowsy thoughts and dreams about the little girl and the world in which she is growing up.

DEFINITIONS AND EXPLANATIONS

bittersweet (line 36)   A shrub that bears clusters of berries that turn bright orange.

ark (line 45)   The huge boat built by Noah to help two living creatures of every kind survive the Flood.

zebra fish (line 48)   Small tropical fish striped like a zebra. Zebra fish are among the common varieties kept in tropical fish tanks by hobbyists.

pheasant (line 54)   A woodland game bird with brilliant body feathers and long, sweeping tail feathers. It was once the fashion for ladies' hats to be decorated with pheasant tail feathers.

mulch (line 55)   A layer of fallen leaves, branches, and other debris on the surface of the soil.

STUDY QUESTIONS

1. What does the pulse that "counts" the child's blood (line 2) really count? What **figure of speech** is this? Why does the mother hold the pulse?

2. As the mother's mind drifts back and forth between the child and the world of nature outside, it seems haunted by images of uncertainty, pain, danger, catastrophe, and death, all of which are seen as a threat to the child. How does the poet illustrate the mother's troubled thoughts?

Darling, life is not in my hands;
life with its terrible changes
will take you, bombs or glands,
your own child at
your breast, your own house on your own land.   35
Outside the bittersweet turns orange.
Before she died, my mother and I picked those fat
branches, finding orange nipples
on the gray wire strands.
We weeded the forest, curing trees like cripples.   40

Your feet thump-thump against my back
and you whisper to yourself. Child,
what are you wishing? What pact
are you making?
What mouse runs between your eyes? What ark   45
can I fill for you when the world goes wild?
The woods are underwater, their weeds are shaking
in the tide; birches like zebra fish
flash by in a pack.
Child, I cannot promise that you will get your wish.   50

I cannot promise very much.
I give you the images I know.
Lie still with me and watch.
A pheasant moves
by like a seal, pulled through the mulch   55
by his thick white collar. He's on show
like a clown. He drags a beige feather that he
        removed,
one time, from an old lady's hat.
We laugh and we touch.
I promise you love. Time will not take away that.   60

3. What catastrophe does the mother think about in lines 45–49? How does the thought of catastrophe make her feel?

4. How does the mother try to shake off the mood and comfort herself and the child with a joke, a gesture, and a promise?

5. What is the meaning of the title of the poem?

WRITING

Parents often worry a great deal about their children. Write an essay describing the concerns you would have as a parent raising a child in today's world. How would you deal with the issues that worry you?

Values

1. Memorable lines Continue to add to your collection of memorable or quotable lines. From the poems in this unit, select two passages of one line or several lines. The basis of your selection may be strength of image, music of line, depth of emotion, appeal of theme, or any combination of these. Write the passages in your notebook with title and author. Memorizing the lines will give you added pleasure.

2. Briefly review the poems in this unit. Then, answer the following questions:

    a. How does "I taste a liquor never brewed" emphasize joy in the beauty of nature as a value for living?

    b. How does "On Hearing a Symphony of Beethoven" offer the beauty of music as an escape from the pain of life?

    c. How are "To a Waterfowl" and "The Creation" expressions of spiritual and religious faith?

    d. Which poem from this unit seems to you to be the best statement of love as a value? Why?

    e. Which poem from this unit made the deepest personal impression on you? Why?

3. Show your knowledge of terms in poetry. Here are five short passages from the poems in this unit. Choosing from the list of terms that follows, name the term applicable to the passage and explain why the passage is an example of the term you selected.

        apostrophe   **metonymy**
        imagery   **personification**
        symbolism

    a. "Where the wave leaps in the
       Wind and rejoices"
       —Archibald MacLeish: "Poem in Prose"

b. "I hold the pulse that counts your blood."
   —Anne Sexton: "The Fortress"

c. "Sweet sounds, oh, beautiful music, do not cease!"
   —Edna St. Vincent Millay: "On Hearing a Symphony of Beethoven"

d. "Then the green grass sprouted,
   And the little red flowers blossomed,"
   —James Weldon Johnson: "The Creation"

e. "And miles to go before I sleep."
   —Robert Frost: "Stopping by Woods on a Snowy Evening"

4. Review your knowledge of vocabulary by choosing the numbered word or phrase whose meaning is closest to the underlined word.

   a. benign   (1) confused   (2) kindly   (3) precious
                  (4) bright   (5) competent

   b. billows   (1) clouds   (2) succeeds   (3) covers
                  (4) waves   (5) entices

   c. celestial   (1) heavenly   (2) detailed   (3) monetary
                  (4) lucid   (5) like cellophane

   d. imperially (1) harshly   (2) specifically   (3) slowly
                  (4) dynamically   (5) majestically

   e. lucre   (1) hard work   (2) dialect   (3) coat
                  (4) money   (5) speech defect

   f. The movie star wanted to renounce fame and fortune and become a recluse.
           (1) give up   (2) garner   (3) accumulate
           (4) attract   (5) decline

   g. After a hard day in the Oval Office, the President wanted to repose quietly in his study.
           (1) dine   (2) review important papers
           (3) sleep soundly   (4) rest
           (5) discuss matters of state

   h. Though the question was difficult to answer, the response sounded plausible.
           (1) incorrect   (2) acceptable   (3) marginal
           (4) inviolate   (5) exact

i. The terrorists' plot to bomb key New York sites was <u>thwarted</u> thanks to excellent work by the F.B.I.
  (1) discovered   (2) untangled   (3) deplored
  (4) created   (5) frustrated

j. Though classical music can be passionate, intense and exciting, it can also be <u>tranquil</u>.
  (1) loud   (2) enjoyable   (3) serene
  (4) remarkable   (5) creative

5. Poems and paintings   Poets and painters are artists who have much in common. Study each of the reproductions of paintings that follow. Examine the image carefully. Just what do you see? What feelings does the image arouse in you? What mood or idea does the picture suggest? If a person or persons appear, try to flesh out in your mind their background and character. Is rhythm, metaphor, or symbol important in the picture? After you have studied each picture in this way, select the one that you associate most powerfully with one of the poems in this unit. Be ready to discuss or write about your choice and the reasons for it.

Optional: Select one picture that inspires you to write your own poem and write the poem.

THE SCREEN PORCH
Fairfield Porter. *1964.*
Whitney Museum,
New York.
Oil on canvas. 79½ × 79½ in. Lawrence H. Bloedel Bequest 77.1.41.

TREE PLANTING GROUP   Grant Wood. *1937.*
Whitney Museum, New York. Lithograph. Sheet: 11⅞ × 16 in.
Image: 8⁷⁄₁₆ × 10⅞ in. Gift of Arthur G. Altschul 72.78.

DRAGON   Leo Katz. *1966.*
Whitney Museum, New York.
Lithograph. Sheet: 30 × 22¼ in. Image:
25¼ × 17⅝ in. Gift of Dr. and Mrs. Bela
Schick 66.87.

FLOWER MARKET David Park. *1955. Whitney Museum, New York.*
Oil on canvas. 34½ × 43 in. Lawrence H. Bloedel Bequest 77.1.39.

THE LORD IS MY
SHEPHERD
Thomas Hart Benton.
1926. Whitney Museum,
New York. Tempera on
canvas. 33¼ × 27⅜ in.
Purchase 31.100.

This Land of Ours

The character of our nation is influenced not only by its diverse population, but by its geography, its landforms, and its climate. Before there was a United States of America, the land was here to give its character to the nation that would develop.

An ocean apart from Europe, the "new world" was vast, rich, and infinitely varied. It was filled with fertile plains, rivers, lakes, and harbors, with mighty mountain ranges, with forests, with wildlife, with a wealth of natural resources, and with great oceans on its eastern and western shores.

This land of ours existed in its raw, glorious natural form long before the artificial boundaries of states, cities, and towns were imposed upon it. The Rocky Mountains, the Grand Canyon, the Great Lakes, the Everglades, Mount St. Helens, Old Faithful, the Mississippi River, and the Hudson River were here in all their impressive, awe-inspiring beauty.

The land is the unique setting for the unique American nation. This land shaped the nation's history, ideas, and customs. Out of this land grew the nation's cities, towns, villages, farmlands, parks, highways, and monuments.

The poems in this unit are about this land of ours and what has sprung from it.

THE GIFT OUTRIGHT
Robert Frost

The land was ours before we were the land's.
She was our land more than a hundred years
Before we were her people. She was ours
In Massachusetts, in Virginia,
But we were England's, still colonials,   5
Possessing what we still were unpossessed by,
Possessed by what we now no more possessed.
Something we were withholding made us weak
Until we found out that it was ourselves
We were withholding from our land of living,   10
And forthwith found salvation in surrender.
Such as we were we gave ourselves outright
(The deed of gift was many deeds of war)
To the land vaguely realizing westward,
But still unstoried, artless, unenhanced,   15
Such as she was, such as she would become.

DEFINITIONS AND EXPLANATIONS

Outright (title)   Complete; without reservations.

deed (line 13)   A legal document stating a transfer of property.

deeds (line 13)   Acts of courage.

realizing (line 14)   Coming into full reality.

unstoried (line 15)   Without a history.

artless (line 15)   Simple and natural.

unenhanced (line 15)   Not made greater or richer.

At the inauguration ceremony for President John F. Kennedy in 1961, perhaps the most stirring moment of all came when eighty-seven-year-old Robert Frost, his white hair tossed by a cold winter wind, stood and recited this poem for the occasion. In this poem, Frost seemed to have in mind a thought that appears in the poem only by suggestion. The thought is that the land of America was the one proper place for the development of the ideas and ideals of America. The land was like a great, rich farm for growing democracy and liberty, waiting only to be cultivated.

STUDY QUESTIONS

1. Before the American Revolution, how was it true that "The land was ours . . . before we were her people" and that we possessed "what we still were unpossessed by"?

2. What were we "withholding" that "made us weak" (line 8)?

3. How is the usual process of people dealing with land, owning it, and trans ferring ownership by sale or gift reversed in lines 9–13?

4. How is line 13 a play on words?

5. Did we give ourselves to the land only once or many times? Explain. What is suggested about the process of the development of a democracy?

6. How were we and the land different when first "we gave ourselves outright" from what we are now?

7. Why is the wording of the last line especially strong?

WRITING

According to the poem, how did the land play a role in the development of the American nation? What was the role of the people in that development? How are the two interrelated?

MUSIC

1. Listen to "America the Beautiful" by Katherine Lee Bates and "God Bless America" by Irving Berlin. What point do these two songs make about America? How do they relate to the message of "The Gift Outright"?

2. Antonin Dvorak, though from Central Europe (then Bohemia), had a special place in his heart for American culture. Listen to his *New World Symphony*, and write a short story or poem to one of the movements.

THE FLOWER-FED BUFFALOES
Vachel Lindsay

The flower-fed buffaloes of the spring
In the days of long ago,
Ranged where the locomotives sing
And the prairie flowers lie low:—
The tossing, blooming, perfumed grass   5
Is swept away by the wheat,
Wheels and wheels and wheels spin by
In the spring that still is sweet.
But the flower-fed buffaloes of the spring
Left us, long ago.   10
They gore no more, they bellow no more,
They trundle around the hills no more:—
With the Blackfeet, lying low,
With the Pawnees, lying low,
Lying low.   15

Over the past decades, many natural resources of the United States have been developed for commercial use. Similarly, in the nineteenth century, the bison, or buffalo, were brutally pushed from the Plains to make room for locomotives and settlers from the east. The same thing happened to the American Indian population. Vachel Lindsay bemoans this along with the senseless destruction of the natural resources of the Great Plains.

STUDY QUESTIONS

1. What are the **connotations** of the words ''flower-fed buffaloes of the spring''? How is the impression of the buffalo created by this phrase different from the impression of the buffalo that many people have?

2. What has taken the place of the buffalo on the prairie lands? What has replaced the prairie grass? What other change has taken place?

3. What are the ''Wheels and wheels and wheels'' that ''spin by'' (line 7)?

4. How does the poet echo the sound of the **rhythm** of the wheels in lines 7 and 8?

5. Where does the poet use **repetition** of mournful phrases to express his feelings about what once was and is now gone? Why does he use this device?

6. This poem tells of the passing of the buffalo, the prairie grass, the Blackfeet and the Pawnees. Yet how are they and all they represent still with us?

WRITING

There are areas of the United States in which the beautiful natural resources still remain relatively untouched. Nevertheless, some individuals advocate the development of these lands for commercial use. Discuss this issue in some depth, taking a clear stand one way or the other.

A BLESSING

James Wright

Just off the highway to Rochester, Minnesota,
Twilight bounds softly forth on the grass.
And the eyes of those two Indian ponies
Darken with kindness.
They have come gladly out of the willows   5
To welcome my friend and me.
We step over the barbed wire into the pasture
Where they have been grazing all day, alone.
They ripple tensely, they can hardly contain their
    happiness
That we have come.   10
They bow shyly as wet swans. They love each other.
There is no loneliness like theirs.
At home once more,
They begin munching the young tufts of spring in the
    darkness.
I would like to hold the slenderer one in my arms,   15
For she has walked over to me
And nuzzled my left hand.
She is black and white,
Her mane falls wild on her forehead,

continued

James Wright is a poet who believes that human expansion encroaches upon and contaminates the pure state of nature. In his poetry, we see a healthy appreciation for and love of nature combined with an anger at the restrictions that humanity places upon it. As a writer who sympathizes with the exploited and downtrodden, Wright expresses his disillusionment with ''man's inhumanity to man'' with exquisite imagery and select language.

DEFINITIONS AND EXPLANATIONS

bounds (line 2)   Moves by leaping or jumping.

forth (line 2)   To move out into view as in ''to go forth.''

ripple (line 9)   To rise and fall in small waves.

tufts (line 14)   Bunches of grass or vegetation growing closely together.

nuzzled (line 17)   Rubbed or touched with the nose.

mane (line 19)   The long and heavy hair that grows on the neck of mammals such as the horse and the lion.

STUDY QUESTIONS

1. What is the opening mood of the poem? How do lines 1–4 establish it?

2. Why might the poet have chosen Indian ponies?

3. How is the barbed wire used as a **symbol**? How does this relate to the poet's use of Indian ponies?

4. How does the poet convey the loneliness of the ponies? Why are they lonely? Why is there ''no loneliness like theirs''?

5. Why are the ponies compared to ''wet swans''? What similarities can you see between these two different kinds of animals? How do the phrases ''ripple tensely'' and ''bow shyly'' express different emotions?

6. How does the speaker react to the ponies? How do they react to him? Why?

7. Why does the poet make one of the ponies ''black and white'' whose ''mane falls wild on her forehead''?

And the light breeze moves me to caress her long ear   20
That is delicate as the skin over a girl's wrist.
Suddenly I realize
That if I stepped out of my body I would break
Into blossom.

8. How does the speaker use a **simile** to describe the pony's ear? What effect does this create? How appropriate is it in relation to the poem's overall point and tone?

9. Lines 23–24 create a beautiful **metaphoric image** which suggest that the human soul is a blossoming flower. What does the poet mean when he uses this metaphor to conclude the poem? (Think in terms of peace and being one with nature.)

WRITING

1. This poem has several elements that reflect human intrusion into the natural order of things. In a well-developed paragraph, tell how the poet shows this intrusion and explain how effective you believe his presentation is. Support your view with specific details.

2. Imagery is used quite effectively in this poem. Choose two images which the poet employs. For each, describe the image in detail and then explain how it is used to create a specific effect on the reader.

3. Think of a time when you saw something beautiful and awe inspiring in nature that was tainted by pollution. Write in your journal a description of what you saw and explain how you felt when you saw it.

MUSIC

Listen to a recording of "The Swan" from Saint-Saens's *Carnival of the Animals*. How does the cello convey the movement of the swan? How could it be used to convey, too, the movement of the ponies? Compare this to typical horse music such as the finale to the *William Tell Overture* by Rossini or the "Light Cavalry Overture" of von Suppe. How could this contrast reflect the conflict within the themes of freedom vs. captivity and nature vs. mankind? Write a paragraph or two explaining the comparisons in detail.

LILACS

Amy Lowell

Lilacs,
False blue,
White,
Purple,
Color of lilac,   5
Your great puffs of flowers
Are everywhere in this my New England.
Among your heart-shaped leaves
Orange orioles hop like music-box birds and sing
Their little weak soft songs;   10
In the crooks of your branches
The bright eyes of song sparrows sitting on spotted
        eggs
Peer restlessly through the light and shadow
Of all Springs.
Lilacs in dooryards   15
Holding quiet conversations with an early moon;
Lilacs watching a deserted house
Settling sideways into the grass of an old road;
Lilacs, wind-beaten, staggering under a lopsided
        shock of bloom
Above a cellar dug into a hill.   20
You are everywhere.
You were everywhere.
You tapped the window when the preacher preached
        his sermon,
And ran along the road beside the boy going to
        school.
You stood by pasture-bars to give the cows good
        milking,   25

continued

New England was the first of all the lands in which the roots of the United States took hold and flourished. The great ports and harbors, the rivers and forests, the biting winters, brilliant autumns, and lovely springs of New England energized the region's farming, fishing, and industry. The spirit of enterprise, independence, and freedom, all the basic traits of the American character, thrived there. Amy Lowell captures the many facets of New England by using the lilac as a centerpiece and symbol—the lilac that in May decorates every corner of New England with its color and fragrance.

DEFINITIONS AND EXPLANATIONS

Lilacs (title)   A shrub that grows widely in New England, as well as elsewhere in the world. It is loved for the beauty and fragrance of its blooms, which grow in great heavy clusters or puffs in many shades of blue, lavender, purple, and white. In New England, the lilac blooms in May, wild, in front yards, and in gardens. Almost every house has some of its cut blooms in a vase.

orioles (line 9)   Small birds with bright orange or yellow feathers with black markings.

flaunted (line 28)   Showed off proudly.

Custom Houses (line 29)   The buildings housing the customs offices, where taxes on imported goods are collected.

sandal-wood (line 30)   A hard sweet-smelling wood from Asia, used in fine cabinetmaking.

quill (line 31)   A large, stiff feather, commonly used years ago as a pen.

greenhouses (line 50)   Buildings whose roofs and sides are made mostly of glass, used for the cultivation of delicate or out-of-season plants; hothouses.

Pashas (line 60)   A Turkish title of high rank or honor.

reticent (line 62)   Not given to much talking; silent; reserved.

candid (line 63)   Honest; outspoken.

State Houses (line 82)   The official buildings of the state government.

Charters (line 82)   Legal documents founding some of the New England colonies and giving them a degree of self-government.

thrush (line 85)   A large group of songbirds that includes the robin, the bluebird, and the woodthrush.

1. Why did the poet choose the lilac as a **symbol** of New England? How does she use the symbol to create scenes of New England's nature? To give typical small scenes of everyday New England life and activity? To weave **allusions** to New England's geography and history into the poem?

2. How was the lilac able to persuade "the housewife that her dish pan was of silver/And her husband an image of pure gold" (lines 26–27)?

3. Why are Custom Houses (lines 29–30) significant in the story of New England? Why are the clerks called "Paradoxical" (line 37)?

4. How is **personification** used in the **image** in lines 50–52?

5. What is suggested about the origin of the lilac in lines 58–60? What contrast is brought out in the lines that follow?

6. Explain in detail the **image** in lines 65–67. How has the lilac become "friendly to a house-cat and a pair of spectacles"?

7. Explain the meaning of the **image** in lines 93–94, "May is a full light wind of lilac/From Canada to Narragansett Bay."

WRITING

The poem is written in free verse, but its marked rhythms are lyrical, songlike, and lovely. What rhythmic refrain occurs three times in the poem? How are these lines made distinctive and emphatic? What other examples of repetition are there that add to the haunting lyricism of the poem? Give two examples of lines whose musical quality is enhanced by alliteration.

You persuaded the housewife that her dish pan was
    of silver.
And her husband an image of pure gold.
You flaunted the fragrance of your blossoms
Through the wide doors of Custom Houses—
You, and sandal-wood, and tea,   30
Charging the noses of quill-driving clerks
When a ship was in from China.
You called to them: ''Goose-quill men, goose-quill
    men,
May is a month for flitting,''
Until they writhed on their high stools   35
And wrote poetry on their letter-sheets behind the
    propped-up ledgers.
Paradoxical New England clerks,
Writing inventories in ledgers, reading the ''Song of
    Solomon'' at night,
So many verses before bed-time,
Because it was the Bible.   40
The dead fed you
Amid the slant stones of graveyards.
Pale ghosts who planted you
Came in the night-time
And let their thin hair blow through your clustered
    stems.   45
You are of the green sea,
And of the stone hills which reach a long distance.
You are of elm-shaded streets with little shops where
    they sell kites and marbles,
You are of great parks where everyone walks and
    nobody is at home.
You cover the blind sides of greenhouses   50
And lean over the top to say a hurry-word through
    the glass
To your friends, the grapes, inside.

continued

Lilacs,
False blue,
White,   55
Purple,
Color of lilac,
You have forgotten your Eastern origin,
The veiled women with eyes like panthers,
The swollen, aggressive turbans of jeweled Pashas.   60
Now you are a very decent flower.
A reticent flower,
A curiously clear-cut, candid flower,
Standing beside clean doorways,
Friendly to a house-cat and a pair of spectacles,   65
Making poetry out of a bit of moonlight
And a hundred or two sharp blossoms.

Maine knows you,
Has for years and years;
New Hampshire knows you,   70
And Massachusetts
And Vermont.
Cape Cod starts you along the beaches to Rhode
     Island;
Connecticut takes you from a river to the sea.
You are brighter than apples,   75
Sweeter than tulips,
You are the great flood of our souls
Bursting above the leaf-shapes of our hearts,
You are the smell of all summers,
The love of wives and children,   80
The recollection of the gardens of little children,
You are State Houses and Charters
And the familiar treading of the foot to and fro on a
     road it knows.
May is lilac here in New England,
May is thrush singing "Sun up!" on a tip-top ash-
     tree,   85

May is white clouds behind pine-trees
Puffed out and marching upon a blue sky.
May is green as no other,
May is much sun through small leaves,
May is soft earth,   90
And apple-blossoms,
And windows open to a South wind.
May is a full light wind of lilac
From Canada to Narragansett Bay.

Lilacs,   95
False blue,
White,
Purple,
Color of lilac.
Heart-leaves of lilac all over New England,   100
Roots of lilac under all the soil of New England,
Lilac in me because I am New England,
Because my roots are in it,
Because my leaves are of it,
Because my flowers are for it,   105
Because it is my country
And I speak to it of itself
And sing of it with my own voice
Since certainly it is mine.

NORTH COUNTY
Sherley Anne Williams

The freeway is a river
of light rounding the base of
Mt. Soledad, its distant
drone a part of the night. I've
watched in the darkness as the   5
river dimmed to the fitful
passing of solitary
cars and heard the coyotes
in the canyon crying their
survival to the strange land.   10

I booted up one day, walked
out across the mesa that
fronts along my place till the
land was a shallow cup around
me and the houses were lost   15
in the distance on its
rim. The plants were the only
life I saw—muted greens dry
browns bursts of loud purple and
lighter blues, brilliant in the   20
spring light; something rustled the
undergrowth; a jet murmured
in the softly clabbered sky.

The Indian dead are here
buried beneath Spanish place   25
names and the cities of the
pioneers and the droning
silence is witness to what
each has claimed, what each owned.
My father's grave is here some   30
where his tale lost like that jet
in clabber his children
scattered along the river
voices singing to the night.

Often, in this land of ours, we pay a price for progress in the form of the destruction of natural resources and environments. "North County" describes how modern civilization has encroached on the land once belonging to American Indians. The poem also notes the progression of land use or ownership from American Indians, to the Spaniards, to the pioneers, to modern Americans. It is interesting that Sherley Anne Williams, a black poet from California, is speaking here with the voice of an American Indian lamenting the loss of a world unspoiled by technology.

DEFINITIONS AND EXPLANATIONS

Mt. Soledad (line 3)   A mountain near the city of Soledad in California. Soledad is located near Monterey.

drone (line 4)   A steady, monotonous humming sound.

mesa (line 12)   Spanish for "table"; mesa also refers to a high, raised, flat landscape with sharply dropping sides.

clabbered (line 23)   Looking like the pattern that forms in sour milk that has curdled.

clabber (line 32)   Sour milk that has curdled.

STUDY QUESTIONS

1. Why is the freeway compared to the flowing of a river?

2. What effect does the **repetition** of the "c" sound have in lines 8 and 9?

3. Why is the mesa described by the speaker as a "shallow cup"?

4. What contrasts does the speaker make between nature and artificial intrusions? Are they effective? Explain.

5. What effect is created by the use of the **oxymoron** "droning silence" in lines 27 and 28?

6. What progression of ownership is described in lines 24–29?

7. How do lines 30–34 describe the father's life story?

WRITING

A number of other poems in this book lament the intrusion of modern life on the environment. Select two and, in a well-developed essay, compare and contrast how these poems and "North County" treat the same theme.

OREGON WINTER

Jeanne McGahey

The rain begins. This is no summer rain,
Dropping the blotches of wet on the dusty road:
This rain is slow, without thunder or hurry:
There is plenty of time—there will be months of rain.
    Lost in the hills, the old gray farmhouses   5
Hump their backs against it, and smoke from their
        chimneys
Struggles through weighted air. The sky is sodden
        with water,
It sags against the hills, and the wild geese,
Wedge-flying, brush the heaviest cloud with their
        wings.
    The farmers move unhurried. The wood is in,   10
The hay has long been in, the barn lofts piled
Up to the high windows, dripping yellow straws.
There will be plenty of time now, time that will smell
        of fires,
And drying leather, and catalogues, and apple cores.
    The farmers clean their boots, and whittle, and
        drowse.   15

The lives of many Americans change in a regular rhythm according to the seasons. But, in each section of the country, the seasons are different, bringing different conditions that create different feelings and moods, requiring different responses. This poem is about winter in the farmlands of Oregon.

STUDY QUESTIONS

1. What is the chief characteristic of the Oregon winter? Describe it in detail through references to the poem.

2. How are the farmhouses **personified** in lines 5–6?

3. What are the tasks the farmers have completed in preparation for winter?

4. What are the predominant smells in the farmhouses during winter? How do the farm people spend their time?

5. What is the mood of the Oregon winter as expressed by the poem? How does it compare to the mood of the winter you know?

WRITING

Suppose an artist were to paint a picture depicting Oregon winter. What color or colors would predominate? What are some of the visual details that would appear in the picture? Explain in a well-developed paragraph.

NOMAD EXQUISITE

Wallace Stevens

As the immense dew of Florida
Brings forth
The big-finned palm
And green vine angering for life,

As the immense dew of Florida   5
Brings forth hymn and hymn
From the beholder,
Beholding all these green sides
And gold sides of green sides,

And blessed mornings,   10
Meet for the eye of the young alligator,
And lightning colors
So, in me, come flinging
Forms, flames, and the flakes of flames.

In the varied geography of America, Florida is unique, with its semitropical climate and lush native vegetation. Hundreds of years ago, Ponce de Leon sought the fountain of youth in Florida. Today, several million Americans live there, vacation there, retire there. Perhaps they wish to escape the harshness of winter. Perhaps, like Ponce de Leon, they hope to find health and long life in the warm climate. Or perhaps they just want to revel in Florida's own particular beauty.

DEFINITIONS AND EXPLANATIONS

Nomad (title)   A wanderer.

Exquisite (title)   Being highly sensitive; having exceptional awareness of beauty or perfection.

Meet (line 11)   Fitting; suitable.

STUDY QUESTIONS

1. What does the title tell you about the speaker?

2. How is the repeated phrase "immense dew" used to characterize the climate of Florida?

3. How is the tropical lushness of the scene suggested?

4. How is the word "angering" in the phrase "green vine angering for life" (line 4) used as an **image**? What **figure of speech** is this?

5. How does the brilliant scene affect the beholder emotionally?

6. In your opinion, what do the last two lines of the poem (lines 13–14) mean?

WRITING

Have you ever felt passionately about a particular place? Why? Describe the place in detail, tell your feelings about it, and explain them clearly.

MUSIC

The British composer Frederick Delius wrote the *Florida Suite*. Listen to the piece and explain what aural picture the music creates of Florida. Compare it to the word picture created by Wallace Stevens.

PURITAN SONNET

Elinor Wylie

Down to the Puritan marrow of my bones
There's something in this richness that I hate.
I love the look, austere, immaculate,
Of landscapes drawn in pearly monotones.
There's something in my very blood that owns   5
Bare hills, cold silver on a sky of slate,
A thread of water, churned to milky spate
Streaming through slanted pastures fenced with
    stones.

I love those skies, thin blue or snowy gray,
Those fields sparse-planted, rendering meager
    sheaves;   10
That spring, briefer than apple-blossom's breath,
Summer, so much too beautiful to stay,
Swift autumn, like a bonfire of leaves,
And sleepy winter, like the sleep of death.

DEFINITIONS AND EXPLANATIONS

Puritan (title)   The Puritans were among the earliest settlers of New England. They emphasized strictness in their moral and religious beliefs and simplicity, plainness, and even self-denial in their lifestyle. The Puritan heritage runs through the American character as an important strain.

austere (line 3)   Very simple; severe; lacking in richness or abundance.

immaculate (line 3)   Pure; without flaw or fault.

spate (line 7)   A flood.

fenced with stones (line 8)   This phrase refers to the same stone walls or "fences" that inspired Frost's "Mending Wall."

sheaves (line 10)   The bundles into which stalks of grain, corn, etc. are gathered and tied during the harvest.

The attractions of the mild climate of the "sunbelt"—Florida, Southern California, Arizona, and similar regions of the country—have caused great changes in American population distribution and in the economy. Nevertheless, many people still prefer the atmosphere of New England. For example, see what the speaker of this sonnet has to say.

STUDY QUESTIONS

1. How does the first line tell you how deeply the speaker feels about her heritage?

2. In line 2, what does the phrase "this richness" tell you about the probable locale of the speaker?

3. What are some of the features of the landscape preferred by the speaker as described in lines 4–8?

4. What adjectives (in addition to "austere" and "immaculate," for example) does the speaker use to describe her Puritan preferences in geographical surroundings?

5. What colors and tints has the speaker "painted" into the poem to express her preferences?

6. Which characteristic of New England is described in the last four lines of the poem?

7. How are each of the four seasons described by **metaphor** in lines 11 and 12 and **simile** in lines 13 and 14?

8. Is this an English or an Italian **sonnet**? How do you know?

WRITING

Which way does your own preference in climatic surroundings lean, toward that of "Nomad Exquisite" or that of "Puritan Sonnet"? Why?

MUSIC

Charles Ives's *Three Places in New England* was written to capture the mood of Putnam's Camp in Redding, Connecticut, the Housatonic River in Stockbridge, Massachusetts, and a sculpture in the Boston Commons. Listen to the three short movements and describe them in writing. What does each piece suggest about New England? Do they express the same feelings as Elinor Wylie's poem? Explain.

259

SMOKE ROSE GOLD

Carl Sandburg

The dome of the capitol looks to the Potomac river.
    Out of haze over the sunset,
    Out of a smoke rose gold:
One star shines over the sunset.
Night takes the dome and the river, the sun and the
       smoke rose gold,   5
The haze changes from sunset to star.
The pour of a thin silver struggles against the dark.
A star might call: It's a long way across.

On the banks of the Potomac River, our nation's capital was built amid a serene and majestic geographical setting. The great dome of the Capitol rises above the area, dominating the scene. Nearby stands the Supreme Court building. The Washington Monument and the Lincoln and Jefferson memorials are at water's edge. This setting, an unusual marriage of natural and architectural beauty, is a symbol of America, its strength, its riches, and its historic dedication to human dignity and freedom. This poem, in a few simple strokes, captures the reality and spirit of the nation's capital and its quiet dignity.

STUDY QUESTIONS

1. At what time of day does Sandburg choose to open the poem? Which two words express the quality of the light? Why do you think Sandburg chose that time of day and that quality of light?

2. What colors appear in the poem? What **connotations** do these colors have for you?

3. What two physical features of the capital city appear in the poem? Why do you think Sandburg has chosen only these two features? Why has he emphasized the setting of air, light, and sky rather than buildings or people?

4. What change in the scene takes place?

5. How is the "star" in the last line used as a **symbol**? What do you think is the meaning of the sentence "It's a long way across."?

WRITING

The Washington Monument and the Lincoln Memorial have been the sites of many protests, demonstrations, and gatherings about "hot" political and social issues. Why would these locations be chosen so frequently by groups of people who wish to make a point?

MUSIC

This poem celebrates Washington, D.C. as a symbol of democracy and hope. One president who also symbolizes hope and courage is Abraham Lincoln. Aaron Copland's *Lincoln Portrait* is a musical poem about Lincoln accompanied by spoken narration and quotations from his speeches. Do you think the piece is a powerful tribute to Lincoln? Why or why not? How effectively does it capture his essence?

from *JOHN BROWN'S BODY*
Stephen Vincent Benét

You took a carriage to that battlefield.
Now, I suppose, you take a motor-bus,
But then, it was a carriage—and you ate
Fried chicken out of wrappings of waxed paper,
While the slow guide buzzed on about the war   5
And the enormous, curdled summer clouds
Piled up like giant cream puffs in the blue.
The carriage smelt of axle-grease and leather
And the old horse nodded a sleepy head
Adorned with a straw hat. His ears stuck through it.   10
It was the middle of hay-fever summer
And it was hot. And you could stand and look
All the way down from Cemetery Ridge,
Much as it was, except for monuments
And startling groups of monumental men   15
Bursting in bronze and marble from the ground,
And all the curious names upon the gravestones. . . .

So peaceable it was, so calm and hot,
So tidy and great-skied.
        No men had fought   20
There but enormous, monumental men
Who bled neat streams of uncorrupting bronze,
Even at the Round Tops, even by Pickett's boulder,
Where the bronze, open book could still be read
By visitors and sparrows and the wind: 25
And the wind came, the wind moved in the grass,
Saying . . . while the long light . . . and all so
    calm . . .

continued

The Vietnam Memorial in Washington, D.C. is a moving monument to the tens of thousands of Americans who lost their lives in Southeast Asia. Visited by many thousands each year, the memorial stimulates reflection and deep thought. In Pennsylvania another monument commemorates the battle of Gettysburg. What do the shrines in Washington and Gettysburg mean to the thousands who visit each year? Do they feel the incredible courage of the soldiers? Do they thrill to the causes that were at stake? Or, is their visit merely a day's outing, a social amusement, just something to do? Benét's poem is a reaction to a visit to Gettysburg.

DEFINITIONS AND EXPLANATIONS

Gettysburg   The Battle of Gettysburg took place on July 1, 2, and 3 in 1863. This Pennsylvania battleground marked the high point of Lee's invasion of the North and the turning point of the Civil War. Two parallel ridges run south from Gettysburg—Seminary Ridge to the west and about a mile to the east across open fields, Cemetery Ridge. The Confederate Army took positions on Seminary Ridge, and the Union Army, under General Meade, took defensive positions along Cemetery Ridge. At the northern flank of Cemetery Ridge are two hills, Cemetery Hill and Culp's Hill. At the southern flank are two other hills, Little Round Top and Big Round Top. These hills, overlooking the Union forces on Cemetery Ridge, were strategically important to the Union defenses. On July 2, Southern troops attempted to take Little Round Top, but the defenses were reinforced at the last moment and the Confederate attack was repulsed, with sharpshooters of the 20th Maine Regiment playing a key role in the fierce fighting. An attack on the two hills to the north was also repulsed. An advance on the Union center gained ground but was finally repulsed. On July 3, Lee ordered a direct frontal attack across the open fields by the Virginians under General Pickett, with some support from other troops. Pickett's men lay behind Seminary Ridge ready for their advance. Shortly after 1 P.M., Confederate cannons launched a withering barrage against the Union positions. The fire was returned by the Union artillery. After two hours, the barrage suddenly stopped. Pickett's men moved out and began their advance across the open fields. For a few moments, a strange hush fell across the battleground as the gray ranks, flags flying, marched forward. Then the Union artillery opened fire, blowing great holes in the exposed ranks. The Southerners kept coming until they advanced within range of murderous rifle fire. A few hundred survivors reached and charged the Union lines and fought hand to hand in a

''Pickett came
And the South came
And the end came,   30
And the grass comes
And the wind blows
On the bronze book
On the bronze men
On the grown grass,   35
And the wind says
'Long ago
Long
Ago.' ''

Then it was time to buy a paperweight   40
With flags upon it in decalcomania
And hope you wouldn't break it, driving home.

hopeless struggle. They died or surrendered or ran. The Battle of Gettysburg was over. When the artillery duels, the gunfire, the hand-to-hand combat, the attacks and counterattacks were done, Lee had lost 28,000 men, Meade 23,000.

Pickett's boulder (line 23) A large granite rock, now marked with a plaque, stands at the high point of the charge of Pickett's men into the Union lines.

decalcomania (line 41) More commonly known now as a "decal," a decalcomania is a design or print that can be transferred from the special paper on which it comes to some other surface.

STUDY QUESTIONS

1. How do you know that the speaker is recalling a visit to Gettysburg, years earlier when he was young? What do lines 1–12 suggest are some of the speaker's memories about his trip? What do these memories tell you about the meaning of this memorial to the young visitor?

2. In lines 12–25, the speaker describes the former battlefield using such adjectives as "peaceable," "calm," and "tidy," while referring to "the curious names upon the gravestones." He describes the monument dramatically in lines 20–22. How does the poet suggest an **ironic** contrast between the terrible human reality of the battle and the meaning of the shrine to the speaker?

3. What is the message of the wind?

4. How is the poem's **irony** brought to a climax in the last three lines?

WRITING

1. In his "Gettysburg Address," Lincoln said

. . . in a larger sense, we cannot dedicate, we cannot consecrate, we cannot hallow this ground. The brave men, living and dead, who struggled here have consecrated it far above our poor power to add or detract. The world will little note nor long remember what we say here, but it can never forget what they did here. . . .

In your opinion, do the words of this poem affirm or deny Lincoln's statement? Explain in detail.

2. How do you feel about the monuments, shrines, and memorials that mark the American story on American land? Do they serve effectively to keep alive the meaning of great events and great individuals in history, or are they empty, hollow gestures, mere commercial tourist attractions? Explain your view, supporting it, if possible, with references to any visits you may have made to such memorials.

CHICAGO
Carl Sandburg

Hog Butcher for the World,
Tool Maker, Stacker of Wheat,
Player with Railroads and the Nation's Freight
    Handler;
Stormy, husky, brawling,
City of the Big Shoulders: 5

They tell me you are wicked and I believe them, for I
    have seen your painted women under the gas
    lamps luring the farm boys.
And they tell me you are crooked and I answer: Yes,
    it is true I have seen the gunman kill and go free
    to kill again.
And they tell me you are brutal and my reply is: On
    the faces of women and children I have seen the
    marks of wanton hunger.
And having answered so I turn once more to those
    who sneer at this my city, and I give them back
    the sneer and say to them:
Come and show me another city with lifted head
    singing so proud to be alive and coarse and
    strong and cunning.   10
Flinging magnetic curses amid the toil of piling job on
    job, here is a tall bold slugger set vivid against
    the little soft cities;
Fierce as a dog with tongue lapping for action,
    cunning as a savage pitted against the wilderness,
        Bareheaded,
        Shoveling,
        Wrecking,   15
        Planning,
        Building, breaking, rebuilding,

continued

Of the achievements and developments in our nation, none is more phenomenal than our great cities, each a unique product of its own geography and location. Each is a great center of vitality, culture, and commerce. Each is a marvel of achievement and a concentration of problems. "Chicago" is one of the best known of American city poems and paints a portrait of a colorful, diverse city.

EXPLANATION

Chicago (title) is located approximately at the center of the distribution of the nation's population, and it is ideally situated at the crossroads of the nation's industry, agriculture, and commerce. It has become one of the major livestock and meat-packing centers, railroad centers, and one of the most important grain markets in the entire world. Its airport, O'Hare, is one of the busiest in the nation. It can boast one of the tallest buildings in the world, the Sears Tower. Nevertheless, especially during the prohibition era, Chicago was also notorious as the city where the crime czars like Al Capone operated freely and corruption prevailed. Also, Upton Sinclair, in *The Jungle*, uncovered the unsanitary conditions and the corruption in the meat-packing industry at the turn of the century.

STUDY QUESTIONS

1. How does Sandburg **personify** Chicago in lines 4 and 5, line 10, line 11, and in lines 20 and 21? What characteristics of the city are suggested by these personifications? How are these same characteristics expressed in the style of the opening **stanza**, the **imagery**, the capitalized nouns and adjectives, the line lengths, and the **rhythms**? How would you recite the stanza aloud? What other part of the poem has a style and effect similar to that of the first stanza?

2. What problems of the city are mentioned? The poem was written in 1914. If the poem were to be written today, how would the list of problems be different? What similarities would there be?

3. "To those who sneer" the speaker would "give them back the sneer" (line 9). In the next line, how does the poet answer the critics of Chicago? What, in your opinion, is "the terrible burden of destiny" referred to in line 19?

Under the smoke, dust all over his mouth, laughing
    with white teeth,
Under the terrible burden of destiny laughing as a
    young man laughs,
Laughing even as an ignorant fighter laughs who has
    never lost a battle,   20
Bragging and laughing that under his wrist is the
    pulse, and under his ribs the heart of the people,
        Laughing!
Laughing the stormy, husky, brawling laughter of
    Youth, half-naked, sweating, proud to be Hog
    Butcher, Tool Maker, Stacker of Wheat, Player
    with Railroads and Freight Handler to the
    Nation.

Choose the city or town that you live in or one that you know very well. Write a short poem in free verse in the style of the opening stanza of "Chicago" about the place you have selected.

THE PURSE-SEINE

Robinson Jeffers

Our sardine fishermen work at night in the dark of
      the moon; daylight or moonlight
They could not tell where to spread the net, unable to
      see the phosphorescence of the shoals of fish.
They work northward from Monterey, coasting Santa
      Cruz; off New Year's Point or off Pigeon Point
The look-out man will see some lakes of milk-color
      light on the sea's night-purple; he points, and
      the helmsman
Turns the dark prow, the motorboat circles the
      gleaming shoal and drifts out her seine-net. They
      close the circle   5
And purse the bottom of the net, then with great
      labor haul it in.

        I cannot tell you
How beautiful the scene is, and a little terrible, then,
      when the crowded fish
Know they are caught, and wildly beat from one wall
      to the other of their closing destiny the
      phosphorescent
Water to a pool of flame, each beautiful slender body
      sheeted with flame, like a live rocket
A comet's tail wake of clear yellow flame; while
      outside the narrowing   10
Floats and cordage of the net great sea-lions come up
      to watch, sighing in the dark; the vast walls of
      night
Stand erect to the stars.

continued

The speaker in this poem describes two scenes. The first is of sardine fishermen at work off the coast of central California, one of the prime sardine fisheries of the world. The second scene is of a city in the same region, seen from a mountaintop at night. The speaker sees an analogy between the two scenes, an analogy that leads him to a conclusion about the meaning of our big cities to the lives of the people within them.

DEFINITIONS AND EXPLANATIONS

Purse-Seine (title)   A net used to entrap schools of small fish such as the sardine. The cord from which the net is hung is strung with floats. The bottom of the net is strung with lead weights. When a school is sighted, the fishing boat runs the cord of the net around the school in a great circle, the weights carry the net down, and the fish are encircled in a wall of net. The net is pulled shut at the bottom by a drawstring called the purse line, and the fish are entrapped and ready to be hauled aboard the boat.

phosphorescence (line 2)   The quality of shining or giving off light without heat. Dying fish and decaying wood are often phosphorescent.

galaxies (line 14)   Clusters of millions of stars, like the Milky Way.

luminous (line 15)   Bright; radiant.

insulated (line 17)   Separated or shut off from.

STUDY QUESTIONS

1. How do the fishermen first spot the school of sardines?

2. Why is it a "great labor" (line 6) to haul the net in?

3. What two opposite words does the speaker use to describe his reactions to the scene of the trapped fish? Why does he have these two reactions?

4. What are some of the phrases describing light and dark and brilliant color that the speaker uses? How are the **connotations** and associations the speaker makes to these brilliant colors the opposite of their usual connotations and associations?

5. Explain the **metaphor** in lines 11–12. How is the night like walls?

Lately I was looking from a night mountain-
top
On a wide city, the colored splendor, galaxies of
light: how could I help but recall the seine-net
Gathering the luminous fish? I cannot tell you how
beautiful the city appeared, and a little terrible.   15
I thought, We have geared the machines and locked
all together into interdependence; we have built
the great cities; now
There is no escape. We have gathered vast
populations incapable of free survival, insulated
From the strong earth, each person in himself
helpless, on all dependent. The circle is closed,
and the net
Is being hauled in. They hardly feel the cords
drawing, yet they shine already. The inevitable
mass-disasters
Will not come in our time nor in our children's, but
we and our children   20
Must watch the net draw narrower, government take
all powers—or revolution, and the new
government
Take more than all, add to kept bodies kept souls—or
anarchy, the mass-disasters.

These things are Progress;
Do you marvel our verse is troubled or frowning,
while it keeps its reason? Or it lets go, lets the
mood flow
In the manner of the recent young men into mere
hysteria, splintered gleams, crackled laughter.
But they are quite wrong.   25
There is no reason for amazement: surely one always
knew that cultures decay, and life's end is death.

6. What is the parallel to the fishing scene the speaker sees as he looks down on the city from a mountaintop at night? How is his reaction similar?

7. According to lines 16–18, how does the speaker feel about the "interdependence" of the people in the cities? Why are the city people incapable of "free survival," according to the speaker?

8. How does the "verse" in line 24 keep "its reason" though "troubled or frowning"? (The verse refers to the speaker here. This is an example of **metonymy**.)

WRITING

To what extent are your own feelings about the trapped sardines and the people in cities in agreement with the feelings of the speaker in this poem? What do you think Carl Sandburg, the author of "Chicago" would say? Explain in a short essay.

THE CITY
Ogden Nash

This beautiful ditty
Is, for a change, about the city,
Although ditties aren't very popular
Unless they're rural and not metropular.

Sentimentalists object to towns initially   5
Because they are made artificially,
But so is vaccination,
While smallpox is an original creation.

Artists speak of everything urban
As the W.C.T.U. speaks of rye and bourbon,   10
And they say cities are only commercial marts,
But they fail to realize that no marts, no arts.

The country was made first,
Yes, but people lived in it and rehearsed,
And when they finally got civilization down,   15
Why, they moved to town.

City people always want the most faucets
And the comfortablest caucets,
And labor-saving devices in their kitchenette,
And at the movies, armchairs in which to set.   20

Take country people, they suffer stoically,
But city people prefer to live unheroically;
Therefore city dentistry is less painful,
Because city dentists find it more gainful.

continued

In "The Purse-Seine," Robinson Jeffers expresses a pessimistic attitude about our big cities. In this poem, Ogden Nash writes with his usual light, sharp, and witty touch to express a different attitude about the city.

DEFINITIONS AND EXPLANATIONS

ditty (line 1)   A short, usually light, poem or song.

metropular (line 4)   This is a typical coined Nash word, for the sake of humorous rhyme. The actual word from which "metropular" is coined is metropolitan, which means "pertaining to a big city."

Sentimentalists (line 5)   People who tend to be influenced by unrealistic emotions.

urban (line 9)   Having to do with the city or city life; the opposite of rural.

W.C.T.U. (line 10)   The Women's Christian Temperance Union has favored the prohibition of the drinking of any alcoholic beverage.

marts (line 11)   Certain forms of words like e'er (ever), o'er (over), ere (before), thee (you) appeared commonly in older, traditional poetry. "Mart" for market is in that category. Used in a poem written in modern language and style, such words are humorously incongruous.

caucets (line 18)   Nash has humorously misspelled corsets to give the appearance of an exact rhyme with "faucets."

stoically (line 21)   Bearing pain or difficulty without showing any emotional reaction; unemotionally.

querulous (line 25)   Complaining.

queasy (line 25)   Particular as to taste or preference.

perpetually (line 32)   Continuously.

STUDY QUESTIONS

1. According to the first **stanza**, why is this kind of poem unpopular? In what areas of the country might it be more popular?

2. According to the second **stanza**, many people prefer nature and the natural to human-created things and institutions. How does Nash proceed to puncture that belief?

City people are querulous and queasy,　　　　　　25
And they'd rather die than not live easy
And if they did die, they'd find fault
If they weren't put in an air-conditioned vault.

Yes, indeed, they are certainly sissies,
Not at all like Hercules or Ulysses,　　　　　　30
But because they are so soft,
City life is comfortable, if not perpetually, at least oft.

3. How, according to the poem, do artists feel about the city? What practical arguments does Nash bring up? How does he use rhyme to make his point?

4. What are some of the advantages of the city suggested humorously in lines 17–24? How is **synecdoche** used humorously in these lines?

5. How is **hyperbole** used humorously in lines 25–28?

6. When Nash uses the words ''sissies'' and ''soft'' in the last **stanza**, does he do so with **connotations** of approval or disapproval? What is the humor of the word ''oft'' in the last line?

WRITING

The speakers of ''Chicago,'' ''The Purse-Seine,'' and ''The City'' have expressed three attitudes toward the cities that have developed in our country. Which point of view do you personally prefer? Which of the poems did you like best for its language and style?

MUSIC

1. ''The City'' gently satirizes the frenzy and excitement of any big city. In some ways, Nash sees the city as a circus. Listen to a recording of circus music and marches. How do they express excitement and frenzy? Would the music make an appropriate accompaniment to the poem? Why or why not?

2. You may also wish to listen to the song ''New York, New York'' from Leonard Bernstein's *On the Town* (lyrics by Betty Comden and Adolph Green). How does the song describe the frenzy of a great city like New York? How does the music capture the excitement of a city?

This Land of Ours

1. Memorable lines Continue to add to your collection of memorable or quotable lines. From the poems in this unit, select two passages of one line or several lines. The basis of your selection may be strength of image, music of line, depth of emotion, appeal of theme, or any combination of these. Write the passages in your notebook with title and author. Memorizing the lines will give you added pleasure.

2. Briefly review the poems in this unit. Then, answer the following questions:

a. How does *John Brown's Body* raise questions about the significance of physical memorials and monuments?

b. How is "Chicago" a song of praise for the vitality of a great city?

c. How do "Nomad Exquisite" and "Puritan Sonnet" contrast regions of our country?

d. How does "Smoke Rose Gold" describe our nation's capital and what it symbolizes?

e. How do "The Purse-Seine" and "The City" express opposite points of view about the same thing?

3. Show your knowledge of terms in poetry. Here are five short passages from the poems in this unit. Choosing from the list of terms that follows, name the term applicable to the passage and explain why the passage is an example of the term you selected.

imagery   **simile**
hyperbole   **symbolism**
personification

a. "Lilacs in dooryards
   Holding quiet conversations with an early moon;"
   —Amy Lowell: "Lilacs"

b. "And if they did die, they'd find fault
   If they weren't put in an air-conditioned vault."
   —Ogden Nash: "The City"

c. "The rain begins. This is no summer rain,
   Dropping the blotches of wet on the dusty road:"
   —Jeanne McGahey: "Oregon Winter"

d. "Swift autumn, like a bonfire of leaves,"
   —Elinor Wylie: "Puritan Sonnet"

e. "A star might call: It's a long way across."
   —Carl Sandburg: "Smoke Rose Gold"

4. Review your knowledge of vocabulary by choosing the numbered word or phrase whose meaning is closest to the underlined word.

a. candid   (1) outspoken   (2) tasty   (3) awkward
              (4) colorful   (5) careful

b. elegance   (1) hostile attitude   (2) fluency   (3) dignity of
              style   (4) difference   (5) delight in life

c. immaculate (1) internal   (2) slight   (3) unkempt
              (4) significant   (5) pure

d. insulated (1) stubborn   (2) separated   (3) tidy
              (4) internal   (5) exploded

e. luminous   (1) bright   (2) clear   (3) lucrative
              (4) hardworking   (5) dimly lighted

f. "It is meet that you receive a severe sentence," said the judge.
              (1) found   (2) important   (3) established
              (4) fitting   (5) advisable

g. Moving from place to place, the nomad never found one steady
   home.
              (1) wanderer   (2) explorer   (3) police officer
              (4) inventor   (5) painter

h. The hardworking student perpetually earned high grades.
              (1) occasionally   (2) definitely   (3) frequently
              (4) seldom   (5) continuously

i. The quiet student was <u>reticent</u> in class, though she was quite lively with her friends.
      (1) not talkative   (2) excited   (3) exhausted
      (4) determined   (5) merely competent

j. The family reacted <u>stoically</u> to the tragedy.
      (1) joyfully   (2) angrily   (3) quickly
      (4) temperamentally   (5) unemotionally

5. Poems and paintings Poets and painters are artists who have much in common. Study each of the reproductions of paintings that follow. Examine the image carefully. Just what do you see? What feelings does the image arouse in you? What mood or idea does the picture suggest? If a person or persons appear, try to flesh out in your mind their background and character. Is rhythm, metaphor, or symbol important in the picture? After you have studied each picture in this way, select the one that you associate most powerfully with one of the poems in this unit. Be ready to discuss or write about your choice and the reasons for it.

Optional: Select one picture that inspires you to write your own poem and write the poem.

SPRING ON THE HILLSIDE   Wanda Gag. *1935.*
Whitney Museum, New York. Lithograph. Sheet: 11¼ × 15¹⁵⁄₁₆ in.
Image: 9 × 11¾ in. Purchase 36.169.

MERCED RIVER, YOSEMITE VALLEY   Albert Bierstadt.
The Metropolitan Museum of Art, Gift of the sons of William Paton, 1909.

**OVERHANGING CLOUD
IN JULY**
Charles Burchfield. *1947/59.*
Whitney Museum, New York.
Watercolor on paper. 39½ ×
35½ in. Purchase, with funds
from the Friends of the
Whitney Museum of American
Art. 60.23.

281

MIDNIGHT RIDE OF PAUL REVERE Grant Wood. *1931.*
The Metropolitan Museum of Art, Arthur H. Hearn Fund, 1950.
Courtesy of Associated American Artists.

TIMES SQUARE SECTOR
Howard Cook. *1930.*
Whitney Museum, New York.
Etching. Sheet, irregular: 13⅞ ×
11½ in. Plate: 11¹³⁄₁₆ × 9⅞ in. Gift
of Associated American Artists.
77.17.

Good Times/ Bad Times

The world in which we live is made up of contrasts, of good and bad, of happiness and sadness. Outside circumstances can bring many bad experiences into peoples' lives. Natural disasters and the social problems that plague our society today make us realize the frailty of our own existence. The disappointments we all experience, the broken hearts, the loss of loved ones, the loneliness, and the sadness can lead us to reflect on our lives. Yet, when we think realistically, we realize the bad times that are a natural part of our existence are often balanced by good times.

There are times of fun and joy, of satisfaction and fulfillment. There is growing up, there are holidays, there is singing, dancing, and music, and there is love. We experience great elation when we accomplish something new or when we triumph over adversity. We are proud when something important happens, and we are delighted when we achieve success through honest hard work.

The poems in this unit are about some of the bad times and some of the good times.

ANNABEL LEE
Edgar Allan Poe

It was many and many a year ago,
   In a kingdom by the sea,
That a maiden there lived whom you may know
   By the name of Annabel Lee—
And this maiden she lived with no other thought   5
   Than to love and be loved by me.

She was a child and *I* was a child,
   In this kingdom by the sea,
But we loved with a love that was more than love—
   I and my Annabel Lee—   10
With a love that winged seraphs of Heaven
   Coveted her and me.

And this was the reason that, long ago,
   In this kingdom by the sea,
A wind blew out of a cloud by night   15
   Chilling my Annabel Lee;
So that her highborn kinsmen came
   And bore her away from me,
To shut her up in a sepulchre
   In this kingdom by the sea.   20

The angels, not half so happy in Heaven,
   Went envying her and me:—
Yes! that was the reason (as all men know,
   In this kingdom by the sea)
That the wind came out of the cloud, chilling   25
   And killing my Annabel Lee.

continued

Of all our writers, Poe is noted for creating a melancholy mood and for expressing despair. One of his best-known poems in this vein is "Annabel Lee." Like that other great tragic love story, *Romeo and Juliet*, this is a tale of two very young people who love passionately and, because of external forces, end in tragic death. In this poem, the story is highly romantic and imaginative, with a mysterious, unreal quality. Its expression of melancholy is crystal clear, however. Its mood is achieved as much through the music of the words as through their meaning.

DEFINITIONS AND EXPLANATIONS

seraphs (line 11)   Angels.

coveted (line 12)   Envied.

highborn (line 17)   Of noble birth; belonging to the aristocracy or royalty.

kinsmen (line 17)   Relatives.

sepulchre (line 19)   Tomb.

dissever (line 32)   Cut apart; separate.

night-tide (line 38)   Nighttime.

STUDY QUESTIONS

1. Examine the curious "facts" of the story. When did the events take place? Where? What is Annabel Lee's family background? What can you infer about the speaker's background? What was the physical cause of Annabel Lee's death? What does the speaker suggest was the real cause? In what way are the speaker and Annabel Lee not separated? What kind of "facts" are these? What tone do they create?

2. If this highly imaginative story had a parallel in the poet's real experience, what guesses can you make about some of the facts of that experience?

3. How is the melancholy mood expressed though word-music? Which sound is repeated many times in the end **rhymes?** How does the poet use **internal rhyme?** How does he use word and phrase **repetitions?**

4. In keeping with the "facts" of the story, the **diction** of the poem creates a mood that is both melancholy and unearthly. Which are the phrases whose **denotation, connotation,** and **imagery** contribute to the mood?

5. How does the speaker cope with his loss?

But our love, it was stronger by far than the love
   Of those who were older than we—
   Of many far wiser than we—
And neither the angels in Heaven above   30
   Nor the demons down under the sea,
Can ever dissever my soul from the soul
   Of the beautiful Annabel Lee:—

For the moon never beams without bringing me
    dreams
   Of the beautiful Annabel Lee;   35
And the stars never rise but I see the bright eyes
   Of the beautiful Annabel Lee;
And so, all the night-tide, I lie down by the side
Of my darling, my darling, my life and my bride,
   In her sepulchre there by the sea—   40
   In her tomb by the side of the sea.

WRITING

1. There is no physical description of the two lovers of the story. How do you visualize them in your imagination? Give as complete a description as possible.

2. How do you explain the deep and wide appeal of tales of young, pure love coming to a tragic end, as in ''Annabel Lee'' and *Romeo and Juliet*?

MUSIC I HEARD FROM YOU
Conrad Aiken

Music I heard with you was more than music,
And bread I broke with you was more than bread;
Now that I am without you, all is desolate;
All that was once so beautiful is dead.

Your hands once touched this table and this silver,   5
And I have seen your fingers hold this glass.
These things do not remember you, beloved,—
And yet your touch upon them will not pass.

For it was in my heart you moved among them,
And blessed them with your hands and with your
      eyes;   10
And in my heart they will remember always,—
They knew you once, O beautiful and wise!

"**A**nnabel Lee" tells an imaginary, highly romantic tale of the heartbreak of love lost. However, that particular kind of loss has a counterpart in real experience, as reflected by the words of this poem. Here an answer is given to an important question: How does a person feel when he or she is separated from one who is dearly loved?

DEFINITION

desolate (line 3)   Lonely; dreary.

STUDY QUESTIONS

1. The speaker is addressing another person. How is the speaker talking to the "you" of the poem? What was the probable relationship between the two people? What has probably happened to the "you"?

2. What can you infer from the poem about the former lifestyle of the two people?

3. What two specific experiences that the couple shared are mentioned? What do the phrases "more than music" and "more than bread" tell you about the relationship?

4. How have the mind and heart of the speaker been affected by the loss of the loved one? To what extent do you think this reaction is common among people who are separated from a loved one?

5. How do you think the speaker will behave in the face of the tragic loss?

WRITING

1. Do you find this poem or "Annabel Lee" a more moving expression of the heartbreak of love lost? Why?

2. A few years have passed and the speaker of "Music I Heard with You" meets and falls in love with another woman. He writes an entry in his diary telling about her. Write the entry.

MUSIC

This poem speaks about loneliness and loss. The aria "My Man's Gone Now" from George Gershwin's *Porgy and Bess* also deals with loneliness and loss. How does "My Man's Gone Now" express the feelings of Serena, the character who sings this song at her husband's wake? What musical devices are used to express the character's pain?

WATER
Robert Lowell

It was a Maine lobster town—
each morning boatloads of hands
pushed off for granite
quarries on the islands,

and left dozens of bleak   5
white frame houses stuck
like oyster shells
on a hill of rock,

and below us, the sea lapped
the raw little match-stick   10
mazes of a weir,
where the fish for bait were trapped.

Remember? We sat on a slab of rock.
From a distance in time,
it seems the color   15
of iris, rotting and turning purpler,

but it was only
the usual gray rock
turning the usual green
when drenched by the sea.   20

The sea drenched the rock
at our feet all day,
and kept tearing away
flake after flake.

One night you dreamed   25
you were a mermaid clinging to a wharf-pile,
and trying to pull
off the barnacles with your hands.

We wished our two souls
might return like gulls   30
to the rock. In the end,
the water was too cold for us.

It is a tragedy when one lover loses another. It is also tragic when love itself goes sour. Why might this happen? What is the result?

DEFINITIONS

quarries (line 4)   Places where stone is excavated for building or other purposes.

weir (line 11)   A stake fence built in an inlet of the sea for trapping small fish.

STUDY QUESTIONS

1. In the first **stanza,** what are "boatloads of hands"? What work are they going to do? What feelings and associations does the **image** create? How are these feelings and associations continued in the images of the second and third stanzas?

2. In the first three **stanzas,** the mood established by the **images** is expressed directly in such words as "granite," "bleak," "stuck," "rock," "raw," and "trapped." Which words continue that mood in the remainder of the poem?

3. The two important people in the poem are the speaker and the person spoken to. What was the probable relationship between the two at first? Then what happened? Why do you suppose they came to the Maine lobster town? What was the result of their visit? Which lines **metaphorically** summarize the result?

4. The poet ends many of his lines with **near-rhymes** arranged in no particular pattern. Examples of near-rhymes include "hands"—"islands," and "bleak"—"stuck"—"rock." Give two other examples of near-rhymes. How is this technique suitable to the meaning of the poem?

WRITING

In your opinion, who is worse off, the speaker of this poem or the speakers of "Annabel Lee" and "Music I Heard with You"? Explain.

PITY ME NOT
Edna St. Vincent Millay

Pity me not because the light of day
At close of day no longer walks the sky;
Pity me not for beauties passed away
From field and thicket as the year goes by;
Pity me not the waning of the moon,   5
Nor that the ebbing tide goes out to sea,
Nor that a man's desire is hushed so soon,
And you no longer look with love on me.
This have I known always: Love is no more
Than the wide blossom which the wind assails,   10
Than the great tide that treads the shifting shore,
Strewing fresh wreckage gathered in the gales:
Pity me that the heart is slow to learn
What the swift mind beholds at every turn.

When a person has a painful experience, he or she may feel depressed for some time afterwards. Eventually, the pain subsides and a more balanced outlook on life returns. Sometimes, the pain is so bad that the depression continues, making all experiences seem painful. This kind of depression is very severe because the person begins to react to everything with a feeling of hopelessness.

DEFINITIONS AND EXPLANATIONS

thicket (line 4)   A thick growth of underbrush or small trees.

waning (line 5)   The gradual decreasing

of the visible face of the moon after it has become full.

assails (line 10)   Attacks.

STUDY QUESTIONS

1. What experience has caused the speaker's depression?

2. Which examples from nature does the speaker, in her state of depression, offer to confirm the feeling that nothing good lasts? How would a happy person have reacted to these examples?

3. Use your imagination to describe the **image** created by lines 11 and 12.

4. Which lesson does the speaker say

"the swift mind beholds at every turn"? Do you believe the speaker's statement in line 9 that she has known this lesson always? Why?

5. The speaker asks to be pitied because her heart is slow to learn the lesson mentioned in question 4 above. What does she mean? Why is her heart slow to learn the lesson?

6. How does the poet use **alliteration** in this poem? What is the **verse form**?

WRITING

Write a narrative in which you tell what you foresee in this speaker's future.

RECUERDO
Edna St. Vincent Millay

We were very tired, we were very merry—
We had gone back and forth all night on the ferry.
It was bare and bright, and smelled like a stable—
But we looked into a fire, we leaned across a table,
We lay on a hill-top underneath the moon;   5
And the whistles kept blowing, and the dawn came soon.

We were very tired, we were very merry—
We had gone back and forth all night on the ferry;
And you ate an apple, and I ate a pear,
From a dozen of each we had bought somewhere;   10
And the sky went wan, and the wind came cold,
And the sun rose dripping, a bucketful of gold.

We were very tired, we were very merry,
We had gone back and forth all night on the ferry.
We hailed, "Good morrow, mother!" to a shawl-
     covered head,   15
And bought a morning paper, which neither of us read;
And she wept, "God bless you!" for the apples and pears,
And we gave her all our money but our subway fares.

EXPLANATIONS

Recuerdo (title) This is the Spanish word for "I remember."

ferry (line 2) For many years, a ferry has run from the tip of Manhattan to Staten Island in New York City. It is a scenic, romantic excursion on the water. The salt smell of the sea is in the air Oceangoing vessels, the Statue of Liberty, the magnificent skyline of lower Manhattan, the graceful bridges of the city are all part of the vista. Because of the loveliness of the ride and the low fare, it has been a favorite evening outing for young lovers.

Earlier, you read a poem by Emily Dickinson that described the feeling of sheer, intoxicated joy aroused by the beauty of a summer day. Everyone knows that new love or even infatuation creates the same kind of euphoria, or wild delight and joy in being one's self and in being alive.

STUDY QUESTIONS

1. What is the mood of the lovers as suggested by the first two lines? How had they spent the night? What did they eat?

2. Where are the lovers when dawn comes? How is the dawn described? Using your imagination, describe the scene in detail. Where are the lovers exactly? What are they doing? What else do they, and you, see, smell, and hear in the scene?

3. What do the lovers do when they finally leave the ferry?

4. Why do you think the poet used the word "Recuerdo" rather than "I Remember" as the title?

5. As indicated by the title, the poet is recalling the night in her memory. In your opinion, is it a long time later or fairly soon afterward? What is the mood of the speaker at the time she is remembering? What is your guess as to the place and situation of this remembering?

WRITING

Have you ever taken a trip to a place that has left you with a romantic memory or a special feeling? Describe the trip, the person or people you were with, and the setting in detail. Try to create the same kind of mood that Edna St. Vincent Millay creates in "Recuerdo." If you like, write your response as a poem.

MUSIC

"Recuerdo" is a recollection of a romantic evening on the Staten Island Ferry. Charles Ives's *Central Park in the Dark* is a romantic recollection of an evening in New York's Central Park in which he contrasts the mysterious, calm beauty of the park with the hectic, fast-paced city night life outside the park. How does Ives do this effectively? Did you like the piece? Why or why not?

THIS IS JUST TO SAY
William Carlos Williams

I have eaten
the plums
that were in
the icebox

and which   5
you were probably
saving
for breakfast

Forgive me
they were delicious   10
so sweet
and so cold

$\mathbf{H}$ere is a poem in the form of a simple brief note from one person to another. For all its brevity and simplicity, it is alive, vivid, and somehow very down-to-earth. However, such a note does not occur in a vacuum. It involves two real people and the complexities of the relationship between them. Look beneath the surface. Begin to read the poem more carefully, and you will want to answer some intriguing questions about these two people and their situation.

EXPLANATION

This Is Just to Say   These words serve as both title and first line of the poem.

STUDY QUESTIONS

1. Who is the writer of the note? To whom is it addressed?

2. At what time of day did the eating of the plums probably take place? Why do you think the writer ate them? Where do you think the other person was?

3. The **diction** of the poem is important. In what circumstances would a person usually begin a written message with the words "This is just to say"? Under what circumstances does a person say "Forgive me"? Is this such a circumstance? If not, why were the words used?

4. Why does the writer mention that the other person was probably saving the plums for breakfast and then go on to describe carefully how "delicious," "sweet," and "cold" they were?

5. What do you think was the real message intended by the writer? How do you think the other person will react? What conclusions do you draw about the two people and their relationship?

WRITING

1. This poem consists of only 33 words, 26 of which are of one syllable, and all of which are as simple, direct, and ordinary as words can be. Yet the poem has a powerful impact on most readers and often stirs heated differences of opinion as to what lies behind the words. How do you explain this?

2. You will find it fun to try writing a similar poem. First, think up a situation between any two people—for example, two friends, two members of a family, or a boss and an employee. In that situation, one writes a note to the other. Write the note as a skeleton-bare poem in the style of "This Is Just to Say." Try to make it a poem that will make the reader itch to put flesh on the skeleton.

THE KISS

Sara Teasdale

I hoped that he would love me,
    And he has kissed my mouth,
But I am like a stricken bird
    That cannot reach the south.

For though I know he loves me,   5
    To-night my heart is sad;
His kiss was not so wonderful
    As all the dreams I had.

Young people tend to be idealistic in their expectations, and sometimes they are rudely disappointed when reality turns out to be a little different from their dreams. This can be especially true in romantic relationships, when the difference between being ''in love with love'' and being in love becomes clear.

STUDY QUESTIONS

1. What had the speaker in this poem hoped for? Has that hope been fulfilled?

2. How does the speaker use a **simile** to express her state of mind? What is her state of mind? Why is she feeling this way?

3. In view of the total statement made in the poem, how would you explain the hope the girl had?

4. How old would the speaker most likely be? How deep is her disappointment? What do you think she has learned from her experience?

5. How do you suppose the boy will be affected by all this?

6. Why do you think the poet chose to title this poem ''The Kiss''?

WRITING

1. How common do you feel the kind of experience described in this poem is? Is any permanent damage likely to be involved? How does one feel at the actual time of the disappointment? Why?

2. How effectively has the poet registered a reaction to a kiss? How have you felt when reality has not met your expectations? Why? How have you dealt with it?

MY PAPA'S WALTZ

Theodore Roethke

The whiskey on your breath
Could make a small boy dizzy;
But I hung on like death:
Such waltzing was not easy.

We romped until the pan   5
Slid from the kitchen shelf;
My mother's countenance
Could not unfrown itself.

The hand that held my wrist
Was battered on one knuckle;   10
At every step you missed
My right ear scraped a buckle.

You beat time on my head
With a palm caked hard by dirt,
Then waltzed me off to bed   15
Still clinging to your shirt.

For the young, who are just learning what the game of life is like, even love can have its difficulties, as the girl of "The Kiss" found out. This poem tells about a father's way of expressing his love for his little son, resulting in an experience that had a meaning different for the child from the meaning it had for the father.

STUDY QUESTIONS

1. About how old is the boy in the poem? How do you know?

2. What might the mother have said that triggered the waltz?

3. How do lines 10–14 and your answer to question 2 tell you about the father himself and about his feelings toward his son?

4. Describe the dance and its various effects on the boy.

5. Think about the feelings of the three people during the incident. How did the boy feel? How did the father feel? How did the mother feel? Why didn't she interfere? Should she have interfered? Why or why not?

6. The speaker is not the boy, but the boy grown to manhood and remembering. How does he now view his father? How does the title help you to answer this question? What may have brought this memory into the speaker's mind?

7. You know the speaker's childhood background. What kind of man do you think he has grown to be?

WRITING

Look back at something you recall from your childhood. How do you view it today? How is your view today different from or similar to the view you had as a child at the time the event occurred or shortly after?

MUSIC

Because the father is inebriated his waltz is unsteady and irregular. Listen to the melody, pleasant tonality, and waltz rhythm of the main melody of a traditional waltz such as Johann Strauss's "The Blue Danube." How is this different from the music of Maurice Ravel's "La Valse"? Which would be more likely to accompany the father's "waltz"? Why? Listen to "Saturday Night Waltz" from Aaron Copland's ballet *Rodeo*. Compare it to the Strauss and Ravel selections.

TO AN OLD WOMAN
Rafael Jesús González

Come, mother—
   Your rebozo trails a black web
   And your hem catches on your heels.
You lean the burden of your years
On shaky cane, and palsied hand pushes   5
   Sweat-grimed pennies on the counter.
Can you still see, old woman,
The darting color-trailed needle of your trade?
   The flowers you embroider
   With three-for-a-dime threads   10
Cannot fade as quickly as the leaves of time.
   What things do you remember?
Your mouth seems to be forever tasting
The residue of nectar-hearted years.
Where are the sons you bore?   15
   Do they speak only English now
   And pass for Spaniards?
Did California lure them
To forget the name of *madre*?
   One day I know you will not come   20
   And ask for me to pick
   The colors you can no longer see.
I know I'll wait in vain
   For your toothless benediction.
I'll look into the dusty street   25
Made cool by pigeons' wings
Until a dirty child will nudge me and say:
   "Señor, how much ees thees?"

In Mexican-American society, as in many others, mothers are highly respected and admired. One result of assimilation with mainstream American culture, however, has been a lessening of the regard in which members of past generations are held. In this poem, the speaker looks at an old woman and wonders about her memories and about how, when she dies, a part of him will be lost.

DEFINITIONS AND EXPLANATIONS

rebozo (line 2)   A long scarf worn primarily by Mexican women.

palsied (line 5)   Afflicted with uncontrollable shaking; tremor ridden.

STUDY QUESTIONS

1. What **image** does the speaker create when describing the old woman in the opening lines? What is her occupation?

2. How do lines 8–11 reflect the speaker's attitude about the passage of time? What is the old woman's legacy as time passes?

3. How does the reader know that the old woman lives in the past? How effective is the **image** that describes this?

4. How has America changed the old woman's sons? Is the speaker happy about this? How do you know?

5. How does the speaker describe his acceptance of the woman's eventual death? What mood will he be in?

6. Why are the last two lines of the poem significant?

WRITING

"Europe and America" by David Ignatow is about a parent and a son who have experienced cultural and generational differences. Compare and contrast "To an Old Woman" with "Europe and America" in a thoughtful, analytical essay.

"OUT, OUT—"

Robert Frost

The buzz saw snarled and rattled in the yard
And made dust and dropped stove-length sticks of
    wood,
Sweet-scented stuff when the breeze drew across it.
And from there those that lifted eyes could count
Five mountain ranges one behind the other   5
Under the sunset far into Vermont.
And the saw snarled and rattled, snarled and rattled,
As it ran light, or had to bear a load.
And nothing happened: day was all but done.
Call it a day, I wish they might have said   10
To please the boy by giving him the half hour
That a boy counts so much when saved from work.
His sister stood beside them in her apron
To tell them "Supper." At the word, the saw,
As if to prove saws knew what supper meant,   15
Leaped out at the boy's hand, or seemed to leap—
He must have given the hand. However it was,
Neither refused the meeting. But the hand!
The boy's first outcry was a rueful laugh,
As he swung toward them holding up the hand,   20
Half in appeal, but half as if to keep
The life from spilling. Then the boy saw all—
Since he was old enough to know, big boy
Doing a man's work, though a child at heart—
He saw all spoiled. "Don't let him cut my hand off—   25
The doctor, when he comes. Don't let him, sister!"
So. But the hand was gone already.

continued

There is a side to life, which most of us come to know sooner or later, when death strikes suddenly, unexpectedly, meaninglessly, wastefully. At such a time, the uncertainty and unpredictability that is part of all experience takes a form so fierce and so intense as to be very nearly overwhelming.

DEFINITIONS AND EXPLANATIONS

"Out, Out—" (title) In Shakespeare's tragic play, Macbeth is told the unwelcome and unexpected news of his wife's death. He speaks the following famous lines, from which the title of this poem is taken.

> To-morrow, and to-morrow, and to-morrow
> Creeps in this petty pace from day to day
> To the last syllable of recorded time;
> And all our yesterdays have lighted fools
> The way to dusty death. Out, out, brief candle!
> Life's but a walking shadow, a poor player,
> That struts and frets his hour upon the stage
> And then is heard no more. It is a tale
> Told by an idiot, full of sound and fury,
> Signifying nothing.

rueful (line 19) Mournful.

STUDY QUESTIONS

1. The speaker is an onlooker at the scene. Is he a member of the family or someone else? What is the setting?

2. Look at the first nine lines, in which the speaker watches the boy at work, fixes his attention elsewhere for a moment, and then has his attention redrawn to the boy and the buzz saw. How do the very first words foreshadow danger? What close observations does the onlooker make as he watches the boy at work? Where does his attention then wander? Why is his attention again drawn back to the boy? How does this sequence of events affect the strength of the sense of danger created by the opening words of the poem? How does line 9 reinforce the suspense? Nowhere in these lines is the boy ever mentioned! Why?

The doctor put him in the dark of ether.
He lay and puffed his lips out with his breath.
And then—the watcher at his pulse took fright.   30
No one believed. They listened at his heart.
Little—less—nothing!—and that ended it.
No more to build on there. And they, since they
Were not the one dead, turned to their affairs.

3. What wish does the speaker express in lines 10–11? Do you think he thought of the wish at that moment or later?

4. Who is the "they" in line 10 and the "them" in lines 13 and 14? What happened when the sister announced supper? What was the boy's reaction in the first instant? How do you explain that reaction? What was his next reaction? What was "spilling"? What great fear does the boy have?

5. Describe the scene at the boy's death, beginning at line 28.

6. Macbeth's reaction to his wife's tragic death was that life was very short, a "brief candle," and meaningless, "a tale told by an idiot." What is the reaction to this tragic death as expressed in the last two lines of the poem?

WRITING

Do you know people who have experienced the untimely, tragic loss of a loved one? How did they cope?

LAMENT
Edna St. Vincent Millay

Listen, children:
Your father is dead.
From his old coats
I'll make you little jackets;
I'll make you little trousers   5
From his old pants.
There'll be in his pockets
Things he used to put there,
Keys and pennies
Covered with tobacco;   10
Dan shall have the pennies
To save in his bank;
Anne shall have the keys
To make a pretty noise with.
Life must go on,   15
And the dead be forgotten;
Life must go on,
Though good men die;
Anne, eat your breakfast;
Dan, take your medicine;   20
Life must go on;
I forget just why.

Tragic death can strike the infant, the child, the youth, the young adult. It is hard to say which is the worst for those who are bereaved. This poem tells how a young mother attempts to cope with the death of her husband.

STUDY QUESTIONS

1. How many children are there in this family? What are their names and approximate ages?

2. According to the first line, the mother is speaking to the children. Is she really? Explain.

3. What seems to be the economic status of the fatherless family? What kind of thoughts chiefly occupy the mother's mind? How do her thoughts reflect both her feeling for her dead husband and her feeling for the living children?

4. Why does the mother say the following?

> "Anne, eat your breakfast;
> Dan, take your medicine;"

5. What emotion is the mother expressing in the last line? How is she dealing with this emotion?

6. What feelings do your have toward this mother? How do you guess the family will fare?

WRITING

How does the sudden loss of a close relative who was very loved affect a family? How does it affect an individual? Write a short story or poem in which you show a young person grappling with the confusing and conflicting emotions of such a terrible loss. First, identify the emotions for yourself. Then, make sure that they are conveyed with effective and vivid language in your story or poem.

LOST SISTER
Cathy Song

1

In China,
even the peasants
named their first daughters
Jade—
the stone that in the far fields   5
could moisten the dry season,
could make men move mountains
for the healing green of the inner hills
glistening like slices of winter melon.

And the daughters were grateful: 10
They never left home.
To move freely was a luxury
stolen from them at birth.
Instead, they gathered patience,
learning to walk in shoes   15
the size of teacups,
without breaking—
the arc of their movements
as dormant as the rooted willow,
as redundant as the farmyard hens.   20
But they traveled far
in surviving,
learning to stretch the family rice,
to quiet the demons,
the noisy stomachs.   25

2

There is a sister
across the ocean,
who relinquished her name,
diluting jade green

continued

Cathy Song considers herself Chinese-American, though she was born in Hawaii and her grandmother was Korean. In this poem, the speaker contrasts women's lives in America with the lives of their Chinese ancestors. In some ways, she concludes, they are still very similar after all.

DEFINITIONS AND EXPLANATIONS

relinquished (line 28)   Surrendered; given up.

inundate (line 33)   To overwhelm, to flood.

strangulate (line 40)   To choke, to cut off air.

fermented (line 43)   Here, having been chemically changed; roots were often fermented by soaking in liquid preservatives before being eaten.

unremitting (line 64)   Ceaseless, without stopping.

STUDY QUESTIONS

1. Why did the peasants name their first daughters ''Jade''? How did the daughters react to this honor?

2. How is the life of the Chinese woman described? What **images** does the poet use to express this?

3. How did the women manage to have ''traveled far'' nevertheless?

4. How has the sister diluted ''green jade with the blue of the Pacific''? Why is this a **metaphor?**

5. Why are the immigrants compared to ''a tide of locusts''?

6. What benefits do women have in America? How does the second **stanza** show the difficult side of American life for the immigrant? How does the poet use **imagery** and a **simile** in lines 37–40 to convey the loneliness?

7. What point do lines 41–45 make?

8. How does the speaker describe the trials of the immigrant way of life in lines 46–52?

9. How does the speaker **symbolize** the link with China? How does she emphasize its importance?

10. How is the Chinese-American woman like the Chinese woman? Why is the use of the word ''footless'' **paradoxical?** Why has the American left no footprints?

11. Explain the **metaphor** of the last two lines of the poem.

with the blue of the Pacific.   30
Rising with a tide of locusts,
she swarmed with others
to inundate another shore.
In America,
there are many roads   35
and women can stride along with men.

But in another wilderness,
the possibilities,
the loneliness,
can strangulate like jungle vines.   40
The meager provisions and sentiments
of once belonging—
fermented roots, Mah-Jong tiles and firecrackers—
    set but
a flimsy household
in a forest of nightless cities.   45
A giant snake rattles above,
spewing black clouds into your kitchen.
Dough-faced landlords
slip in and out of your keyholes,
making claims you don't understand,   50
tapping into your communication systems
of laundry lines and restaurant chains.

You find you need China:
your one fragile identification,
a jade link   55
handcuffed to your wrist.
You remember your mother
who walked for centuries,
footless—
and like her,   60
you have left no footprints,
but only because
there is an ocean in between,
the unremitting space of your rebellion.

In this poem, jade is used as a metaphor that connects the speaker to her homeland. Choose an object which you feel exemplifies your connection to where you live or where you came from. Write a poem or short story in which the object is used metaphorically as a central device in your work.

THE SLAVE AUCTION
Frances Ellen Watkins Harper

The sale began—young girls were there,
   Defenceless in their wretchedness,
Whose stifled sobs of deep despair
   Revealed their anguish and distress.

And mothers stood with streaming eyes,   5
   And saw their dearest children sold;
Unheeded rose their bitter cries,
   While tyrants bartered them for gold.

And woman, with her love and truth—
   For these in sable forms may dwell—   10
Gaz'd on the husband of her youth,
   With anguish none may paint or tell.

And men, whose sole crime was their
     hue,
   The impress of their Maker's hand,
And frail and shrinking children, too,   15
   Were gathered in that mournful band.

Ye who have laid your love to rest,
   And wept above their lifeless clay,
Know not the anguish of that breast,
   Whose lov'd are rudely torn away.   20

Ye may not know how desolate
   Are bosoms rudely forced to part,
And how a dull and heavy weight
   Will press the life-drops from the heart.

DEFINITIONS AND EXPLANATIONS

stifled (line 3)   Muffled.

unheeded (line 7)   Ignored; not listened to.

tyrants (line 8)   Individuals who use their power brutally and oppressively; here the merciless slave traders.

bartered (line 9)   Traded.

sable (line 10)   The color black.

hue (line 13)   Shade or color.

impress (line 14)   A mark or characteristic.

Frances Ellen Watkins Harper was born in 1825 to "free Negro" parents in Baltimore. Before the Civil War, she became involved in the Underground Railroad and spoke at meetings of antislavery societies. She wrote poetry and prose to much acclaim, and remained involved in early civil rights organizations until her death in 1911. Thus, "Slave Auction" emerges as a statement about slavery from a poet who, though not enslaved herself, was actively involved in the antislavery movement. In this poem, Harper focuses upon the terrible crime of selling human beings and the suffering it causes.

STUDY QUESTIONS

1. The poem is divided into two parts: the first four **stanzas** and the last two stanzas. How does each of the two parts function within the poem's structure?

2. How is each category of person in the sale described? How does this contribute to the description of the whole group as a "mournful band"?

3. Though one could easily expect the mothers to be sad, why does Harper describe their cries as "bitter" (line 7)?

4. Why does the poet make the point that love and truth "In sable forms may dwell"? What does this reveal about attitudes towards blacks during the slavery era?

5. What comparison is made in the last two **stanzas** about separation from loved ones? According to Harper which is worse, to be torn from a living loved one or to bury a dead loved one? Why?

6. Why are the slave traders mentioned only once?

7. How is the form of this poem traditional? What effect is created by the use of the biblical "Ye"?

WRITING

Frances Ellen Watkins Harper paints a description of the slave auction in poetry. Using that description as a foundation, write a prose selection or a short play telling the story of the auction.

MUSIC

The African-American spiritual "Lord, How Come Me Here" describes the feelings of a slave singing to God about his misery. What questions does the slave ask? How does the slave feel? How does the hushed intensity of the melody reinforce the feeling expressed by the words?

SUMMER REMEMBERED
Isabella Gardner

Sounds sum and summon the remembering of
    summers.
The humming of the sun
The mumbling in the honey-suckle vine
The whirring in the clovered grass
The pizzicato plinkle of ice in an auburn   5
uncle's amber glass.
The whing of father's racquet and the whack
of brother's bat on cousin's ball
and calling voices call-
ing voices spilling voices. . .   10

The munching of saltwater at the splintered dock
The slap and slop of waves on little sloops
The quarreling of oarlocks hours across the bay
The canvas sails that bleat as they
are blown. The heaving buoy bell-   15
ing HERE I am
HERE you are HEAR HEAR

listen listen listen
The gramophone is wound
the music goes round and around   20
BYE BYE BLUES   LINDY'S COMING
voices calling calling calling

continued

For some children, summer can be a joyous time of the family's being together, of vacations at the shore or mountains, of games and sports, of relaxation and fun. For a child, time hardly exists, and the delicious summer seems to last forever. But that is an illusion. Summer ends. The child grows up. For the adult, time moves faster and faster. The adult remembers the seemingly endless summer of childhood, sadly.

DEFINITIONS AND EXPLANATIONS

pizzicato (line 5)   The plucking of the strings of a violin or other stringed instrument with the fingers instead of running the bow across the strings.

auburn (line 5)   Reddish brown (referring here to suntan).

sloops (line 12)   Small, one-masted sailboats.

gramophone (line 19)   A hand-wound record player of years ago.

Bye Bye Blues Lindy's Coming (line 21)   These are the titles of two popular songs of the 1920's.

wantonly (line 25)   Freely, unrestrainedly; wastefully.

familial (line 25)   Belonging to or involving the family.

chidingly (line 26)   In the manner of scolding or rebuking.

sacks (line 27)   Plunders; loots; lays waste.

STUDY QUESTIONS

1. How does the poem show that the summer is remembered mainly by sound?

2. How do the named sounds convey a clear picture of the remembered setting? What is the locale? What people are present? What sort of house do they probably occupy? How spacious are the grounds?

3. How does the poet use **onomatopoeia**, **alliteration**, and **repetition** to make the poem effective? What overall emotional tone is set and expressed by the use of these devices?

4. To whom is the speaker addressing the words ''HEAR'' and ''listen'' in lines 17 and 18? What is their purpose?

"Children!   Children!   Time's Up
Time's Up"
Merrily sturdily wantonly the familial voices   25
cheerily chidingly call to the children   TIME'S UP
and the mute children's unvoiced clamor sacks the
        summer air
crying Mother   Mother   are you there?

5. Who is saying "Time's Up" in lines 23 and 24? How is the same sentence picked up in line 26 with a different meaning?

6. Why are the children mute and their clamor unvoiced (line 27)? What feeling is the speaker expressing when she says that the "unvoiced clamor sacks the summer air"?

7. What is the real feeling behind the question in the last line of the poem?

WRITING

Do you have a vivid memory of a delightful time from your childhood that you recall with a mixture of pleasure in the memory and sorrow at time's passing? What is the memory? Describe it in detail (in either poetry or prose). Include your emotional reactions.

MUSIC

"Summertime" from George Gershwin's *Porgy and Bess* is a classic musical encapsulation of the mood of summer. How does the music reflect the laziness of a summer day? What do the words say about summer? Compare this to the feelings about summer expressed in "Summer Remembered."

TOO BLUE
Langston Hughes

I got those sad old weary blues.
I don't know where to turn.
I don't know where to go.
Nobody cares about you
When you sink so low.   5

What shall I do?
What shall I say?
Shall I take a gun and
Put myself away?

I wonder if   10
One bullet would do?
Hard as my head is,
It would probably take two.

But I ain't got
Neither bullet nor gun—   15
And I'm too blue
To look for one.

Everybody gets blue once in a while. Sometimes this melancholy mood comes as a result of some small disappointment; sometimes, perhaps, as a result of natural rhythms of emotional ups and downs. Maybe we even enjoy feeling sorry for ourselves occasionally. The fact that we all experience these periods of emotional downs probably accounts, at least in part, for the existence and enduring popularity of the form of American music known as "Blues." This music both expresses and gives relief to the melancholy mood. Here is a poem that is about being blue and is itself a piece of Blues music.

STUDY QUESTIONS

1. Try reading the whole poem aloud to make it sound like a Blues song. You will have to experiment with vocal expression and intonation. Try several readings until you are satisfied that your vocal expression and intonation are in the Blues manner.

2. How does the use of "sad old weary" in line 1 establish the tone of the poem?

3. What specific effects of feeling blue are given in the first **stanza?** How do you explain these effects? Is it true that "Nobody cares about you/When you sink so low"?

4. Is the speaker seriously contemplating suicide? How do you know?

WRITING

Compare this poem to "Richard Cory" in terms of theme, message, language, and poetic form. Which poem is more effective for you? Why?

MUSIC

Look up the words of any popular Blues song, old or new. How do they compare to the words of "Too Blue"? Try fitting the words of "Too Blue" to a Blues tune that you know or an original one you can improvise yourself. What is the real message of this poem and of Blues music?

JAZZ FANTASIA
Carl Sandburg

Drum on your drums, batter on your banjoes,
sob on the long cool winding saxophones.
Go to it, O jazzmen.

1

Sling your knuckles on the bottoms of the happy
tin pans, let your trombones ooze, and go husha-
husha-hush with the slippery sand-paper.

2

Moan like an autumn wind high in the lonesome tree-
tops, moan soft like you wanted somebody terrible, cry
like a racing car slipping away from a motorcycle cop,
bang-bang! you jazzmen, bang altogether drums, traps,
banjoes, horns, tin cans—make two people fight on the
top of a stairway and scratch each other's eyes in a
clinch tumbling down the stairs.

3

Can the rough stuff . . . now a Mississippi steamboat
pushes up the night river with a hoo-hoo-hoo-oo . . .
and the green lanterns calling to the high soft stars
. . . a red moon rides on the humps of the low river
hills . . . go to it, O jazzmen.

4

EXPLANATION

Jazz Fantasia (title) Two of the great forms of American music, jazz and Blues, originated in the South from the folk music of the slaves brought here from Africa. Jazz is thought to have originated specifically in New Orleans, which certainly became the world capital of jazz. The early jazz musicians did not play from written scores, and in their improvisations, they gave full and free expression to deeply felt emotions and moods. Among the great names of jazz are Louis Armstrong and Duke Ellington. A fantasia is a musical composition of no fixed form or a medley of tunes.

Nothing has wider appeal to our emotions than our favorite music, whether popular or classical. We listen to our own favorites of past and present on radio and television (MTV), as well as on records, tapes, and compact discs. We remember for a long time the words and tunes of songs from different times in our lives. Why? The sound of music is a pleasure in itself, a form of relaxation and entertainment. Also, these songs are a release for us; they give expression to our own inexpressible longings, sorrows, joys, angers, and hopes. They make us aware that we are not alone in these feelings. This poem is about one of the greatest forms of American music, and it helps to explain what the music says and does for us.

STUDY QUESTIONS

1. What musical instruments do the jazzmen of this group use?

2. What specific emotions and moods does the speaker urge the jazzmen to reflect in their music? Why does the speaker so urge them?

3. Select lines at which you think certain instruments would predominate. Where would the saxophone predominate? The drums and traps? The trombone?

4. How does Sandburg use **onomato-poeia** and **alliteration** to reflect the sound of the music he is writing about? How does he use **rhythm** in his **free-verse** lines for the same purpose?

5. Repeat for this poem the experiment in reading aloud for musical effect that you tried with "Too Blue."

6. How do you explain the wide and deep appeal that jazz, blues, rock, heavy metal, ballads, and other forms of popular music have had for the American audience? What is your own favorite song? Why?

WRITING

What similarities are there between the appeal of poetry and the appeal of songs? What differences are there?

MUSIC

Listen to a selection of jazz pieces by such artists as Wynton Marsalis, Benny Goodman, Miles Davis, or others. A good source for recordings is *The Smith-sonian Collection of Classic Jazz*. How does the music make you feel? How well does Sandburg capture the spirit of jazz in the poem?

THE FACT
Dave Etter

The going-home sun
smiles my railroad eyes.

I run a rough stick
across the last picket fence.

Under our tulip tree   5
you wait in the yellow dust
smoothing a lilac dress.

I touch my arms, my chest,
watch my moving feet.

I have to know it's me,   10
really me, always.

There is a mood that is the opposite of being blue. It isn't named for a color, but it is a time when we are full of the joy of being alive, when we are happy with everything and everyone around us, and, above all, delighted to be ourselves. In this tiny gem of a poem, the speaker's own gladness is so bright it shines on us.

DEFINITION

tulip tree (line 5)   A tree of the magnolia family, with large, tulip-shaped, greenish-yellow blossoms.

STUDY QUESTIONS

1. What is the "going-home sun"? How does this first line create an opening note of gladness and brightness by using **image** and **connotation?**

2. What is the actual effect on the speaker's eyes that is described in the second line? How does this line continue the note of brightness and gladness?

3. What is the "rough stick" of line 3? How do lines 3 and 4 suggest the presence of bright light? How is **near-rhyme** used within the **image** of these lines to add to the note of lively, sharp brightness?

4. What does the speaker see as he comes close to home (lines 5–7)? How are these lines emphasized by the **stanza** arrangement? What feelings are suggested to you by the stanza?

5. What does the speaker do? What are the feelings that lie behind this action?

6. This very short, seemingly simple poem tells you directly and implies a good deal about two people. Tell everything you know about them.

WRITING

The title of this poem is deceptively simple. In a short essay, explain it as fully as possible, noting its literal and figurative meanings.

IN EXTREMIS

John Updike

I saw my toes the other day.
I hadn't looked at them for months.
Indeed, they might have passed away.
And yet they were my best friends once.

When I was small, I knew them well.   5
I counted on them up to ten
And put them in my mouth to tell
The larger from the lesser. Then

I loved them better than my ears,
My elbows, adenoids, and heart.   10
But with the swelling of the years
We drifted, toes and I, apart.

Now, gnarled and pale, each said, *j'accuse!*—
I hid them quickly in my shoes.

When we are in a supremely happy mood, laughter comes easily. We are ready to see humor all about us. The speaker of this poem looks at his toes, has a little joke about them, and shares it with us.

EXPLANATIONS

In Extremis (line title)   This Latin phrase means "at the extremity or far end"; it is commonly used more specifically to mean "near death."

j'accuse (line 13)   These French words for "I accuse" were the dramatic title of an essay by the French writer Émile Zola, which was of historical importance in the famous Dreyfus case.

STUDY QUESTIONS

1. The title is a pun, a play on the two meanings of the Latin phrase. Explain the pun. How is it carried into the poem?

2. In what well-known way were his toes the speaker's "best friends once" (line 4)? What does he humorously suggest have replaced the toes as close friends?

3. Explain the humor, also involving puns, of lines 11 and 12.

4. How are the toes humorously personified in line 13? What is their accusation? Why does the speaker hide them in his shoes? How does the **rhyme** add to the humor of the final **couplet**?

WRITING

Are toes an especially suitable subject for good-natured humor such as this? Why? Choose another part of the body or item of dress or other everyday object that would have been a good subject for humorous exaggeration. Write a humorous poem about it.

Good Times/Bad Times

1. Memorable lines Complete your collection of memorable or quotable lines. From the poems in this unit, select two passages of one line or several lines. The basis of your selection may be strength of image, music of line, depth of emotion, appeal of theme, or any combination of these. Write the passages in your notebook with title and author. Memorizing the lines will give you added pleasure.

2. Briefly review the poems in this unit. Then, answer the following questions:

a. Which ''good time'' poem affected you the most? Why?

b. Which ''bad time'' poem affected you the most? Why?

c. How does the age of the speaker create a special perspective in ''My Papa's Waltz''?

d. Why are the memories in ''Recuerdo'' so special?

e. How are sound effects especially important in ''Jazz Fantasia''?

3. Show your knowledge of terms in poetry. Here are five short passages from the poems in this unit. Choosing from the list of terms that follows, name the term applicable to the passage and explain why the passage is an example of the term you selected.

alliteration   **onomatopoeia**
internal rhyme   **personification**
near-rhyme

a. ''For the moon never beams without bringing me dreams''
—Edgar Allan Poe: ''Annabel Lee''

b. ''white frame houses stuck
like oyster shells
on a hill of rock,''
—Robert Lowell: ''Water''

c. "Pity me not because the light of day
   At close of day no longer walks the sky;"
   —Edna St. Vincent Millay: "Pity Me Not"

d. "Sweet-scented stuff when the breeze draws across it."
   —Robert Frost: "Out, Out—"

e. "The whirring in the clovered grass"
   —Isabella Gardner: "Summer Remembered"

4. Review your knowledge of vocabulary by choosing the numbered word or phrase whose meaning is closest to the underlined word.

a. rueful   (1) tired   (2) incoherent   (3) mournful
             (4) inexorable   (5) disappointing

b. assails   (1) goes boating   (2) slows down   (3) walks
             (4) quickens   (5) attacks

c. auburn   (1) combustible   (2) reddish brown   (3) naive
             (4) dark blue   (5) calming

d. coveted   (1) envied   (2) denied   (3) covered
             (4) enclosed   (5) explained

e. desolate (1) destroyed   (2) dynamic   (3) demented
             (4) distinguished   (5) dreary

f. The members of the law firm wanted to dissever the links among them.
   (1) reinforce   (2) confirm   (3) separate
   (4) castigate   (5) resolve

g. Though the old woman's sons and daughters had moved away, a familial relationship still existed between them.
   (1) belonging to the family   (2) disregarding family ties
   (3) familiar   (4) fractious   (5) competitive

h. According to the news report, the invading army sacks a town and then leaves it to burn.
   (1) patronizes   (2) rejuvenates   (3) explores
   (4) infiltrates   (5) plunders

i. After the singer reached her prime, her powers began waning all too quickly.
   (1) developing   (2) decreasing   (3) evolving
   (4) emerging   (5) changing

j. The question read, "In which novel by F. Scott Fitzgerald did Nick and Daisy spend money wantonly?"
   (1) tastefully   (2) carefully   (3) prudently
   (4) wastefully   (5) too quickly

5. Poems and paintings Poets and painters are artists who have much in common. Study each of the reproductions of paintings that follows. Examine the image carefully. Just what do you see? What feelings does the image arouse in you? What mood or ideal does the picture suggest? If a person or persons appear, try to flesh out in your mind their background and character. Is rhythm, metaphor, or symbol important in the picture? After you have studied each picture in this way, select the one that you associate most powerfully with one of the poems in this unit. Be ready to discuss or write about your choice and the reasons for it.

Optional: Select one picture that inspires you to write your own poem and write the poem.

DUST, DROUGHT AND DESTRUCTION William C. Palmer. *1934.*
Whitney Museum, New York. Egg tempera on composition board. 24 × 30 in. Purchase 34.22.

THE SILENT SEASONS—FALL
Will Barnet. *1967.*
Whitney Museum, New York.
Oil on canvas. 43½ × 33 in.
Purchase, with funds from Mr. and
Mrs. Daniel H. Silberberg. 73.48.

STRING QUARTETTE   Jack Levine.
The Metropolitan Museum of Art, Arthur H. Hearn Fund, 1942.

331

STILL LIFE Harley Perkins. *1926. Whitney Museum, New York.*
Oil on canvas. 20 × 24 in. 31.315.

SELF-PORTRAIT
Bradley Walker Tomlin. *1932.*
Whitney Museum, New York.
Oil on canvas. 17 × 14 in. Gift of
Henry Ittleson, Jr. 55.28.

Study the pictures that follow as you studied those in each Unit Review. Your teacher will give you the specific assignment though the following ideas will serve as guidelines. Depending on your teacher's instructions, you can work on this project alone or in groups. You may also wish to present an oral report to the class. If you are preparing a portfolio, you may wish, after revisions, to place this project in the portfolio.

1. Select a painting that personally appeals to you most strongly. Decide on two poems that appeal to you most strongly. In a carefully planned composition, explain the appeal that the painting and the poems have for you.

2. Select a painting that you feel makes a strong comment on one of the unit themes developed in this book. Write a carefully planned essay in which you first tell what the comment of the painting is and then compare or contrast the comment of the painting with the comment of two of the poems in the unit.

3. Paintings and poems often strongly establish a single mood or emotion. Select one painting that seems to you to establish a single mood or emotion. In a carefully planned composition, discuss the mood or emotion established by the painting and two poems that establish a similar mood or emotion.

4. Paintings and poems often create a fictional character or personality about whom we are told a little directly and about whom we are told a lot more by the power of the imagination. In a carefully planned composition, discuss three such characters or personalities, one from a painting and two from poems you have studied.

5. Poems and paintings often create a setting—a physical background of place and time. In a carefully organized composition, select and discuss three such settings, one from a painting, two from poems.

GOOD EVENING MR. SMALLWEINER, SR.
Tommy Dale Palmore. *1971. Whitney Museum, New York.*
Synthetic polymer on canvas. 48 × 60 in. Gift of Benjamin D. Bernstein.
72.8.

FAMILY   Charles H. Alston. *1955.*
Whitney Museum, New York.
Oil on canvas. 48¼ × 35¾ in. Purchase,
with funds from the Artists and
Students Assistance Fund. 55.47.

OFFICE IN A SMALL CITY   Edward Hopper. *1953.*
The Metropolitan Museum of Art, George A. Hearn Fund, 1953.

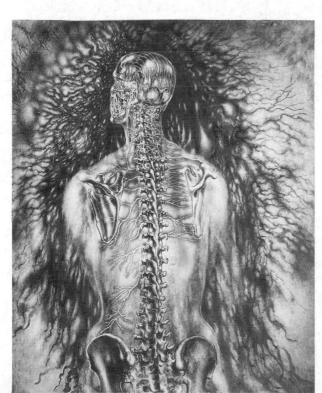

ANATOMICAL PAINTING
Pavel Tchelitchew. *1946.*
Whitney Museum, New York.
Oil on canvas. 56 × 46 in. Gift of
Lincoln Kirstein. 62.26.

WAR SERIES: BEACHHEAD **Jacob Lawrence.** *1947.*
Whitney Museum, New York. Egg tempera on composition board. 16 × 20 in.
Gift of Mr. and Mrs. Roy R. Neuberger. 51.13.

INDIAN ENCAMPMENT **Unknown American artist.**
c. 1850–75. Whitney Museum, New York. Oil on canvas. 27¾ × 35¾ in. Gift of
Edgar William and Bernice Chrysler Garbisch. 68.89.

FAMILY PORTRAIT
Marisol. *1961.*
Whitney Museum, New York.
Lithograph. Sheet: 29¹/₁₆ × 23⅛ in.
Image: 26³/₁₆ × 20¹³/₁₆ in. Gift of
Rock-Hil-Uris, Inc. 63.101.

THE UNTILLED FIELD **Peggy Bacon.** *1937.*
Whitney Museum, New York. Pastel on paper. Sight: 19⅛ × 25¼ in. Gift of
Mr. and Mrs. Albert Hackett. 52.29.

THE PIER Glenn O. Coleman. *Whitney Museum, New York.*
Pastel on paper. Sight : 14⅞ × 18 in. Gift of Samuel S. Goldberg. 50.19.

PORTRAIT OF A LIVING ROOM
Dorothy Varian. *1944.*
Whitney Museum, New York.
Oil on canvas. 40 × 30 in.
Purchase. 45.7.

A READER'S GUIDE
TO POETIC TERMS AND DEVICES

Alliteration is the repetition of initial consonant sounds. Alliteration occurs in such names as Woodrow Wilson, Charlie Chaplin, Billy Budd, Simple Simon, Greta Garbo, and in such common expressions as "safe and sound," "rags to riches," "tip to toe," "do or die." The repetitions create a design or pattern of sounds that lends emphasis to the words and is memorable to the ear. In poetry, alliterated sounds blend artistically with other sounds, with word meaning, with **image** to create the total meaning effect of the poem. The following stanza from Coleridge's "The Rime of the Ancient Mariner" tells how the mariner's ship has been sailing before a brisk fresh wind and is suddenly totally and helplessly becalmed. It is a fine illustration of the artistic use of an interplay of alliterative sounds.

> "The fair breeze blew, the white foam flew,
> The furrow followed free;
> We were the first that ever burst
> Into that silent sea."

Other examples are

> "The blazing brightness of her beauties beam"
>
> Edmund Spenser

> "Peter Piper picked a peck of pickled peppers"
>
> Anonymous

> "Ay, they heard his foot upon the stirrup
> and the sound of iron on stone
> And how the silence surged softly backward,
> When the plunging hoofs were gone."
>
> Walter de la Mare

Allusion is a brief reference to a person, a place, an event, or to well-known words. An allusion may be drawn from history, literature, geography, the Bible, mythology, or any other area of knowledge. The author expects the reader to recognize the allusion and get the full meaning suggested by the brief word or phrase. For example, suppose a newspaper editorial says that a new law will open a Pandora's box. If you know the story of Pandora from Greek mythology, you know that the editorial is saying that the new law will let loose many unforeseen and unmanageable problems and difficulties. In the stanza below, from a poem about the spider, full understanding of the lines depends on an understanding of the allusion to Euclid, the "father" of plane geometry.

> "He does not know he is unkind,
> He has a jewel for a mind
> And logic deadly as dry bone
> This small son of Euclid's own."
>
> Robert P. Tristram Coffin

The full meaning of the following lines from "Grass" depends on the allusions to Austerlitz and Waterloo, two crucial, bloody battles of the Napoleonic Wars.

> "Pile the bodies high at Austerlitz and Waterloo.
> Shovel them under and let me work—
> I am the grass; I cover all."
>
> Carl Sandburg

Ambiguity is the presence of two or more possible meanings or interpretations. A simple and familiar form of ambiguity is the *pun*, in which the double meaning of a word is played on for humorous effect. "What has four wheels and flies? A garbage truck." Shakespeare played on the meanings of words at a somewhat higher and sometimes more serious level. In *Romeo and Juliet*, Mercutio, a lighthearted person, lies mortally wounded and says, "Ask for me tomorrow, and you shall find me a *grave* man." Othello, insanely jealous of his wife Desdemona, decides to kill her by suffocating her with a pillow as she lies sleeping. First, he lowers the light of the lamp by her bedside; then, after giving her the kiss of death, he places the pillow on her face to snuff out her life. These two actions are accompanied by the words, "Put out the light, and then put out the light." In poetry, titles, single words, lines, the identity of the speaker, even the circumstances, can be ambiguous. Ambiguity can also be regarded as a general characteristic of poetry because meaning in poetry is often multileveled, suggested, and open-ended. In this sense, poetry simply parallels real experience in which meaning is more often ambiguous than it is clear and simple, which is why we have so much difficulty in learning from history, making good laws, and finding clear-cut answers to personal problems and the problems of society.

Analogy is a comparison between two things that are actually alike in many respects. For example, an analogy is often made between the way electricity flows through a wire and the way water flows through a pipe. An analogy is a *literal comparison* as opposed to the **figurative** comparisons made in **simile, per-**

sonification, and **metaphor.** When scientists perform experiments on labora-
tory animals to learn about human beings, they are depending on analogies
between humans and animals to draw conclusions applicable to both.

Anapestic foot. See **Meter.**

Anticlimax is the deliberate leading up to a big letdown, for the sake of humor
or **irony,** as in the following example:

> "And there, there overhead, there, there hung over
> Those thousands of white faces, those dazed eyes,
> There in the starless dark, the poise, the hover,
> There with vast wings across the canceled skies,
> There in the sudden blackness, the black pall
> Of nothing, nothing, nothing—nothing at all."
>
> Archibald MacLeish

Antithesis is the placing together of contrasting ideas, often for the sake of
irony, as in the following example:

> "O God! that bread should be so dear,
> And flesh and blood so cheap!"
>
> Thomas Hood

Apostrophe is the addressing of words to someone absent or something non-
human as if it were present or human. The following are examples:

> "Thou, too, sail on, O Ship of State!
> Sail on, O Union, strong and great!"
>
> Henry Wadsworth Longfellow

> "O wind, rend open the heat,
> cut apart the heat,
> rend it to tatters."
>
> H.D.

> "O black and unknown bards of long ago,
> How came your lips to touch the sacred fire?"
>
> James Weldon Johnson

Assonance is the repetition of vowel sounds, as in the expression "fit as a fid-
dle" and in the following examples:

> "The greatest and richest good,
> My own life to live in,
> This she has given me—
> If giver could."
>
> Archibald MacLeish

The following passage is an example of a rich, musical interlacing of assonance with **alliteration** and **consonance** and other **sound effects.**

> "How to keep—is there any any, is there none such, nowhere
> known some, bow or brooch or braid or brace, lace,
> latch or catch or key to keep
> Back beauty, keep it, beauty, beauty, beauty . . . from
> vanishing away?"

Gerard Manley Hopkins

Blank verse is poetry written in lines of **iambic pentameter** without **rhyme.** (Blank verse should not be confused with **free verse.**) What is generally recognized as the greatest poetry of the English language—the tragedies of Shakespeare and the epics of John Milton—is written in blank verse. Some memorable examples follow.

> "A mind not to be chang'd by place or time.
> The mind is its own place, and in itself
> Can make a heaven of hell, a hell of heaven."

John Milton

> "A dungeon horrible on all sides round
> As one great furnace flamed; yet from those flames
> No light; but rather darkness visible
> Served only to discover sights of woe,
> Regions of sorrow, doleful shades . . ."

John Milton

> ". . . Besides, this Duncan
> Hath borne his faculties so meek, hath been
> So clear in his great office, that his virtues
> Will plead like angels, trumpet-tongued, against
> The deep damnation of his taking-off"

William Shakespeare

In this book, Robert Frost's " 'Out, Out'—" is written in blank verse.

Cacophony is a combination of sounds that are harsh and grating in effect. The poet will deliberately make use of cacophonous sounds to support an unpleasant mood, idea, or **image,** as in the following examples:

> "The old South Boston Aquarium stands
> in a Sahara of snow now. Its broken windows are boarded.
> The bronze weathervane cod has lost half its scales.
> The airy tanks are dry."

Robert Lowell

"Bent double, like old beggars under sacks,
Knock-kneed, coughing like hags, we cursed through sludge."

Wilfred Owen

"The buzz saw snarled and rattled in the yard."

Robert Frost

Connotation is the overtone of meaning suggested by a word or words beyond their dictionary meaning. For example, the words "horse" and "steed" denote the same animal. However, "steed" has romantic and historical connotations that "horse" does not. Words like "doubloon," "corsair," and "cutlass" have connotations that "coin," "sail ship," and "knife" do not. The connotations of "filet mignon" and "champagne" are different from those of "steak" and "beer." Snakes and turtles are both reptiles; the connotations of "snake" and "turtle" are entirely different. Connotation is an important resource of the poet in creating a language of rich multidimensional meaning to parallel the complexity of human feeling and human experience.

Consonance is the repetition of final consonant sounds, as in such expressions as "la_st_ but not lea_st_," "fir_st_ and foremo_st_," "par_k_ and lo_ck_," "o_dds_ and en_ds_," and in the following examples from poetry:

"I saw his cropp_ed_ haircut go under.
I leap_t_, and my steep body flash_ed_"

James Dickey

"Our throa_ts_ were tight as tournique_ts_,
Our feet were bound with splin_ts_, but now,
Like convalescen_ts_ . . ."

Karl Shapiro

Couplet is a pair of rhyming lines. The most widely used couplet is the heroic couplet, written in **iambic pentameter.** An entire poem can consist of couplets, or a couplet may occur only occasionally, or it may occur in a single instance in a poem, usually for emphasis, as in the last two lines of the **English sonnet.** Geoffrey Chaucer introduced the heroic couplet into English poetry, most notably in his *Canterbury Tales.* Another English poet, Alexander Pope, used the heroic couplet to create memorable, often quoted, proverb-like lines.

"And, spite of pride, in erring reason's spite,
One truth is clear, Whatever is, is right."

"Hope springs eternal in the human breast:
Man never is, but always to be blest."

As a very young girl, the American poet Edna St. Vincent Millay wrote the fine poem "Renascence" in couplets of iambic tetrameter.

"The world stands out on either side
  No wider than the heart is wide;
  Above the world is stretched the sky—
  No higher than the soul is high."

Dactylic foot. See **Meter.**

Denotation is the dictionary meaning of a word, the thing or situation the word specifically refers to. The words "you" and "thou" have the same denotation, but the **connotations** have different flavors. The word "home" denotes the place where you live but has strong emotional connotations. In ordinary language—prose—the stress in word use is on denotation, in poetry, on connotation.

Diction is the careful choice of words employed by the poet. Diction may be employed to suit the character of the speaker, the mood or tone of the poem, or to create other effects desired by the poet. In the following lines, Ogden Nash mixes highly formal language and slang for humorous effect.

"And I shall even add to it by stating
    unequivocally and without restraint
  That you are much happier when you are happy
    than when you ain't."

In the following lines from a poem by Philip Booth, the speaker is stopped in his automobile by the gates of a railroad crossing and watches and counts as the cars of a long freight train rattle by. The words of the poem are entirely the names seen on the cars, the types of cars, and the speaker's counting, as the train flashes by.

"B & M boxcar,
  boxcar again,
  Frisco gondola,
  eight-nine-ten
  Erie and Wabash,
  Seaboard, U.P.,
  Pennsy tank car,
  twenty-two, three"

The diction of these lines captures the speaker's visual experience; their **rhythm,** the speaker's auditory experience.

Dramatic monologue is a poem in which the speaker, a specific person other than the poet, is talking to one or more listeners who are present, but not heard from. In this book, the following poems are examples of the dramatic monologue or variations of it: "The Unknown Citizen," "To James," and "Recuerdo." The dramatic monologue is not to be confused with the **soliloquy,** in which a specific person, other than the poet, is thinking aloud, putting his or her inner thoughts into words. The soliloquy is not addressed to another character, simply made available to the audience or reader. "Summer Remembered" is an example of the soliloquy form.

End rhyme. See **Rhyme.**

English sonnet. See **Sonnet.**

Euphony is a combination of sounds that are pleasant and smooth in effect. The poet makes use of euphonious sounds to support a pleasant or sensual mood, idea, or **image,** as in the following examples:

> "Fluxions of yellow and dusk on the waters
> Make a wide dreaming pansy of an old pond in the
>   night."

Carl Sandburg

> "With jellies soother than the creamy curd,
> And lucent syrops, tinct with cinnamon;
> Manna and dates, in argosy transferred
> From Fez; and spicéd dainties, every one,
> From silken Samarcand to cedared Lebanon."

John Keats

Extended metaphor. See **Metaphor.**

Figurative language (Figure of Speech) is a way of using words so that they mean something other than what they seem to say, and in which the intended meaning is clear. If a person says, "My heart is broken," everyone will understand that these words are not to be taken literally. Everyone will understand that the words mean "I am deeply sad." Other common and readily understood examples of figurative language occur in such statements as: "They were sweating blood." "It was raining cats and dogs." "All hands on deck." "A new broom sweeps clean." The poet uses fresh, original figures of speech to make powerful use of language, to enrich and extend meaning. The important figures of speech or forms of figurative language include **simile, metaphor, personification, synecdoche, metonymy, hyperbole, paradox, apostrophe, irony.**

Free verse is poetry that is written in a loose **rhythm** instead of **meter** (regular rhythm) and usually has no **rhyme.** The lines of free verse vary greatly in length. Although the "Psalms" and the "Song of Solomon" of the King James Bible are written in a form resembling free verse, free verse did not become established in poetry until relatively recently. Walt Whitman, with his *Leaves of Grass,* introduced free verse to American poetry, after which it became firmly established as a poetic form in the writing of such poets as Amy Lowell, Carl Sandburg, and e e cummings.

Haiku is a poetic form that originated in Japanese literature, consisting of a total of seventeen syllables divided into three lines of five, seven, and five syllables respectively. The haiku is typically simple and delicate, as in the following example:

> "All the world is cold . . .
>   My fishing-line is trembling
>   In the autumn wind"

Buson

Hyperbole is deliberate exaggeration to emphasize a truth, as when a person says, "You could have knocked me over with a feather," and in the following examples from poems:

> "And my fingertips turned into stone
>   From clutching immovable blackness."

James Dickey

> "And I will luve thee still, my dear,
>   Till a' the seas gang dry."

Robert Burns

Iambic foot. See **Meter.**

Imagery (Image) is the use of words to recreate the sense impressions of actual experience. Verbal imagery most often is visual, but imagery also includes words of sound, smell, taste, and touch. The following lines about racing yachts present precise visual images of the scene:

> "Mothlike in mists, scintillant in the minute
>
> brilliance of cloudless days, with broad bellying sails
> they glide to the wind tossing green water
> from their sharp prows while over them the crew crawls
>
> ant-like . . ."

William Carlos Williams

Sound images dominate the following stanza:

> "The ice was here, the ice was there,
>   The ice was all around:
>   It cracked and growled, and roared and howled
>   Like noises in a swound!"

Samuel Taylor Coleridge

The sight and feel of the tropical sun beating down on a motionless ship come alive in the following stanza:

"All in a hot and copper sky,
The bloody Sun, at noon,
Right up above the mast did stand,
No bigger than the Moon."

Samuel Taylor Coleridge

Imagery may be *literal*, directly describing sense experiences, as in the following lines:

"Under our tulip tree
    you wait in the yellow dust
    smoothing a lilac dress."

Dave Etter

Imagery is also often the strength of the figurative comparisons of **simile, metaphor,** and **personification,** as the similes of the following lines illustrate:

"Our dried voices, when
    We whisper together
    Are quiet and meaningless
    As wind in dry grass
    Or rats' feet over broken glass
    In our dry cellar."

T. S. Eliot

Readers of poetry must be alert to images and respond to them sensitively. Careful readers of poetry will not only see, hear, feel, taste, and smell the sense impressions of the poem, but will add to them whatever is consistent to make the image even more complete. For example, readers of the last two lines of the passage above by T. S. Eliot will not only hear the sound of the rats' feet brushing the glass, but also they will be in the dark gloom of the cellar, see the scurrying grey forms and the vague shapes of discarded junk in the dark, and smell the dusty, mouldy cellar smell. An important part of the richly suggested meaning of poems is grasped by the readers' active and exact response to both the literal and figurative images.

Internal rhyme. See Rhyme.

Irony may occur in two forms. In its verbal form, it is the use of words to mean the opposite of what they say. If the weather has been wet and cold for days and someone says, "Well, another perfect day," the words are used ironically, as everyone will understand. When Siegfried Sassoon, in a poem about war, writes "Does it matter?—losing your sight? . . ./There's such splendid work for the blind," he is writing ironically. The second form of irony is dramatic irony or irony of situation. The contradiction between the outward and inward circumstances of Richard Cory's life is dramatic irony. In Randall Jarrell's poem

"Losses," it is ironic that death-dealing bombers are tenderly given girls' names. In Carl Sandburg's "Mr. Attila," the contradiction between the professor's harmless appearance and personal behavior and his work on the atom bomb is ironic. Emily Dickinson pinpoints the irony of a blindly conformist society in "Much Madness is divinest Sense." Verbal irony sometimes takes specific forms as in **paradox, antithesis,** and **oxymoron.**

Italian sonnet. See **Sonnet.**

Line. In ordinary language, or prose, words are written or printed according to the meaning or thought. The main divisions or units, therefore, are sentences or paragraphs. Line beginnings and endings have no significance; they are determined mechanically by fixed margins on the page. In poetry, patterns of sound are important, and line beginnings and endings are determined by patterns of sound. The line is a basic unit of the pattern of sound. In traditional or regular poetry, each line has a fixed number of syllables and a fixed **meter,** or arrangement of those syllables. If **rhyme** is present, it reinforces the sound pattern established by the line. In **free verse,** the pattern of sound is reflected in a loose or irregular **rhythm,** and the number of syllables in a line varies. More often than not, the thought divisions of a poem do not correspond to the line endings. In reading poetry aloud, it is important to read according to meaning, and not make a full stop at the end of each line unless the thought requires it. The music of the sound pattern will make itself felt through the thought pattern.

Lyric. A lyric is a short songlike poem expressing personal feelings. Portions of many poems have lyrical or songlike qualities. A good example of a lyric is Ben Jonson's "Drink to Me Only with Thine Eyes."

Metaphor is usually defined as an implied comparison (no "like" or "as" is used, as they are in simile) between two unlike things. Real understanding of metaphor needs a fuller explanation. Look at a commonly used metaphorical statement. One student says to another, "The exam was a piece of cake." Obviously this is not a literal statement. The exam does not actually consist of a piece of cake. Moreover, the purpose of the speaker is not to tell anything about the factual substance of the exam. The purpose is to convey some specific essential characteristic of the exam realized in the experience of the speaker. In that experience, the exam was of such character as to be pleasantly and easily disposed of, "eaten up." The image of the piece of cake being so eaten is used to express the character of the exam in the experience of the speaker. From this example, we can learn that the purpose of a metaphor is to convey the speaker's feelings about a specific essential characteristic of a real thing. That purpose is accomplished by presenting an **image** of another and a different thing that vividly expresses the characteristic and the speaker's perception of it. To put this another way, a metaphor has two terms: a *literal* thing and a figurative image that brings out a feeling about the *literal* thing. The following examples of common metaphors will illustrate.

"Life is a bowl of cherries."

"We drove over a washboard road."

"The angry cop came up to us, breathing fire."

The writer of a metaphor works with two terms in mind. The first term is the original literal thing the writer wants to tell us something about. In the examples we have looked at, these are the exam, life, the road, the cop. The second term is the imaginative image that conveys the writer's feeling about some characteristic of the original term: eating a piece of cake, a bowl of cherries, a washboard, a dragon breathing fire. It is important to notice that the writer of the metaphor does not always spell it out completely. For example, "piece of cake" is only part of the image. It is necessary to complete the image by seeing a person pleasantly munching on a piece of cake and disposing of it quickly and easily. "Breathing fire" is only part of the image, and it is necessary to see the fierce and threatening dragon that is breathing fire. Moreover, the formula "*a* is *b*" does not always occur. The phrase "washboard road" condenses the formula. The good reader of poetry must be alert to the facts that the presence of a metaphor is not always spelled out and that a full figurative image is given only through the suggestion offered by a part of the image. Here is one example of a metaphor from a poem in this book, "The Skater of Ghost Lake:"

"Kneeling in snow by the still lake side,
 Rising with feet winged, gleaming, to glide."

In these lines the poet metaphorically compares ice skates to wings on the feet. The imaginative/image suggests the speed and flowing grace with which the skater moves. From the suggestion of the word "winged," the reader must complete the picture of the graceful, easy strides of the skater and get the feeling of the sudden power the skates have given to the skater. The metaphor is highly condensed. The lines do not say "her skates were wings." Skates are not even mentioned. The good reader, however, will see the complete metaphor as it is suggested in the phrase "feet winged." Most metaphors are brief. Sometimes, however, a single metaphor will be developed through many lines or even through a whole poem. Such extended metaphors occur in several of the poems in this book. For example, in "Underwater," the comparison of the sea beneath the surface to a cathedral is extended through much of the poem. In "To James," the comparison of life to a footrace is the thrust of the whole poem.

Meter. English words are made up of units of sound called syllables. The core of every syllable is a vowel sound. When English words of two or more syllables are spoken, one syllable is accented by raising the pitch and volume of voice

slightly and holding the sound slightly longer, as in the following examples
(¯ = accented, ˘ = unaccented):

tŏ dāy

yēs tĕr dăy

tŏ mōr rŏw

One-syllable words are accented or not according to meaning.

Ī ăm bŏss.

Ĭ ā̄m bŏss.

Ĭ ăm bō̄ss.

In ordinary speech, there is an irregular and usually accidental pattern of accented and unaccented syllables which lends speech a degree of rhythmic sound. In **free verse,** the pattern of accented and unaccented syllables is arranged to create a freely flowing, but definite, **rhythm.** In traditional poetry, words are arranged in a fixed pattern of accented and unaccented syllables called meter. Meter has two fixed units. The first unit is the **foot,** or pattern of accented and unaccented syllables followed in the poem. The basic feet are the following:

Examples	*Name of foot*	*Name of meter*
iň-sīst dĭ-vīde rĕ-mōve	**iamb**	**iambic**
pōr-tiŏn ār-rŏw fūl-lў	**trochee**	**trochaic**
cŏn-třa-dīct iň-tĕr-rūpt aš-cĕr-tāin	**anapest**	**anapestic**
stīm-ŭ-laře āp-pĕt-iře yēs-tĕr-dăy	**dactyl**	**dactylic**

The second unit is the **line,** measured by the number of feet in it.

monometer (one foot)
dimeter (two feet)
trimeter (three feet)
tetrameter (four feet)
pentameter (five feet)
hexameter (six feet)
heptameter (seven feet)
octameter (eight feet)

The meter most commonly used is iambic and the most common line length is pentameter. The following are some examples of metric patterns:

Iambic tetrameter
"Ŏ bēautĭfŭl fŏr spācĭoŭs skīes"

Iambic trimeter
"Fŏr āmbĕr wāves ŏf grāin"

Iambic pentameter
"Thĕ wōrk ŏf hūntĕrs īs anŏthĕr thīng"

Iambic dimeter
"Yŏur grīef aňd mīne
Mŭst intĕrtwīne"

Trochaic tetrameter
"Sūrgeŏns mūst bĕ vērȳ cārefŭl"

The purpose of the foregoing discussion is to provide a brief introduction to meter. It is not necessary to have this technical knowledge to understand and appreciate a poem fully. Nor should meter have any more than a background function in the reading of a poem aloud. Poems should be read according to meaning and not in a singsong patter that seeks to stress the meter.

Metonymy is a figure of speech in which the name of a thing is substituted for the name of something closely associated. When we ask, "Have you read Shakespeare?" we are substituting the name of the author for his works. When we say, "The pot is boiling," we are substituting the name of the container for the liquid contents. Other common examples of metonymy are "old salt" for sailor, "the crown" for a king, and "the oval office" for the President. In the following lines, "coroner," an official associated with death, is substituted, in an example of metonymy that is also **understatement,** for mass killing in war.

"One simple thought, if you have it pat,
Will eliminate the coroner"

Ogden Nash

Near-rhyme. See **Rhyme.**

Octet. See **Sonnet.**

Onomatopoeia. Some words that name sounds also imitate the sound they name in their own sound. This quality is called onomatopoeia. Examples of onomatopoetic words are "cock-a-doodle-doo," "quack," "hiss," "buzz," "bang." Onomatopoetic effects can also be gained by **alliteration** or other combinations of sounds in words that are not themselves onomatopoetic, as in the following examples:

"The moan of doves in immemorial elms,
And murmuring of innumerable bees."

Alfred, Lord Tennyson

"I heard them blast
The steep slate-quarry, and the great echo flap,
And buffet round the hills, from bluff to bluff."

Alfred, Lord Tennyson

"Crisp is the whisper of long lean strides"

William Rose Benét

Oxymoron is a concise **paradox** in which two successive words seemingly contradict each other: "living death," "successful failure," "thunderous silence," "sweet sorrow."

Paradox is a seeming contradiction that reveals an underlying truth, as in the following examples:

"Yet each man kills the thing he loves"

Oscar Wilde

"The only way to get rid of a temptation is to yield
to it."

Oscar Wilde

"The more things a man is ashamed of, the more
respectable he is."

George Bernard Shaw

Personification is a special kind of **metaphor** in which an idea, object, or animal is given human characteristics. The tendency to personify is deeply rooted in us. The ancient Greeks personified various aspects of nature in their humanlike gods. We refer to "Mother Nature" and "Old Man River." In the following lines, gasoline pumps are personified as basketball players:

"Flick stands tall among the idiot pumps—
Five on a side, the old bubble-head style,
Their rubber elbows hanging loose and low."

John Updike

Pun. See **Ambiguity.**

Quatrain is a **stanza** of four lines. It is the most common stanza form in English poetry, often used in ballads and long narrative poems. Well-known poems written in quatrains are Coleridge's "The Rime of the Ancient Mariner," Gray's

"Elegy in a Country Churchyard," and Fitzgerald's "The Rubaiyat of Omar Khayyam," the last of which includes the following familiar quatrain:

> "A Book of Verses underneath the Bough,
> A Jug of Wine, a Loaf of Bread—and Thou
> Beside me singing in the Wilderness—
> Oh, Wilderness were Paradise enow!"

Poems in this book written in quatrains include "The Skater of Ghost Lake," "Atomic," "Richard Cory," "I taste a liquor never brewed," "Water," and "The Slave Auction."

Refrain is a line that is repeated in a poem for musical and mood effect. In Millay's "Recuerdo," the line "We were very tired, we were very merry" occurs as a refrain at the beginning of each **stanza.**

Repetition. See **Sound effects.**

Rhyme is the repetition of the sounds of the final accented syllables of two or more words. This repetition usually occurs at the ends of lines (**end rhyme**). Sometimes the repetition occurs within a line (**internal rhyme**). Examples of rhyming words are "June"-"moon," "nation"-"inflation," "relax"-"attacks," "through"-"blue." End rhymes can be arranged in various patterns, called the **rhyme scheme.** The letters of the alphabet are used to code the rhyme scheme. A **couplet,** two rhyming lines, is coded *aa*:

> "Indeed, everybody wants to be a wow, *a*
> But not everybody knows exactly how." *a*
>
> Ogden Nash

A **quatrain** in which alternating lines rhyme is coded *abab*:

> "Whenever Richard Cory went down town, *a*
> We people on the pavement looked at him: *b*
> He was a gentleman from sole to crown, *a*
> Clean favored, and imperially slim." *b*
>
> Edwin Arlington Robinson

A variety of more intricate rhyme schemes is possible. The rhyme scheme of the following **stanza** of six lines is *abcbdd*:

> "Life has loveliness to sell— *a*
> All beautiful and splendid things, *b*
> Blue waves whitened on a cliff, *c*
> Climbing fire that sways and sings, *b*
> And children's faces looking up *d*
> Holding wonder like a cup." *d*
>
> Sara Teasdale

Internal rhyme creates an especially rich musical effect.

> Ah, distinctly I <u>remember</u> it was in the bleak <u>December</u>   *a*
> And each separate dying <u>ember</u> wrought its ghost upon
>   the floor.   *b*
> Eagerly I wished the <u>morrow</u>; vainly I had sought
>   to <u>borrow</u>   *c*
> From my books surcease of <u>sorrow</u>—sorrow for
>   the lost Lenore   *b*
>
>   Edgar Allan Poe

Sometimes poets use rhymes that are not perfect, but approximate. Such rhymes are called **near-rhymes.** Near-rhymes include **assonance** ("mix"-"tick," "how"-"loud") and **consonance** ("just"-"last," "mend"-"band") and words with various other kinds of sound similarity. The following are examples of near-rhyme.

> "Wherever she is it is now.
>   It is here where the apples <u>are</u>:
>   Here in the <u>stars</u>,
>   In the quick <u>hour</u>."
>
>   Archibald MacLeish

> "Your feet thump-thump against my <u>back</u>
>   and you whisper to yourself. Child,
>   what are you wishing? What <u>pact</u>
>   are you making?"
>
>   Anne Sexton

> "For the lime-tree is in <u>blossom</u>
>   And one small flower has dropped upon my <u>bosom</u>."
>
>   Amy Lowell

> "The whiskey on your breath
>   Could make a small boy <u>dizzy</u>;
>   But I hung on like death:
>   Such waltzing was not <u>easy</u>."
>
>   Theodore Roethke

Rhythm is all around us and within us. There is rhythm in the rising and setting of the sun, in birth and death, in the flow of tides, in the coming and going of the seasons. There is rhythm in the beating of our hearts, in our breathing, in our sleeping and waking, in our walking. There is rhythm in music, in dance, in painting, in architecture. There are also rhythms in the sounds of language to reinforce the moods, ideas, and images expressed by the words of poems. Poets use **alliteration, assonance, consonance, rhyme,** and other kinds of repetition to create rhythms. In traditional verse, poets use **meter,** a fixed pattern of accented and unaccented syllables in lines of fixed length, to create rhythm. In **free verse,** poets use an arrangement of lines of irregular length to create loosely flowing rhythms or cadences, reinforced by other kinds of repetitions and patterns of **sound effects.** The following passage illustrates the way the rhythms of free verse reflect the mood of sorrow and mourning in a poem about the death of Lincoln.

> "When lilacs last in the dooryard bloom'd,
>   And the great star early droop'd in the western sky
>   in the night,
>   I mourn'd, and yet shall mourn with ever-returning spring.
>
>   Ever returning spring, Trinity sure to me you bring,
>   Lilac blooming perennial and drooping star in the west,
>   And thought of him I love."

Walt Whitman

The stricter, pounding rhythms of lines that are metrical and rhymed can also be strongly effective in reinforcing the mood and meaning of the words of a poem.

> "It matters not how strait the gate,
>   How charged with punishments the scroll,
>   I am the master of my fate;
>   I am the captain of my soul."

William Ernest Henley

Sestet. See **Sonnet.**

Simile is a figure of speech similar to **metaphor** in which an imaginative image is used to express a feeling about an essential characteristic of a literal thing. Since the words "like" or "as" are used in a simile, this figure of speech is usually more apparent than metaphor. In the following simile, the poet compares the houses in a village on the Maine coast to oyster shells to express the hard, cold, lifeless, unattractive appearance of the houses.

> "White frame houses stuck
>   like oyster shells
>   on a hill of rock"

Robert Lowell

The poet views children's faces as a cup full to the brim with the wonder of innocence in the following simile:

> "And children's faces looking up
>   Holding wonder like a cup."

Sara Teasdale

The swift movement of a hammer gives the impression that the forked claws move with the darting speed of the tongue of a snake.

> "With the claws of my hammer glistening
> Like the tongue of a snake."

Amy Lowell

Simile is usually defined as the expressed comparison of two unlike things. More accurately, simile uses an imaginary image that expresses the poet's feeling about some characteristic of a literal thing. Robert Lowell's simile uses oyster shells to express his feeling about the houses as lifeless, hard, and cold.

Soliloquy. See **Dramatic monologue.**

Sonnet is an important, traditional form of poem, which conforms to a strict structure. A sonnet consists of fourteen lines of **iambic pentameter** and has one of two **rhyme schemes.** The **Italian** or Petrarchan sonnet rhymes *abbaabbacdcdcd* (sometimes *cdecde*). The **English** or Shakespearean sonnet rhymes *ababcdcdefefgg* (three **quatrains** of alternating rhyme and a concluding **couplet**). The English sonnet often follows a structure in which the first eight lines (**octet**) develop the statement of a problem and the last six lines (**sestet**) lead to the resolution of the problem, a resolution that is finalized in the concluding **couplet.** The most famous sonnets are in the sonnet sequence of Shakespeare. Elizabeth Barrett Browning's "Sonnets from the Portuguese" is another noteworthy sequence of love sonnets. Among American poets, Edna St. Vincent Millay is most noted for her sonnets, several of which are included in this book.

Sound effects. Sound is important in our spoken language. When we are angry, we shout. When we speak words of tender love, we whisper. When we are excited, we raise the pitch of our voices; when sad, we lower the pitch. When we give commands, we use short, crisp emphatic words, carefully stressing every syllable. The human voice has been described as the most complex and remarkable of all musical instruments. We make some sounds, the vowels, using only various shapes of our open mouths through which the vibrations of our vocal chords are projected. We make the consonant sounds by using various combinations of positions of tongue, teeth, lips, and palate to form an amazing variety of sound-producing openings or partial openings. For such consonants as *p, t, s, f, k,* we use only expelled breath. For *b, d, z, v, g, j, l, m,* we use the vibrations of our vocal chords. Some sounds can be held indefinitely—all the vowel sounds and *l, m, n, s, r.* Some sounds can only be uttered and finished—*d, t, b, k, g.* Some sounds are soft and liquid—*l, r, m.* Some sounds are hard and explosive—*k, b, d.* The poet makes artistic use of all the aspects of the sound effects of speech to reinforce the mood and meaning of the words. He uses **rhythm, rhyme, assonance, consonance, alliteration, repetition.** The poet also uses other combinations of sound which somehow have a musical

effect that intensifies meaning but are as hard to define or explain as music itself
is. Here are some examples.

> "The world is charged with the grandeur of God.
> It will flame out, like shining from shook foil;
> It gathers to a greatness, like the ooze of oil
> Crushed...."

Gerard Manley Hopkins

> "When the hounds of spring are on winter's traces,
> The mother of months in meadow or plain
> Fills the shadows and windy places
> With lisp of leaves and ripple of rain"

Algernon Charles Swinburne

> "Not in vain the distance beacons. Forward, forward
> let us range,
> Let the the great world spin forever down the ringing
> grooves of change."

Alfred, Lord Tennyson

> "A poem should be palpable and mute
> As a globed fruit,
>
> Dumb
> As old medallions to the thumb"

Archibald MacLeish

Stanza. In a metrical poem, the stanza is the largest unit of **rhythm.** Each stanza
contains a fixed number of lines and a fixed **rhyme scheme** that is usually re-
peated in all the other stanzas. For example, "Richard Cory" consists of four
quatrains in **iambic pentameter** with lines of alternating rhymes: *abab cdcd efef
ghgh*. In **free verse,** the poem may be divided into stanza sections determined
by the poet according to mood, idea, rhythmic pattern, or other factor.

Symbol. We often use concrete objects as symbols for larger ideas or feelings.
A snake symbolizes evil, snow symbolizes purity, and a dove symbolizes peace.
In poetry, a word or a phrase used as a symbol stands for more than it says.
Sometimes, a whole poem is symbolic and stands for more than it says. In "The
Great Scarf of Birds," the flock and its movement seem to symbolize the awe-
some and mysterious ways of nature. The poem "Underwater" may symbolize
the violence that lurks in the dark recesses of the human psyche, of which we
are ashamed when it is exposed to the light. In "Water," the cold Maine water
symbolizes the failure of love. General characteristics of poetry are its sugges-
tiveness and its indirectness which make possible the expression of complex
feelings and experiences in a few words. Symbolism like **metaphor, imagery,**

ambiguity, and **allusion** is a powerful instrument for the expression of large worlds of meaning in a few words.

Synecdoche is a figure of speech in which a part of a thing is spoken of as representing the whole thing. When we use "pigskin" for football and when we speak of "heads" of cattle, we are using synecdoche. In the line "when dawns were young" from "The Negro Speaks of Rivers" the word "dawns" is used to stand for all of time of which dawns are only one part.

Trochaic foot. See **Meter.**

Understatement is a form of **irony** or humor that depends on deliberately representing something as much less than it really is. Mark Twain's remark is a well-known example: "The reports of my death are greatly exaggerated."

Verse form is any one of a number of fixed traditional patterns of a whole poem. The **sonnet** is the best known of these. The limerick is a familiar form used mainly for light verse. The nine-line Spenserian **stanza** and the **quatrain** written in lines of **iambic tetrameter** with various **rhyme schemes** (*abcb, abab*) are other traditional verse forms.

INDEX OF AUTHORS

INDEX OF TITLES